Almanac for the Anthropocene

Salvaging the Anthropocene
Stephanie Foote, Series Editor

aLmanac
FOR THE
anTHROPOCene

a compendium of soLarpunk futures

edited by

phoebe wagner

and BRONTË CHRISTOPHER WIELAND

West Virginia University Press
Morgantown

ISBN 978-1-952271-50-2 (paperback) / 978-1-952271-51-9 (ebook)

Library of Congress Control Number: 2022016229

Book and cover design by Than Saffel / WVU Press.
Front cover typeface is Suspicion Regular by Kai-Cong Fam, distributed under the SIL Open
Font License.

CONTENTS

Part 3

Community

Part 4

Ingenuity

The Situation So Far

Phoebe Wagner and Brontë Christopher Wieland

This book is about hope, resistance, and transformation, but first it's necessary to recognize the stakes. Reviewing the climate crisis has a purpose: to clearly understand the need for a radical, anticapitalist, decolonial transformation. Far from a prescriptive, didactic utopian ideology and aesthetic, solarpunk aspires to a world rooted in community and honoring all peoples— human and nonhuman. Solarpunks are also dedicated to adapting theory to local reality: the goal isn't simply to install solar panels on every roof but to examine community needs and respond in accordance with those needs, working within the community to make it better for all. Being a solarpunk means understanding and working through the Anthropocene's despair; it means taking a cold, hard look at the facts and still finding hope.

We *know* the climate crisis is already here. With our different ways of knowing: planting diverse crops, the strange weather, the last time deep snow came, the horror of heat, the desperation of cold, the missing bees, the rise of deer ticks, the migration of birds, the increased ferocity of hurricanes and devastation of wildfires, the faltering jet stream, the erosion of coastal islands, the images of a near-iceless Arctic, the continued unseasonable rainfall or perpetual drought, the dead elm trees, the missing bats. And yet we live in collective denial, as teenage climate activist Greta Thunberg—a leader of the School Strike for Climate—describes it: "If [climate change] was really happening, we wouldn't be talking about anything else. As soon as you'd turn on the TV, everything would be about that. Headlines, radio, newspapers, you would never read or hear about anything else, as if there was a world war going on."[1] The denial feels surreal. To go to work, to go to class, to start the car, to eat ramen. It all hurts. It's a double life. What has been destroying the planet slowly (by human standards of time) is no longer slow. It's coming hard and fast and *we know*. It won't be a surprise, like in so many end-times movies (though perhaps something will thaw from the permafrost, or nanoplastics will cause mass sterilization). We keep arriving at the same destructive actions over and over without opportunity for change due to the chokehold of the oil elites. In the Global North, to truly live a sustainable life within this system requires such huge degrees of privilege and property that few have that option, and those who make the choice are considered more than a bit odd. Too often, these sustainable lifestyles end with the individual rather than scale to a societal or communal change.

A solarpunk imagines new futures in the shadow of and in opposition to environmental collapse, then works to create those futures. A solarpunk doesn't just have ideas and beliefs; a solarpunk enacts. On paper, being a solarpunk might sound like being a Marxist, a municipalist, or another ideology entirely. Yet a different kind of necessity turns solarpunk thought into action: namely, extinction. A solarpunk might approach a problem with the following questions: How do my actions impact my human and nonhuman community? What intentionality fuels this issue? Does the following action dismantle a damaging system like capitalism, white supremacy, or colonialism? Does this action produce radical care of self and others? Does this action overcome the cultural desire to consume?

In other words, being a solarpunk is not just about solar. Neither is it Woodstock for the new millennium. The emphasis on *solar* reminds us of environmental interconnectedness (or, as Anna Tsing would call it, entanglement). Human-nonhuman-sunlight-nightlight-mineral-oil-ocean-and-and-and. It's a nice idea—and plenty of advertisements capitalize off connection—but the climate crisis demonstrates this connectedness on the grandest scale available for humans.

Solarpunk grew to life online in 2008[2] but became more widely recognized with the publication of *Solarpunk: Histórias ecológicas e fantásticas em um mundo sustentável*, edited by Gerson Lodi-Ribeiro, in 2012 and Adam Flynn's "Solarpunk: Notes toward a Manifesto" in 2014. Returning to the collective roots of cyberpunk, the first solarpunks gravitated to online spaces to build their lifestyle. A consistent interest in community, green spaces, and practical but pleasant art nouveau design defined early solarpunk, though the community debated how these elements would be included in deserts or less hospitable climates. Foundationally, solarpunk rejected the dystopian hopelessness of speculative literature trending after 9/11. This rejection of dystopia did not mean embracing utopia, however. Rather, solarpunks aimed for something in the middle, such as the ambiguous utopias of Ursula K. Le Guin's work. The goal of solarpunk was not to dream of perfect worlds but to strive for something sustainable and just in the Anthropocene.

Meanwhile, cyberpunk and steampunk represent the most commonly known -punk genres. Both impacted solarpunk in separate ways. Writers like

Philip K. Dick and William Gibson constructed the cyberpunk genre amid the early days of hacking and the late days of punk music. Dystopias, misfits, and technology combined to imagine a bleak future and dark commentary on the present. Harrison Ford stalking through the rain in *Blade Runner* (1982) cemented the aesthetic in the popular imagination, much to the dismay of actual cyberpunks. Leaving the dystopic behind, the most salvaged aspects of cyberpunk come from antigovernment sentiment and transformative technology. In 2013, Victoria Blake described the current state of the genre: "[Cyberpunk] was, and it is, an aesthetic position as much as a collection of themes, an attitude toward mass culture and pop culture, an identity, a way of living, breathing, and grokking our weird and wired world."[3] Indeed, cyberpunk often feels the most countercultural even though it has been subsumed by mass media.

The origins of steampunk are more tangled, as no signifying novel encompasses the genre, though William Gibson and Bruce Sterling's *The Difference Engine* (1990) comes close. The more commonly recognized steampunk aesthetic shouldn't be confused with the heart of the genre, which remains punk. Jess Nevins defines the revolutionary side as undermining Victorian ideals:

> Steampunk, like all good punk, rebels against the system it portrays (Victorian London or something quite like it), critiquing its treatment of the underclass, its validation of the privileged at the cost of everyone else, its lack of mercy, its cutthroat capitalism. Like the punks, steampunk rarely offers a solution to the problems it decries—for steampunk, there is no solution—but for both punk and steampunk the criticism must be made before the change can come.[4]

Steampunk literature continues, but where the genre thrives is the do-it-yourself movement. Always an important aspect of steampunk, the gears-and-brass-clockwork style remains a costume attraction at conventions and is consumed via craft-store shelves. Ann VanderMeer sees this contemporary crafting as a success of the genre rather than something to be ignored: "Let's use *creative play* to look at creation, invention."[5] Unlike cyberpunk, steampunk usually remains in the past or in a revisionist future (what if steam power replaced oil?). This looking backward can create a more critical awareness rather than just a fantasy. While cyberpunk looks ahead to a bleak future, steampunk looks behind to the origins of that bleakness. Indeed, VanderMeer describes the politics of steampunk: "Just as traditional science fiction uses the future to discuss issues that concern us now, Steampunk fiction can use the past (or alternate pasts) to bring to light issues that we might otherwise have trouble discussing. . . . How else can we make positive change without understanding our past?"[6] From the compost pile of these two genres, solarpunk begins to have a frame: to reject the dystopian leanings of both cyberpunk and steampunk but retain the anticapitalist and creative energy both aspired to.

Currently, the -punk genre has fractured into dozens of subcultures, many focused on social justice or environmental issues: salvagepunk, silkpunk, dieselpunk, ecopunk, and more. While each contains its niche and, if literary-based, its signature author (such as Neon Yang and their Tensorate novella series for silkpunk), no other -punk has risen to the prominence of cyberpunk or steampunk. A common criticism of these new genres is why should they be considered punk at all, especially as there are so many. Some of this resistance comes from the old guard, such as Gardner Dozois, who comments: "Assuming that we ever hear anything about solarpunk again; remember the few months a couple of decades back, before it was exiled to the graveyard of dead genre sub-classifications, when everybody was briefly talking about 'cowpunk'?" Another common criticism returns all the way to Bruce Sterling's original cyberpunk publication *Cheap Truth* and its demise after *Time* featured cyberpunks: " 'I hereby declare the revolution over. Long live the provisional government.' "[7] In other words, cyberpunk was no longer punk enough to deserve the classification. While a genre should never worry about *deserving* a title, any genre that represents anticapitalism and promotes inclusive community seems pretty punk. The idea of authenticity haunts the punk scene in all its forms, but as Ivan Gololobov writes, "Regular subversion of meanings, elements of self-destruction, self-abasement, nihilism, the clear anti-foundationalist stance and revolutionizing potential of punk, all make it difficult to locate something uncontroversially authentic."[8] That being said, solarpunk remains largely unconcerned with whether the genre should or shouldn't claim punk. From the beginning, the focus has been on creating something sustainable with real-world applications. This focus on action separates solarpunk from other genres. From its inception, solarpunk was and is a transformative response to the climate crisis.

While environmental discussions seem stuck in certain circles, often academic or activist, a solarpunk belongs to no one group. They could be the literature professor or the biologist or the videogame designer or the houseless activist or the McDonald's cashier. Rather than focusing on a specific discipline, a solarpunk can observe community needs and consider how their talents and passions might best aid that community in reaching a more sustainable future.

Mutual aid and mutual benefit with human and nonhuman life is central to solarpunk.

A final note: solarpunk should be fun. There's a reason it first came out of online communities and speculative fiction rather than academia or Washington, DC. Yes, it's about radical care and intentional community, but we need to *live* those ideals, and fun is integral to the goal.

To that end, we (Phoebe and Brontë) edited the first general solarpunk anthology in English, hoping to explore the depth and breadth the genre could offer. *Sunvault: Stories of Solarpunk & Eco-Speculation* (2017) defined solarpunk as "the stories of those inhabiting the leverage points, the crucial moments when great change can be made by the right people with the right tools. Stories of the peoples living during tipping points, and the spaces before and after them, the stories of those who fought to effect change and seek solutions, even if it was too late."[9] After successful crowdfunding, the anthology expanded to include poetry and line art. The pieces collected in the anthology ranged from asteroid mining to near-future activism. While *Sunvault* retained the breadth of a general introduction to the genre, that very generalness still made the genre hard for newcomers to grasp. Since solarpunk's inception, the impacts of the climate crisis have crystalized and provided a clearer sense of the responses needed, both individual and collective. Within that focus, solarpunk can become more clearly defined: solarpunks treat today as the first day of the future, not just acknowledging the climate crisis and systems of oppression but also asking, in true punk fashion, what are we going to do about it?

The Future of Solarpunk

When considering the future of ecocriticism in 1996, Cheryll Glotfelty asked, "For how can we solve environmental problems unless we start thinking about them?"[10] Solarpunk, and the mission of this book, takes the next step—how can we imagine, create, and then enact solutions to environmental problems? How can we build systems to uphold and maintain these changes? Change must happen in the next ten years, which means we've run out of time to start thinking. We must fully commit to the doing. While solarpunk literature aims at shaping hopeful and sustainable futures on the page, the online community often discusses what it would take to reach such reforms, creating a gap between the solarpunk conversation and the literature—though some stories do feature practical discussions. Rather than anthologizing solarpunk in academia, this book hopes to close that gap between speculation and action. Since *Sunvault*, another independent publisher, World Weave Press, has published three solarpunk anthologies focusing on responses to seasonal change (summer and winter, specifically) and multispecies cities. Several books have included solarpunk as a marketing tool, but the lack of radical environmental awareness in the texts makes them appear like greenwashing. While many authors in the solarpunk community are in the process of writing novels, the most signature text remains Cory Doctorow's *Walkaway* (2017), though not published under the genre label. That being said, solarpunks and eco-futurists have claimed the novel, even producing a handbook on how to walk away from capitalist society.

The future of solarpunk would transcend literature, the humanities, the academy to become a way of interacting with the world. As solarpunk doesn't exist in institutions, we collaborate around common ideas, online platforms, community needs, and activism. It must be more than a lifestyle, which is too easy to co-opt into consumeristic greenwashing. Currently, the community is largely unshaped and emerging, but solarpunks will make changes to their home, their yard, their community, their labor, and their consumption not because it will help stave off the climate crisis but because it is a healthier way to live with the world. Solarpunks will normalize nontraditional and communal living, will seek active decolonization and food sovereignty, will live models of balance rather than models of growth, will build infrastructures of resistance and sustainability. A goal of this almanac is to not only inspire such changes but also demonstrate how to actualize change. The pandemic and social unrest after the murder of George Floyd show that the world is restless for change at a large scale. These changes will be made not out of guilt or fear but out of hope that we can renew relationships with the human and nonhuman peoples around us and learn to honor, rather than exploit, them.

As stated earlier, to be solarpunk is also to be anticapitalist, but what do we mean by capitalism? We do not mean simply an economic system. Capitalism in the United States was foundationally connected to colonialism and geno-cide of Indigenous people. Capitalism as an economic system has always been deemed a sign of progress, modernity, and rationalization, thereby dehuman-izing anyone who did not practice that system, particularly Indigenous people around the globe. So when we say capitalism, we also mean colonialism. In the United States, capitalism is also directly rooted in slavery. Tricia Hersey reminds us that the capitalism of genocide and slavery is the same capitalism functioning today. Hersey argues that capitalistic grind culture is rooted in "my ancestors on those plantations, that they were human machines, they were one of capitalism's first experiments."[11] So when we say capitalism, we mean the United States building a country founded on slavery. In environmental litera-ture and criticism, the connection between environmental degradation and capitalism is often at the forefront, but we must remember the other systems of oppression that capitalism funds, whether it's the militarized police force or extractive oil practices. Nick Estes says it best: "Indigenous ways of relating to human and other-than-human life exist in opposition to capitalism, which transforms both humans and nonhumans into labor and commodities to be bought and sold."[12]

Early solarpunk was necessarily rooted in literature as a means of imagining radically changed systems of knowing and being. In a decentralized society, we envision texts like this almanac connecting like-minded people, much as Edward Abbey's books inspired a generation of environmentalists. But the future of solarpunk steps forward from imagining to doing and living. Future solarpunks will have acknowledged the apocalypse and will transform with the world.

The Uses of This Almanac

With each new climate report, the question (though often formed as a debate) of individual response versus collective (often read as governmental) response overwhelms the environmental discussion. Each side argues the other side is useless because their type of change won't occur for X reason, while the reality of monumental change on both the individual and collective front remains a final, conciliatory response. Rather, this book emphasizes a solarpunk lifestyle that can create community (through online networks, co-ops, communal spaces, art collectives, mutual aid, activism, and so on) in the face of the oncoming crisis. We will focus not only on creating community but on creating systems that operate independently and separately of the current capitalist, white supremacist, colonialist, consumerist systems driving the climate crisis.

Part of the current climate debate revolves around green consumerism—if humanity would just stop buying plastic straws and go organic, a certain number of problems would solved. This option *might* have been viable decades ago, but the required drastic carbon cuts reach beyond such capitalist ideas and are only completable if massive corporate entities and governments make these changes. Buying a way out only continues the destructive patterns of consumerism and materialism. This book investigates changes at a deeper, more fundamental level—founded on anti-racist, decolonial ideas—of our interaction with others.

Similarly, this book isn't searching for the next patent or technological hope but rather explores low-tech as a future option. The climate crisis will not be solved through a technological fix—not because humanity's inventiveness isn't up to the challenge but because current research, patenting, and creation methods all rely on capitalism and, by extension, colonialism and white supremacy. For example, big oil derided global warming in the 1990s while building taller drilling platforms to accommodate sea-level rise. New research in nuclear energy, hydrology, solar, and synthetic meats could all help the situation, but no master fix remains possible through capitalism. In a system that measures success by profit, sustainable relationships with the ecosphere do not make money. As emphasized by Pacific Gas & Electric causing multiple wildfires on the West Coast—including the destruction of Paradise, California, by the Camp Fire—even regulations, fines, and reprimands do not make change when profit exists. Yet solarpunks aren't waiting for the final crumble of capitalism. As the pandemic has shown, particularly in the United States, the drumbeat of the economy will always continue, regardless of the death toll. We must undermine this system in whatever ways we can—particularly by deconstructing white supremacy and through direct decolonial action—while hoping and striving for a postcapitalist society. Solarpunks look to a different future while working in the present.

Appealing to the ethical sensibilities of fossil fuel companies, or big business in general, is not only unviable but has already proven to be a blatant failure—due not to the protesters but to the nonresponse of the companies. The 2016 Dakota Access Pipeline protests at the Standing Rock Sioux Tribe reservation proved a new ground zero for this issue as peaceful protest was met by a brutal and militarized police force, lies from the North Dakota state government, and inaction from President Obama as Democratic leadership spent millions on reelection instead. The number of protests that make national news demonstrates the current engagement with activism across generations, but as Senator Dianne Feinstein made clear to children activists of the Sunrise Movement, neither protest nor scientific data sway either party: "It's not going to get turned around in ten years."[13] While this book will be useful to protest organizers, the recent actions of big businesses and the politicians they support have made it clear different tactics are required. We have yet to see how the summer of protest begun in response to the murder of George Floyd by the Minneapolis Police Department in 2020 will create change, though change has been promised in multiple states, from Minnesota to Pennsylvania. The protests have certainly been successful in changing general ideas around the Black Lives Matter movement and started a national conversation about defunding, disbanding, and abolishing the police—a conversation that seemed beyond the fringe a few years ago. We have also seen universal police brutality against protesters, press, and elected officials. Police have murdered and maimed protesters and allowed racists and fascists to murder and maim protesters.[14] US elected officials have encouraged this violence against peaceful protesters, especially President Trump. As protests continue at the time of this writing, we can only assume this brutality will grow worse, not better. Will the promised change actually occur? At the time of writing, we don't know. We can only continue to keep working.

How to Use This Book

This book hopes to provide a variety of paths to making that holistic change. Like a map with many trails, we expect readers to use what is viable to them in their community and set aside the rest. We framed this book around the manifestation of the climate crisis in the United States, but we hope other solarpunks across the globe will build off this book for their unique situation and community needs. In 2014, Adam Flynn defined solarpunk as a lifestyle focused on "ingenuity, generativity, independence, and community."[15] This book follows that model with four parts based off these ideas (though not in that order). Each part begins with an introduction, written by us, that questions and examines some of the larger solarpunk issues inherent in generativity, independence, community, and ingenuity. These introductions emphasize not just resistance to capitalism and climate disaster on its own but also how solarpunk can be used to resist capitalism structurally. How do we build a system that is inherently (or as close as possible) intolerant of capitalism and our ongoing ecocide? Rather than simply describing forms of resistance, our introductions will question further: How do we write capitalism, white supremacy, and colonialism out of the picture?

Each part is largely autonomous, and readers are welcome to flip to the pieces that sound useful to them. Reading this collection straight through might give a reader the greatest sense of the entangled nature of these ideas, but this book has been designed to be read in whatever order is useful. For example, someone new to solarpunk might want to check out the essays with solarpunk in the title, such as "Solarpunk Is a Verb for Rising" by The Commando Jugendstil and Tales from the EV Studio or "Solarpunk: The Fruitful Revolution" by Connor D. Louiselle. For readers most interested in the do-it-yourself aspect of solarpunk, we recommend skipping right to the end to part 4, Ingenuity, which features practical blueprints and instructions.

Part 1, Generativity, considers how stories, of both the past and the future, have propelled the United States to accept unsustainable consumerism, dragging much of the world with it. Part of transforming the Anthropocene will be the stories we tell moving forward. To generate new histories and alternate futures means to change structures. The generative aspects of solarpunk come not only from our ingenuity but the possibility of generating new forms of thinking, new lifestyles, and new relationships. The part begins with "Solarpunk Is a Verb for Rising" by The Commando Jugendstil and Tales from the EV Studio, an essay that explores the transformative possibilities of solarpunk to fight against inequality and ecofascism in our communities. Margaret Killjoy also considers community in the face of the pandemic. "In Defense of Hope" feels almost like a time capsule coming from April 2020 when the COVID-19 pandemic raged across the world and governments demonstrated their true disinterest in saving lives. Rather, Killjoy takes hope in the mutual aid groups that popped up, the rent strikes, the way communities came together to protect each other. There was, and is, hope in the face of great crisis. Following hope to action, Giulia Lepori and Michał Krawczyk consider how we can feed our imagination while engaging with the more-than-human world. Through a series of informal performative interviews, Lepori and Krawczyk guide the reader around the Thar dö Ling permaculture site. Their interviews with Simona Trecarichi and Danilo Colomela include recipes for compost, how to design a food forest, and permaculture in Italy. Finally, Christoph D. D. Rupprecht provides a garden shed of ideas, terms, and transformative possibilities for readers to explore in their own work and communities. Rupprecht's meditations represent a generative exercise of creating new narratives for communities across time and a new model for futurity that rejects the apocalypse as the end.

The second part focuses on independence. While our introduction explores a wider definition of independence from food sovereignty to abolition, these essays focus on material independence, mainly, how we can design away from our unsustainable power grid and power usage to something more equitable. First, Gabriel Aliaga reminds readers we must consider our mineral footprint. A professional geologist working in the mining industry, Aliaga explains how sustainable technology like solar panels or electric vehicles require materials to be mined, which inevitably impacts the rest of the living world. Instead, he questions our desire for more technology and how that can only lead to more mining. Following that thread, Navarre Bartz explores how designers could reconsider the life span of technology and provides guidelines to help makers rethink their projects. In "How to Build a Solar-Powered Website" by Kris De Decker, we see how sustainability, design, and DIY all come together to make a functioning piece of technology: a website. Decker explains his philosophy for powering his website through solar and provides instructions, examples, and references for others to rethink their designs. Part 2 ends with a more philosophical piece by Craig Stevenson. "Solarpunks See the World: Traversing the World without Destroying It" asks the reader not to abandon travel as inherently unsustainable but rather to redesign our methods of travel, often using slower forms, such as trains. Stevenson reminds us there is much to be learned and communities to be made across cultures, so let's redesign travel.

In preparation for the creation and maintenance of resilient, healthy, and long-lasting communities during and after the Sixth Extinction, part 3, Community, will explore routes toward building sustainable and self-reliant communities. To transform the end of the world, we must reexamine the meaning of intentional community, the focus of part 4. As class separation becomes more evident—whether it's Kanye West paying private firefighters to protect his house or the rise of GoFundMe as an answer to inconceivable medical debt—communities must move beyond monthly potlucks to more radical care for each other. Part of this radical care is pushing against individualism as proposed by capitalism and recognizing that even the human body is not individual but made up of numerous nonhumans. Through exploring ideas of kinship, this part considers how to find justice for human and nonhuman peoples, recognizing that social justice issues like abolishing the police is as much a success for environmental justice as it is for social justice. This part begins with "Science Fiction and Disability: Engage!" by Petra Kuppers, an essay on disability and narrative, which invites the reader to write their own story after Kuppers's prompt. Through the prompt, the reader turned writer is invited to think through what community looks like and is reminded of the violent oppression of disabled communities in the United States. The next essay, by Octavia Cade, takes a solarpunk look at how we can reconsider city design to be multispecies. Green spaces cannot just mean parks but must push deeper to reconsider what might happily live in the plumbing or vacant buildings set for demolition. Similarly, Susan Haris reconsiders community with street dogs in her essay "The Commensal Canine." Haris encourages the reader to shift their ideas of street dogs from pest or pet to Anthropocene adapters. Ultimately, this essay joins Cade's in asking us to reconsider the urban landscape as multispecies rather than humancentric. Part 3 ends with "Solarpunk: The Fruitful Revolution," by Connor D. Louiselle, which tuns the focus to a solarpunk understanding of literature and how solarpunk stories could encourage revolution. This essay returns to Kuppers's point that the stories we tell ourselves shape possibility.

The final part, Ingenuity, focuses on a foundational aspect of solarpunk, and the punk ethos in general: "do it yourself" thinking and action. The climate crisis has already created a narrative of reusing, reclaiming, and self-reliance, but as systems continue to crumble under the increasing stress of climate change, this DIY initiative will grow as modern society is salvaged and transformed. In our introduction, we emphasize that individual action will not save the planet, a common idea that the oil industry tries to push off on consumers—that the climate crisis is caused by your last Starbucks coffee or your neighbor not recycling. But what individual action and DIY action can perpetuate is a different relationship with the living world by sidestepping oppressive systems. This is a privileged response, but learning how to mend, forage food, grow trees, or build multispecies community gardens can all be tools for the community at large and create ways to thrive during the climate crisis. First, Sari Fordham shows how ingenuity can take small shapes by guiding the reader step-by-step through the clothes mending process. Next, Joy Lew and Vance Mullis of Critter Cove Farm demonstrate that the common narrative around how to correctly grow plants isn't the only story available, and they detail how anyone can grow food-bearing trees. Similarly, Michael J. DeLuca guides us through his foraging practices, suggesting we can relearn how to see ourselves as members of a complex and interdependent multispecies community with a long history of finding what we need in the world around us. Part 4 ends with an illustration by Christoph D. D. Rupprecht, Aoi Yoshida, and Lihua Cui, showing how to create a multispecies community garden—a truly solarpunk vision of depicting the present as well as the future and the transformation in between.

Ultimately, our ideas, and ideas contributed by others in this book, will not fit all situations, and anything irrelevant should be disregarded. Not all of this book will work for every person or every place, and that's okay as the climate crisis will impact every community differently. We also want to acknowledge that the language we use in this book will be outdated before it is sent to print, that how we talk about environmental and social justice is a constantly transforming dialogue trapped by our limited English. We have used certain terminology that we do not think is the best choice but is currently one of the only choices, such as Anthropocene, nonhuman, and more-than-human. We look forward to when these terms are replaced with more generous and respectful language.

In the end, being a solarpunk means totally upending the capitalist mode while having fun and keeping the hope. We'll see you out there.

Notes

Phoebe would like to thank Michael P. Branch and Daniel Ryan Morse for their early advice and support of the collection.

1. Greta Thunberg, "The Disarming Case to Act Right Now on Climate Change," *TED*, 2018, https://www.ted.com/talks/greta_thunberg_the_disarming_case_to_act_right_now_on_climate/transcript?language=en.
2. The first reference is generally regarded to be a blog post called "From Steampunk to Solarpunk" by Republic of the Bees on a now-defunct website.
3. Victoria Blake, "Introduction," in *Cyberpunk: Stories of Hardware, Software, Wetware, Revolution, and Evolution*, ed. Victoria Blake (Portland, OR: Underland Press, 2013), 10.
4. Jess Nevins, "The 19th-century Roots of Steampunk," in *Steampunk*, eds. Jeff VanderMeer and Ann VanderMeer (San Francisco: Tachyon Publications, 2008), 10.
5. Ann VanderMeer, "Introduction," in *Steampunk III: Steampunk Revolution* (San Francisco: Tachyon Publications, 2013), 11.
6. VanderMeer, "Introduction," 10.
7. Blake, "Introduction," 10.
8. Ivan Gololobov, "Immigrant Punk: The Struggle for Post-Modern Authenticity," in *Fight Back: Punk, Politics, and Resistance*, ed. The Subcultures Network (Oxford: Oxford University Press, 2017), 77.
9. Phoebe Wagner and Brontë Christopher Wieland, "Introduction," in *Sunvault: Stories of Solarpunk & Eco-Speculation* (Nashville, TN: Upper Rubber Boot Books, 2017), 3.
10. Cheryll Glotfelty and Harold Fromm, eds., *The Ecocriticism Reader: Landmarks in Literary Ecology* (Athens: University of Georgia Press, 1996), xxiv.
11. "Tricia Hersey on Rest as Resistance," *For the Wild with Ayana Young*, June 8, 2020, podcast, 00:07:10–00:07:22, https://forthewild.world/listen/tricia-hersey-on-rest-as-resistance-185.
12. Nick Estes, *Our History Is the Future: Standing Rock Versus the Dakota Access Pipeline, and the Long Tradition of Indigenous Resistance* (New York: Verso, 2019), prologue, Kindle.
13. Olivia Rosane, " 'It's Not Going to Get Turned around in 10 Years': Sen. Feinstein Criticized for Dismissive Attitude to Young Climate Activists," *EcoWatch*, 2019, https://www.ecowatch.com/senator-feinstein-green-new-deal-2629995045.html.
14. Mara Hvistendahl and Alleen Brown, "Armed Vigilantes Antagonizing Protesters Have Received a Warm Reception from Police," *The Intercept*, June 19, 2020. https://theintercept.com/2020/06/19/militia-vigilantes-police-brutality-protests/.
15. Adam Flynn, "Solarpunk: Notes toward a Manifesto," *Hieroglyph*, September 4, 2014, https://hieroglyph.asu.edu/2014/09/solarpunk-notes-toward-a-manifesto/.

PART 1

GENERATIVITY

Not Just Solar: Creating Our Own Powers, Stories, and Spaces

Brontë Christopher Wieland

The creation of a solarpunk worldview requires a complete renegotiation of humanity's relationships with itself, with nature, with nations, with food, fashion, culture, urbanity and rurality, with our collective and individual aspirations and our systems of survival. As part of this reimagining, we must interrogate humanity's role, place, and dominion in the world (particularly as many cultures in the Global North currently understand them), and we must ask ourselves what purpose those factors serve, who benefits from the answers as they are now. Only once that is clear can we move forward and ask those same questions of a solarpunk future.

This reimagining is a daunting task, no doubt. But in the face of global climate disaster, a complete deconstruction and reconstruction of our systems of being is perhaps our only option.

To answer these queries and to usher new answers into existence, all while fighting the despair and ennui that climate activists know is all too pervasive, solarpunk needs a creative, constructive force that propels us forward. A spirit that emphasizes practicality and doability, that traces a path toward the future that is relatable, adaptable, attainable, and accessible. We call this essence *generativity*.

In a broad sense, the solarpunk conceptualization of generativity draws from DIY and maker philosophies. Most solarpunks would agree that if you can make/grow/find/forage/borrow something and you have the means, then there is no need to buy it. But generativity changes the scale. Rather than throwing everything away and starting fresh (a strategy based on the assumption of consequenceless resource extraction), how can we make something new from what we already have on social and global levels? How can we repurpose the tools at our disposal today to build a world that can survive the already-inevitable consequences of climate destabilization and mass extinction? How can we begin rewriting and renewing our relationships to the world around us?

And how can we build resistance to future ecological disasters into the process? The future doesn't exist in a vacuum, and so solarpunk ideas must work from the present forward, acknowledging the realities they are born of.

In a more tangible sense, generativity as a guiding principle of solarpunk is also important because of the movement's explicit opposition to the broad systems of continual, heedless production that define habits of consumption in the Global North (and, all too often, that enable industrial, environmental, and human exploitation in the Global South). The world's current relationship with production is one that standardizes and values *overproduction*, planned obsolescence, constant replacement, discardability, and excess, all of which together have led to massive deforestation, rampant plastic pollution, destruction of water systems and sources, widespread habitat loss, significantly decreased biodiversity, homogenization of global food systems, destruction of local food systems, and so much more. Instead of modern production, which necessitates growth and fails to account for destructive processes and waste, we propose generativity as a creative model that is based on need, sustainability, autonomy, and diversity, that takes into full consideration what is destroyed in order to create as a form of reciprocity, while eschewing assumptions of austerity that often treat social needs like leisure and pleasure as extraneous. In advocating for a model of generativity over productivity, we seek a conscious and mindful balance between what is needful, what is expedient, and what is fun.

The authors in this part will cover different perspectives on generating solarpunk realities, but we also want to address three crucial areas and encourage others to explore and examine these areas as anchors for generative action:

- The weaving of new cultural narratives
- The creation of spaces where solarpunk ideas can thrive
- The generation of power in multiple forms

These three actions form the foundations of solarpunks' attempts to transform their local realities, and while they may seem tasks of a gargantuan magnitude, many groups have already been laying the groundwork for these changes for decades. That is to say: nothing in this book is impossible, not even remotely. We present here starting points, action plans, and proof that even when it feels impossible to gain momentum, there is always a way forward.

Narrative

Many before us, from Edward Said to Robin Wall Kimmerer and Ursula K. Le Guin, have noted the role narrative plays in our relationship to and understanding of our worlds. Every manner of storytelling, from film to folktales and music, both reflects and informs the way we view history, the present day, possible futures, culture, and so on. Stories are, in many ways, a foundation of society, providing large groups of people with easily internalizable and relatively consistent bases of reference. In short, the stories we tell contain deep revelations about our worldviews, our cultural philosophies, and the assumptions we make about reality.

If you were raised in the United States, you most likely know many stories of origin and predestination, from the heroism and martyrdom of the Revolutionary War to settlers invoking manifest destiny to "tame the wilderness" and the unequivocal patriotic unity of World War II. If you're a Christian, you probably know the stories of the Old Testament: the fall from grace, Cain and Abel, David and Goliath. If you're Anishinaabe, you probably know the stories of Nanabozho. If you're Spanish, you probably know the stories of los reyes católicos who drove out the Moorish peoples and "united" Spain. Each example above is just a singular telling among the massive web of stories that inform our cultural identities. Whether these tales are ultimately "true" or not, they are the foundation of what we believe about ourselves and our pasts. But stories like these are more than cultural history. They transmit values, teach morals, and create a fabric for bringing in-groups together.

This effect isn't unique to what we label our mythology, legend, or history. Contemporary forms of storytelling do the same work, though oftentimes less overtly and more passively. Even the most unassuming, unpretentious, "nonphilosophical" movies and TV shows present a specific construction of the world for viewers to become immersed in, and while storytellers are always projecting their ideas and values onto the stories they create, we as listeners are also necessarily absorbing the same right back from them. So it is that, to take a giant of an example, the Marvel Cinematic Universe has come to both define and be defined by what (largely American) audiences view as heroism and struggles against evil and adversity. Similarly, rom-coms shape and are shaped by what we believe about love, sex, and passion. The same for horror and a society's collective fears.

This isn't intentional so much as it is inevitable. We learn from what we experience and what we take in. Consider all the 1980s movies produced in the United States that featured a villain with a Russian accent and a mission to destroy the world, and then consider all the children who grew up *after* the fall of the USSR, *after* the end of the prevailing narrative that the greatest threat to the United States was Russian plots, who still associate the timbre of Russian-tinged English with villainy.

The give-and-take described here creates a kind of feedback loop, a self-reinforcing relationship with lived experience in which cultural biases can become firmly entrenched to the point of becoming "fact" by default. In other words, if we tell ourselves a story enough times, it becomes true. This idea of narrative power to reflect and inform underlies such work as David Graeber and David Wengrow's analysis of the impact of Jean-Jacques Rosseau on our (mis)understanding of humanity's past in their essay "How to Change the Course of Human History" and Edward Said's *Culture and Imperialism* (1994).[1]

Said's theory of Orientalism perhaps deserves a brief explanation here. While ubiquitous in academic circles, the oppression signified by the term Orientalism still thrives today. Said writes: "Orientalism can be discussed and analyzed as the corporate institution for dealing with the Orient [Asia and West Asia]—dealing with it by making statements about it, authorizing views of it, describing it, by teaching it, settling it, ruling over it: in short, Orientalism is a Western style for dominating, restructuring, and having authority over the Orient."[2] While this idea applies to the examples above of who Hollywood might cast as a blockbuster villain, it's just as important to understanding how "Western" countries like the United States, Canada, and the United Kingdom create systems of power through story and knowledge, two major tools.

This phenomenon results in a set of stories and assumptions about oneself that a group accepts as truth. This applies on all levels—individual, familial, local, national, societal, global, etc. But these stories are not immutable. They are not fixed or permanent. These stories can be subverted, rewritten, and unwritten.

As Prasenjit Duara writes, "No movement of major social change has succeeded without a compelling symbology and affective power."[3] If solarpunk's goal is to envision and foment a new green, egalitarian future that addresses and mitigates the threats of climate disaster, it is necessary to examine the larger cultural narratives that are currently driving us through the Earth's sixth mass extinction and then to generate new narratives for a new future.

Space

As crucial as narratives are to codifying a solarpunk ethos, they are only a beginning, and they can't stand on their own in any impactful way. Like a robust rhizome, our narratives and ideas need a carefully calibrated growing medium to thrive in. They need places to be nurtured, developed, evolved, and shared, places to spread from. These spaces can function as test runs and trial grounds for burgeoning ideologies, methods, and structures, and they may become the first spaces where new narratives bridge the gap into lived experience.

Several such community spaces have popped up online, from the early solarpunk tags on Tumblr to the publisher Solarpunk Press, from the monthly #solarpunkchat held on Twitter to Sunbeam.City, a libertarian socialist "democratically-run co-operative of like-minded individuals" that, in 2019, hosted a community of approximately two thousand users through a federated social media platform that uses software such as Mastodon and Pleroma. These spaces have been integral in the generation of solarpunk ideas and practices and in helping the concept of solarpunk reach a broader audience. The success of these efforts is marked by their growth and activity as well as by institutional recognition. In July 2021, Tor.com, one of the largest publishers of speculative fiction in the United States, published the first of two novellas marketed under the solarpunk label.

As of now, there are very few examples, if any, of dedicated and thriving solarpunk associations outside of the internet. We can only speculate, based on the success of digital solarpunk communities, what such groups could accomplish. But seeing as one of the core tenets of solarpunk is practicality and feasible action, we expect solarpunk's transition to a full-fledged physical movement to be a momentous one, marked by a diversity of tactics and a focus on physical, mental, and financial accessibility.

Power

Finally we've arrived at what is perhaps the most obvious and the most frequent question asked in regard to solarpunk. So we should get all our power from solar panels, huh?

No!

Even if we indulged the fantasy that the world could sustainably produce enough solar panels to populate every home and every community with them, we still can't feasibly expect solar panels to power the world the way we're used to. Such a plan would never work in places that receive too much yearly cloud cover, in high-latitude communities, or in heavily forested areas, to name just a few examples. In addition, current large-scale solar technologies rely on centralization and proprietary control, which notably decrease a community's independence and self-reliance. Gabriel Aliaga, in part 2, further reminds us that even our most sustainable technologies rely on massive mining operations. The process of reckoning with this reality will inevitably include reworking our relationships to power in every way.

As we outlined at the beginning of the chapter, generativity is based in need, sustainability, autonomy, and diversity. Communities around the world have widely variable needs that demand a diversity of solutions. We advocate for local answers to energy needs based on what resources are available and accessible to a community. An array of energy solutions also promotes resilience through redundancy. If you're getting all your power from one source, then you're more vulnerable and small failures can have large impacts. When feasible, maintaining multiple sources of power is ideal.

Not only should we not power the world exclusively through solar energy, in this part we propose decentering electricity and combustion as our default modes of power, treating them instead as enhancements to our ability to generate power rather than the source of that ability. In exploring power in this way, we hope to gain an understanding of where the world's rapidly growing consumption of energy is directed and how it can be redirected and reduced by focusing on sustainability. Given the Intergovernmental Panel on Climate Change's assertions that we must globally achieve net-zero annual emissions within thirty years, it is prudent to move efforts beyond energy efficiency and into the reduction of energy use, which is disproportionately concentrated in a small number of countries.[4]

We would also like to examine the generation of power in an institutional sense. A core strategy of solarpunk is creating infrastructure both as resistance to exploitative and oppressive systems and as active replacements for said systems. Rather than from an officiating state, this power emanates from grassroots community organization, directly addressing local needs and desires and dissolving communities' dependence on power structures imposed from the outside. Throughout the book, we refer to strategies and alternative systems that work in counter to the institutional power of states as "dual power," in accord with Murray Bookchin's usage of the term.[5] In this model, grassroots organizations and coalitions build structures of support and governance independent of local, state, and federal governments, and in doing so make hegemonic state powers obsolete.

After more than two decades of climate change apathy and denialism from world governments and major corporations (particularly American), and a much longer history of environmental antagonism from the same bodies, particularly against Indigenous groups. For example, the United States' efforts in the 1800s to eradicate native bison as part of a genocidal crusade against the continent's Indigenous groups, particularly the Plains Nations; the continued destruction of the Amazon rain forest in search of oil and arable land; and the Obama administration's refusal to take definitive action against the Dakota Access Pipeline's route through Standing Rock Sioux territory and the area's primary source of fresh water. It seems obvious to many solarpunks that demanding change of ponderous institutions with vested interests in maintaining a status quo will not yield radical climate action soon enough.[6] Dual power, then, offers an opportunity to generate our own responses to and fortifications against climate destabilization while amassing organizational power to pressure large institutions to act against climate change. Considering the popular statistic that only 100 companies are responsible for over 70 percent of humans' carbon emissions, there are certainly no lasting solutions to climate change that can be implemented on a personal scale, and there ultimately may be none within the global structures currently driving climate change, making the development of robust systems of dual power one of our most urgent priorities.[7]

Efforts to build dual power may take the form of regaining seed and food sovereignty (a movement that, in the US, has largely been stressed by Indigenous peoples whose diverse food systems were often destroyed outright or appropriated and made prohibitively costly in a variation of what's now called the "embrace, extend, and extinguish" strategy) or permaculture, agroforestry, and silvopasture movements; solidarity economics; community implementation of alternative markets and currencies; a culture of member- and worker-owner cooperatives instead of profit-seeking businesses; community-led educational initiatives; meshnets; transformative alternatives to policing; and much more.[8]

These efforts can also take place on many scales: rural neighborhood groups renegotiating their relationship to agricultural methods, town councils and other democratic or consensual municipal levels, confederations and coalitions of groups implementing any combination of the above strategies,[9] and potentially even at city scales. As Mike Childs writes in the foreword to *Sharing Cities: A Case for Truly Smart and Sustainable Cities*, "There is the potential for the world's cities to drive a very different future; a future where cities take their environmental and social responsibilities seriously; a future were cities transform themselves and the rest of the world; a future where cities not only fix themselves but also fix the planet."[10] While we doubt the ability of cities to simply "fix the planet" without entirely eradicating the prevailing systems of exploitation that currently allow them to prosper, a solarpunk future will without question have a distinct and perhaps unrecognizable relationship to urbanity.

Toward Generating Our Own Systems

The pieces in this part cover perspectives on the utility of hope, forging new relationships with and understandings of our surrounding environments, describing foundational terms and concepts to build forward from, and more.

Taken together, they offer us new and important perspectives on moving into a solarpunk future. We encourage readers to take the ideas presented here and make them their own, expand them, and investigate modes of generativity we haven't yet thought of or codified. These pieces cover perspectives on generating our own systems through the stories we tell, our design methodologies, our interactions with local environments, and more.

In "Solarpunk Is a Verb for Rising," The Commando Jugendstil and the collective Tales from the EV Studio write a manifesto about how solarpunk cannot play to a larger entertainment audience. Instead, solarpunk must transfer to local communities and become a tool for those communities. Throughout the essay, the writers generate ideas for equitable change and how to fight back against capitalism. A major tool in that arsenal is narrative, as other writers in this collection argue (such as Petra Kuppers and Connor D. Louiselle in part 3), because narrative in the United States can be so hegemonic, while solarpunk has the opportunity to be as nonhegemonic as possible. The authors point out that solarpunk can be a tool for communities because it can help imagine and reconsider what the future might look like from an anticapitalist and Just Transition standpoint.

Next, Margaret Killjoy's essay "In Defense of Hope" comes from a specific moment in time: April 2020, when COVID-19 cases were rising and there was no vaccine in sight. These were difficult days that will continue until there is a global vaccination response and recognition that everyone deserves equal access to vaccines. Killjoy's essay is situated in a moment that many of us would rather forget, but she points out the hope that foregrounded those early days, such as mutual aid networks and rent strikes. It is still unclear how the pandemic has entirely changed our society, but we echo Killjoy in hoping we will still remember how to care for each other in the deeper ways the pandemic inspired.

"Feeding Imagination" enlarges that network of care to the more-than-human and considers the generativity of soil and feces. Particularly donkey feces. Through the informal interviews conducted and shaped by Giulia Lepori and Michał Krawczyk, the reader is invited to visit the permaculture center Thar dö Ling in Sicily, Italy. In a meditative discussion on compost, the permaculture designers Simona Trecarichi and Danilo Colomela remind us to recognize the entangledness of the living world and how everything from feces to hay to humanity is engaged in that complexity.

Part 1 ends with a collection of "tools" from Christoph D. D. Rupprecht's "A Collective Gardening Shed of Concepts for Planting Solarpunk Futures."

Rupprecht curates a shed of ideas for the reader to choose from, demonstrating there is no singular fix to the climate crisis and its interlinked social justice issues but instead recognizing their entanglement by pairing concepts like solidarity and biocultural diversity. These tools range from tactics of feminist care to the idea of informality when considering a response to an issue.

To begin the book, we wanted essays that excite, that have readers making notes in the margins, imagining how a community could generate new systems in response to oppression. Not every piece in this part will apply to each community or need, but this amalgamation of voices shows the variety of responses from manifesto writing to compost turning.

Notes

1. David Graeber and David Wengrow, "How to Change the Course of Human History," *Eurozine*, March 2, 2018, https://www.eurozine.com/change-course -human-history/.
2. Edward W. Said, *Culture and Imperialism* (New York: Vintage Books, 1994), 3.
3. Prasenjit Duara, *The Crisis of Global Modernity: Asian Tradition and a Sustainable Future* (Cambridge: Cambridge University Press, 2015), 282.
4. Elizabeth Shove, "What Is Wrong with Energy Efficiency?" *Building Research & Information* 46, no. 7 (August 2018): 779–89; "Total Energy Consumption," *Enerdata*, accessed June 12, 2019, https://yearbook.enerdata.net/total-energy /world-consumption-statistics.html.
5. Murray Bookchin, "Thoughts on Libertarian Municipalism," Institute of Social Ecology, accessed June 12, 2019, https://social-ecology.org/wp/1999/08/thoughts -on-libertarian-municipalism/.
6. Roxanne Dunbar-Ortiz, *An Indigenous Peoples' History of the United States* (Boston: Beacon Press, 2014), 142; Rhett A. Butler, "Amazon Destruction," *Mongabay*, April 9, 2019, https://rainforests.mongabay.com/amazon/amazon_destruction.html.
7. Tess Riley, "Just 100 Companies Responsible for 71% of Global Emissions, Study Says," *The Guardian*, July 10, 2017, https://www.theguardian.com/sustainable -business/2017/jul/10/100-fossil-fuel-companies-investors-responsible-71-global -emissions-cdp-study-climate-change.
8. Ava Tomasula y Garcia, "Inside Mexico's Anti-Capitalist Marketplaces," *In These Times*, August 16, 2018, https://www.inthesetimes.com/article/21332/mexico -capitalism-marketplace-alternative-currencies-pesos-economy-profit.
9. For example, see the community organizing group Symbiosis, which is "creating institutions of participatory democracy and the solidarity economy through community organizing, neighborhood by neighborhood, city by city." More information can be found at: https://www.symbiosis-revolution.org/.
10. Duncan McLaren and Julian Agyeman, *Sharing Cities: A Case for Truly Smart and Sustainable Cities* (Cambridge, MA: MIT Press, 2017), vii.

CHAPTER 1

Solarpunk Is a Verb for Rising

The Commando Jugendstil and Tales from the EV Studio

During our discussions on Twitter, the question of how solarpunk can reach a broader community is often asked. One of the solutions offered is that solarpunk should become more mainstream and follow market trends and logics to capture a broader base of content consumers.

Time and time again we have come out in opposition to this notion, and we stand by it.

In this historical, political, and environmental conjuncture, with the climate crisis under way, the rise of global fascism, the destruction of workers' rights, a sweeping global pandemic stemming from climate-wrecking deforestation and supercharged by wrecked welfare systems and for-profit healthcare, and a mental health epidemic rooted in all of the above, we lost the privilege of pretending that we're apolitical; we can't afford the luxury of playing hide-and-seek with social and political issues to appease the market because we have been told that this is what consumers want.

This doesn't mean that solarpunk needs to become prescriptive or "preachy" (which is a problematic term as it's often used to demean works and authors perceived to be too political).

It also doesn't need to model some sort of perfect idealized activism, because this is actually a regressive strategy that is used to derail the efforts of climate activists and make people feel insecure about their actions, and even pull back from efforts, because they cannot physically, financially, or psychologically achieve anything close to perfection.[1]

The idea of "gold star activism" rests heavily on the idea that individuals or consumers can make a difference by adopting ethical lifestyles and consumption choices without addressing the issue that some of these choices are only available to people who are fortunate (or privileged) enough to have disposable income to pay the sustainability premium, which is absolutely not the general case, seeing that many folks work two or three jobs to make ends meet and have to choose between food and heat.

We are indoctrinated to believe that as wealthy and privileged people in the Global North, we are powerful, that our main power rests in our wallets, and that our styles of consumption are an integral part of our identities and of the image we project to the world—which incidentally is why lifestyle branding is such a lucrative activity for corporations.

Some people cannot afford to eat only vegan, organic, sustainable food.

Some people need the much-maligned plastic straws to drink safely because of their medical conditions.

Some people cannot ditch the car because they live in dormitory suburbs with no reliable public transport.

Some people are reluctant to be arrested because they are migrants who risk their right to remain if they incur criminal sentences, or have a justified fear of the police because of how policing is done in their countries of origin, or because they are part of demographics that are at higher risk of police brutality, such as disabled folks, LGBTQIPA+ folks, or communities of color.

That doesn't mean their activism is not valid or that they are not trying hard enough.

We think that if you are lucky enough to be able to do any of the above, you should definitely go for it, because every little bit helps, but individual action is not going to win this fight alone, especially because capitalism is already selling us sustainability as a commodity and a lifestyle choice.

What really matters, the place in which our power really resides, is the fact that we are citizens, that we are part of local communities, of trade unions and collectives and organizations, of neighborhood knitting groups, of Local Exchange Trading Schemes (LETS) where people share their skills and their time in mutual aid and to improve their communities, that we are human beings, integrated in social networks that transcend capitalism, that we are the many and they are the few, and that when we come together we are the tide that no seawall can stop, and that this has always been true, from the first strike in Deir el-Medina in the Late Bronze Age to the popular uprisings that toppled Nazism in northern Italy to the myriad fights for social, economic, and environmental justice that are waged on Earth every day.

The way we see it, to really become a force to be reckoned with, solarpunk needs to become as counterhegemonic as possible, and to do so it needs to move away from the idea that the system we're currently living in is so invincible that the only thing that can topple it is the end of the world as we know it. It needs to base its narratives in near futures in which humanity fights against the climate crisis and reshapes and revolutionizes the system into one that centers the care of humans and nature, rather than narratives in which a lucky few somehow survive the collapse of environmental support systems and society to start afresh. Privileging the latter narratives means admitting that the dichotomy between human society and environment proposed by the greater part of Western thought is right and that harmony with the environment can only be bought at the price of millions of human lives.

Stories are an essential part of how we experience and comprehend the world.[2] While it is quite clear that fiction does not directly translate into reality in a one-to-one fashion, as feared by some critics of transformative works, narratives strengthen or create social and cultural expectations about what people can or cannot, should or should not, do. For example, the classical novels of the eighteenth century, as dissected by Edward W. Said in *Culture and Imperialism* (1993),[3] were based on the assumption of French or English imperial power and used it as a backdrop to the happenings of their protagonists without engaging critically with it, thus strengthening its status as the "natural state of things."

Narratives don't just reflect mores, they also create expectations and associations. Lifestyle branding, the process whereby advertisers tell you a story about what using a product means, has turned brands themselves into narratives of success, wealth, and aspiration to which people can take part through consumption, as Naomi Klein explains in *No Logo* (1990).[4] Brands capitalize on the aspirations of their consumers, telling them that by consuming their product they, too, can be part of something wonderful and bigger than themselves, of an exotic adventure, of a successful team, of a selected group of attractive, empowered individuals. They play up the supposed exclusivity and quality of their products by selecting influential testimonials, whose qualities consumers are supposed to share in by buying the product, when in fact branded products are often made by the same people in the same factories that make off-brand products. What consumers pay for essentially is not the product but the myth.

Associations created by the stories we tell about ourselves and other people have striking real-life consequences. Psychological experiments, detailed by Cordelia Fine in her book *Delusions of Gender* (2010), have shown that focusing on the social/cultural expectations and the narratives inherent in belonging to one or another identity conditions the results of real-life outcomes, like the experimental math tests used in studies like these.[5] In other words, the narrative about women being worse than men at math, once internalized by women, poses a real barrier in their achievements in math tests, either because they expect to fail or because they're so anxious to disprove the myth that their concentration on the task flags, or a combination of both.

Other studies and our own lived experience show that when politicians allow themselves to use dehumanizing, derogatory language and narratives toward marginalized groups, hostile acts and feelings toward these groups increase in the general population.[6] This is particularly evident in the way racist myths about Black men have been used for decades to justify their targeting (and outright murder) by police forces worldwide under the thin guise of "defending law and order."[7] Narratives associating Blackness with drug crime or Islam with terrorism and erosion of various national cultural heritages have been the bread and butter of right-wing parties worldwide, through which they have painted a picture of a society on the brink of chaos, threatened by lawlessness and invasion, which only their strong hand can steer away from catastrophe.[8]

Stories have power, and not just on the present or the past but also on the future. Cory Doctorow and other authors like to think of science fiction as an exercise in prototyping, in design of possible futures.[9] It has long shaped our expectation of outer space and cyberspace, stoked our fear or curiosity toward beings from other planets.

Now as the world wakes up with variable speed to the reality of the climate and biodiversity emergency, different types of stories are emerging on what the future and society look like, but not all of these responses are positive or helpful.

There is a trend in science fiction, and in popular culture in general, to portray grim, cruel, bleak futures and for people to think that those are the best, most profound stories, the ones that stare unflinchingly at the truth. Sad, negative facts and feelings seem more credible, more true, than positive ones. Tragedy is the highest form of literature, comedy the lowest, to say it with good old Aristotle, and the climate emergency makes for some really good tragedy.

Author after author, from Jonathan Franzen to David Wallace-Wells just to mention two of the most prominent ones, queue up in front of the microphones to tell us that it is over.[10] We as a species have collectively messed up because of our inherent moral failures; in hindsight civilization was doomed from the start; everything we ever did was marred by hubris, so really agriculture was the root of all evils and we should have remained hunter-gatherers (even though according to preeminent anthropologists this is a historical misconception).[11] These authors lament that we are all to blame for the disaster we have wrought upon the Earth, so no one is really to blame. It is like Aesop's fable of the scorpion and the frog: human nature is to blame, and there is nothing we can do about it.

The crisis is impossible to solve, so there is no point in trying. Hubris, remember? The most we can do is weather it and try to survive it, somehow, to find joy in the little things and return to that preindustrial, perhaps preagricultural, state of original innocence.

Palingenesis, the idea that the world has to burn to be reborn, purified, from its ashes, always has an appeal, except that if this really happened to the world, lots—and we mean billions—of people will die and even more will become displaced, and there will be uncountable suffering everywhere.

If this doesn't seem bad enough, there is not just climate defeatism and its conflation of extractive capitalism and neocolonialism with human nature to contend with but also the right-wing, nationalist, and identitarian responses to the crisis.

The enmeshment between environmentalism and bigotry is nothing new, and it could be argued that it was foundational for conservationism in the USA.[12] Reaching back to the mythical ahistoric "Indigenous," white-only Europe and into the fascist imaginary of the communion of (white) people with their land, alt-right and identitarian groups are putting forward their own "solutions" to the climate and biodiversity crisis.[13] These solutions frame climate action as a nationalist concern and seek to assuage people's fear of the crisis by promising a safe haven behind national borders—but only for the right categories of people, defined on a racial or nationalistic basis.[14]

Ecofascist discourse is strengthened by the fact that the crisis is creating situations of exceptionality, when decisions need to be taken quickly and people feel at a loss about what to do and what to think and find some safety in letting others, people perceived as decisive and strong, decide for them.

Ethnonationalism gives them a fertile background of narratives over the supposed "invasion" of white-majority countries by immigrants of color and the existential threat they pose to "Western values," whatever they might be, but speculative fiction, especially some of the so-called classics, gives them plenty of narrative ammunition too.

Tom Godwin's "The Cold Equations" (1954),[15] a sci-fi "classic" from the 1950s that the editor, John W. Campbell—who was a horrible, horrible person[16]—really strove to make as abhorrent as possible, is the typical story in which emergency situations force "hard people" (read: cis-het white men) to make "hard choices" for the greater good, and it posits that alternatives are just wishful thinking by liberal bleeding hearts because physics and logic reign supreme and the world is a cold, cruel place.

As Cory Doctorow, James Davis Nicoll, and Marissa Lingen rightfully analyze, "The Cold Equations" is not actually about the inevitability of physics but about unfair, unequal systems built by horrible people who use hard facts/nature/science to justify their cruelty toward other beings in upholding them.[17]

It's a bit like when people use violent metaphors to talk about evolution and praise the ruthless aspects of nature as a model for society, while completely forgetting that the same process that gave us the age-old competition between predator and prey also gave us fungal networks that help trees talk to each other and share nutrients with ailing relatives, or penguins huddling together against the cold, or symbiosis.[18] Pseudo-evolutionary talk focused on concepts such as strength, viciousness, and competition is another huge red flag that we should be mindful of when dissecting narratives about society and environment, as it often has not-so-hidden undertones of ableism, xenophobia, and racism, casting certain categories of people as "weak" and "unfit" to survive, say, a major crisis like the multiple ones we're living through at the moment.

Another example of the value systems that sustain ecofascist imaginaries is *Farnham's Freehold* (1964),[19] another "classic" written by likely crypto-fascist Robert A. Heinlein. With its insistence on "lifeboat rules" as a counter to democratic discussion about choices among a group of postapocalyptic survivors, this story is an example of how emergency situations can and will be used to entrench power by dominant groups and relegate moral choices and democracy to the status of luxuries that society can no longer afford.

Even shying away from extreme examples like this, sci-fi—postapocalyptic sci-fi in particular—has a rich history of every-person-for-themself, leave-the-weak-behind story lines and of valuing characters only if they have some sort of magic power or superhuman ability to compensate for another real or perceived weakness,[20] a penchant that explicitly or implicitly labels some categories of human beings as useless or a drain on resources and singles them out for abandonment or, in the best-case scenario, a tear-jerker self-sacrifice scene to lift any guilt from the abled protagonists' shoulders.

As Naomi Klein explained in her book *The Shock Doctrine* (2007),[21] disasters make societies vulnerable to assaults and appropriation of their resources and structures and to a weakening of democracy to "maintain order" in a situation of emergency, even though it has been demonstrated over and over that societal collapse and *homo homini lupus* situations in the aftermath of a disaster are elite myths and that emergency situations actually spark pro-social behavior in human groups.[22] The pandemic has only confirmed this, with the blooming of pro-social activities aimed at helping the most vulnerable, from hackathons to produce ventilators[23] and face shields[24] to the organization of mutual help groups.[25]

On the other hand, the 2008 financial crisis and the worldwide austerity snap that followed have demonstrated how artificial enforced scarcity can be used to frame some rights and public functions as unaffordable "luxuries" and devalue the rights of marginalized communities and normalize their sacrifice.

In the United Kingdom, austerity has caused about 130,000 preventable deaths in ten years,[26] many of them disabled people whose welfare allowances were drastically reduced or terminated. Looking forward, conservative thinkers have already tried to complain that antidiscrimination rules do not allow "Indigenous Europeans" to keep valuable resources for their own community.[27]

This can only get worse as the climate breaks down further. All the stories that perpetuate the idea that the world is cruel and it should be (but not to people like you, of course, only to people who are different, criminal, or question the "natural rules" on how things should be), that altruism and solidarity are luxuries, and that loyalty and sympathy go to the in-group pave the way for people to expect and perform cruelty in times of crisis. They set up the expectation for who will try to be on the good (loyal, productive, valuable) side of the divide between those who will be allocated resources and those who will be left behind, and to perform and enact this division to gain social brownie points.

To be really impactful and counterhegemonic, solarpunk needs to give people the hope that things can be made better, that yes, the world is unfair, cruel, and full of injustice, but that it doesn't have to be, that it was never meant to be.

Solarpunk needs to believe in the human capacity for compassion and solidarity, for generosity and reciprocity, because these are the traits that helped us get so far,[28] and they are the ones that will get us out of this mess.

It needs to do away with the idea that human nature and capitalist mentality are one and the same, that this mess is a product of our faulty moral nature as a species, or of the inevitability of progress, when it's the consequence of an ideology that prizes greed and profit above all else, especially nature and human lives.[29]

It needs to move beyond the spec-fic staples of the "chosen one" or the "enlightened few" to show that collective action, internationalism, intersectionalism, and solidarity can make a difference, that mass mobilization can topple even the most entrenched inequality, and that no one can do everything, but everybody can do something, together.

It needs to make space not only for our grief and melancholy at what's been lost but for our anger at why and how.

It needs to name names and lay blame where it should be laid.

At present there are well-thought-out plans to make the shift we need to survive this crisis. Green New Deals, Lucas Plans, Transition Initiatives.[30] They are out there and they could solve the climate crisis, austerity, and the rise of fascism all at once, but to do so they need people to back them, to want them, to see that future clearly enough to be willing to fight for it for as long as it takes.

Solarpunk needs to show that the seeds of a new postcapitalist, post-growth, sustainable world already exist in the cracks of the old. It needs to show people that the power of imagination can widen those cracks and create something new and beautiful and fair.

It needs to represent workers organizing to decarbonize and demilitarize their sectors to make them socially useful and beneficial. It needs to show people having meaningful lives and jobs in thriving communities.

It needs to show city dwellers making space for agriculture, environmental restoration, public transport, and affordable, well-insulated housing and community spaces out of the capitalist wasteland of non-places.

It needs to show farmers reclaiming abandoned rural towns and building agro-silvo-pastoral communes.

It needs to show communities reclaiming craft traditions to replace unsustainable industrial processes.

Solarpunk needs to have the Just Transition[31] and its consequences as the meat and bones of its stories and to engage with the choices that we are faced with, between fairness and barbarism, between sharing the bounties of the world equally and hoarding them to survive a bit longer while the world burns, between respecting the Earth, our home and provider, and looting it to the last drop of resources.

It needs to let people see at least a glimpse of the better world that people all over the globe, from schoolkids to the teenage organizers of Fridays for Future, UK Strike for Climate Network, and Youth Strike 4 Climate, just to name a few, to Indigenous leaders, community organizers, and trade union activists, are fighting relentlessly to secure.

It needs to let them believe that this world just beyond the horizon is attainable, there for us if we can make it real.

But that alone is not enough. It is not enough that we sit in our offices or homes and write or that we go to literary and academic conventions to talk about how speculative fiction and solarpunk can be used as design tools.

The experiences of *The Weight of Light* anthology edited by Joey Escherisch and Clark A. Miller (2019),[32] the Berlin Solarpunk Festival,[33] and the Budapest-based Future & Co. interactive theater experience[34] are steps forward, but they are limited to academics and experts, or are finite in time. To really make a difference, solarpunk needs to go out there, into the movements and into the activist spaces, to become permanently embedded in them as a tool in their arsenal to allow people to experiment with ideas around their future, about what a Just Transition would mean to them, about what radical municipalism and direct democracy could look like in practice, and about where the pitfalls and the slippery slopes are, so they can be recognized and avoided.

Solarpunk practitioners need to team up with facilitators, cultural media-tors, and psychologists to engage with marginalized communities and let their voices and their stories be heard.

They need to act as bridges between the general public and environmental and renewable energy scientists and permaculture experts, to make sure that they understand what solutions are available now and what will be available in the future.

They need to go into neighborhood associations, schools, and workplaces and give people the speculative design tools they need to plan and enact their sustainable futures, so that there is no need to choose between the end of the month and the end of the world, as the French *gilets jaunes protestors* felt forced to do.[35]

They need to make sure that communities are the protagonists in their stories, and not just passive subjects of a top-down process of change.

Solarpunk can no longer be an adjective. It needs to be a verb, it needs to be something people do in real life to their cities and schools and workplaces, to the way they produce and distribute goods, to their fields and factories and transport systems.

It needs to be a catalyst for a different way of thinking about what power and community mean.

It needs to be about not the waking but the rising.

We have ten years left to do what no generation before has achieved.

It's now or never.

Notes

1. Emma Marris, "How to Stop Freaking Out and Tackle Climate Change," *New York Times*, January 10, 2020, https://www.nytimes.com/2020/01/10/opinion/sunday/how-to-help-climate-change.html.
2. Robert A. Burton, "Our Brains Tell Stories So We Can Live," *Nautilus* 75 (August 8, 2019), http://nautil.us/issue/75/story/our-brains-tell-stories-so-we-can-live.
3. Edward Said, *Culture and Imperialism* (New York: Vintage Books, 1984).

4. Naomi Klein, *No Logo*, 10th anniversary edition (New York: Fourth Estate, 2010).
5. Cordelia Fine, *Delusions of Gender: The Real Science behind Sex Differences* (London: Icon Books, 2011).
6. Facundo Albornoz et al., "The Brexit Referendum and the Rise in Hate Crime; Conforming to the New Norm," *CeDEx*, 72, https://www.nottingham.ac.uk/cedex /documents/papers/cedex-discussion-paper-2020-12.pdf; Ben Chu, "Normalising Racism in Our Politics Really Does Lead to Hate Crime on Our Streets—Here's How," *The Independent*, September 23, 2018, https://www.independent.co.uk /voices/hate-crime-politics-brexit-eu-referendum-identity-facundo-albornoz -a8549051.html.
7. Beatriz Rios, "Beyond the US: Police Brutality, Structural Racism Are a Problem in Europe Too," *Euractiv*, June 11, 2020, https://www.euractiv.com/section/non -discrimination/news/beyond-the-us-police-brutality-structural-racism-are-a -problem-in-europe-too/.
8. CJ Werleman, "Make Black Lives Matter by Ending the 'War on Drugs,'" *Byline Times*, June 8, 2020, https://bylinetimes.com/2020/06/08/make-black-lives -matter-by-ending-the-war-on-drugs/; Gaby Hinsliff, "The Strange Death of Europe by Douglas Murray Review—Gentrified Xenophobia," *The Guardian*, May 6, 2017, https://www.theguardian.com/books/2017/may/06/strange-death-europe -immigration-xenophobia.
9. Cory Doctorow, "The Unimaginable," *Locus Online*, November 1, 2021, https:// locusmag.com/2021/11/cory-doctorow-the-unimaginable/.
10. Emily Atkin, "Bird Man Cries Wolf," *Heated,* September 9, 2019, http://heated .world/p/bird-man-cries-wolf; Genevieve Guenther, "People Love to Say 'We' Are Causing Climate Change. But Who Is We?" *Slate*, October 10, 2018, http://slate .com/technology/2018/10/who-is-we-causing-climate-change.html; Amy Westervelt, "The Case for Climate Rage," *Popula*, August 19, 2019, https://popula .com/2019/08/19/the-case-for-climate-rage/.
11. David Graeber and David Wengrow, "How to Change the Course of Human History," *Eurozine,* March 2, 2018, https://www.eurozine.com/change-course -human-history/.
12. Jedediah Purdy, "Environmentalism's Racist History," *New Yorker*, August 13, 2015, https://www.newyorker.com/news/news-desk/environmentalisms-racist-history.
13. Sarah Manavis, "Eco-Fascism: The Ideology Marrying Environmentalism and White Supremacy Thriving Online," *New Statesman*, September 2018, https://www .newstatesman.com/science-tech/social-media/2018/09/eco-fascism-ideology -marrying-environmentalism-and-white-supremacy.
14. Susie Cagle, "'Bees, Not Refugees': The Environmentalist Roots of Anti-Immigrant Bigotry," *The Guardian*, August 16, 2019, https://www.theguardian.com /environment/2019/aug/15/anti; Kate Aronoff, "The European Far Right's Environmental Turn," *Dissent*, May 31, 2019, https://www.dissentmagazine.org /online_articles/the-european-far-rights-environmental-turn.
15. Tom Godwin, "The Cold Equations," in *The World Turned Upside Down*, ed. by David Drake (Riverdale, NY: Baen Books, 2004), 445–71.
16. See Cory Doctorow's essay: "Jeannette Ng Was Right: John W. Campbell Was a Fascist," *Locus Online*, November 4, 2019, https://locusmag.com/2019/11 /cory-doctorow-jeannette-ng-was-right-john-w-campbell-was-a-fascist/.
17. Cory Doctorow, "Cold Equations and Moral Hazard," *Locus Online*, March 2, 2014,

http://locusmag.com/2014/03/cory-doctorow-cold-equations-and-moral-hazard/; James Davis Nicoll, "On Needless Cruelty in SF: Tom Godwin's 'The Cold Equations,' " *Tor.com*, April 29, 2019, https://www.tor.com/2019/04/29/on-needless-cruelty-in-sf-tom-godwins-the-cold-equations/; Marissa Lingen, "Beware the Lifeboat," *Uncanny* 29 (August 2019), https://uncannymagazine.com/article/beware-the-lifeboat/.

18. Peter Wohlleben, *The Hidden Life of Trees: What They Feel, How They Communicate—Discoveries from a Secret World* (Vancouver: Greystone, 2016); Kelly Clancy, "Survival of the Friendliest," *Nautilus*, August 22, 2019, http://nautil.us/issue/75/story/survival-of-the-friendliest-rp.

19. Robert A. Heinlein, *Farnham's Freehold* (Riverdale, NY: Baen Books, 2006).

20. Shoshana Kessock, "Disability Erasure and the Apocalyptic Narrative," *Shoshana Kessock* (personal blog), August 28, 2017, https://shoshanakessock.com/2017/08/28/disability-erasure-and-the-apocalyptic-narrative/.

21. Naomi Klein, *The Shock Doctrine: The Rise of Disaster Capitalism* (New York: Picador, 2007).

22. Arkady Martine, "What Really Happens after the Apocalypse," *Tor.com*, March 28, 2019, https://www.tor.com/2018/11/14/what-really-happens-after-the-apocalypse/.

23. Joshua M. Pearce, "A Review of Open Source Ventilators for COVID-19 and Future Pandemics," *F1000Research* 9 (April 2020): 218.

24. "Prusa Face Shield," *PrusaPrinters*, https://www.prusaprinters.org/prints/25857-prusa-face-shield.

25. Francesca Sironi, "A Milano nascono le brigate per aiutare contro il virus: 'È un dovere etico non restare fermi,' " *l'Espresso*, April 1, 2020, https://espresso.repubblica.it/attualita/2020/04/01/news/a-milano-nascono-le-brigate-per-combattere-il-virus-e-un-dovere-etico-non-restare-fermi-1.346439; Angiola Codacci-Pisanelli, "Altruisti organizzati: dal Friuli a Messina la solidarietà contro il coronavirus," *l'Espresso*, March 30, 2020, https://espresso.repubblica.it/plus/articoli/2020/03/30/news/altruisti-organizzati-chi-per-solidarieta-s-ingegna-e-impegna-1.346125; "Find Your Local Group—Covid-19 Mutual Aid," *COVID Mutual Aid*, accessed June 14, 2020, https://covidmutualaid.org/local-groups/.

26. Toby Helm, "Austerity to Blame for 130,000 'Preventable' UK Deaths—Report," *The Guardian*, June 1, 2019, https://www.theguardian.com/politics/2019/jun/01/perfect-storm-austerity-behind-130000-deaths-uk-ippr-report.

27. Portes, Jonathan, "Roger Scruton's Brand of Conservatism Became a Licence for Bigotry," *The Guardian*, January 17, 2020, https://www.theguardian.com/commentisfree/2020/jan/17/roger-scruton-conservatism-bigotry-anti-immigrant.

28. Brian Gallagher, "Humans Are Wired for Goodness," *Nautilus*, August 22, 2019, http://nautil.us/issue/75/story/humans-are-wired-for-goodness.

29. Simon Hannah, "The Fight against Climate Change Is a Fight against Capitalism," *OpenDemocracy*, August 13, 2019, https://www.opendemocracy.net/en/oureconomy/fight-against-climate-change-fight-against-capitalism/.

30. A Green New Deal is a package of economic, social, and political measures aimed at transitioning society from the current fossil fuel and extraction-based model to one based on social, climate, and global justice (see https://gnde.diem25.org/). The Lucas Plan was a bottom-up industrial conversion plan designed by the workers of Lucas Aerospace Combine in the 1970s. "A New Lucas Plan" working group aims to

transfer the spirit and methods of that experience to the climate and ecological emergency, initiating and supporting a just transition for workers and their communities (see https://lucasplan.org.uk/). A Transition Initiative is a local initiative within the framework of the Transition Network, a global movement of communities coming together to reimagine and rebuild the world (see https://transitionnetwork.org/).

31. Just Transition is a conceptual framework originating in the 1990s in which the labor movement captures the complexities of the transition toward a low-carbon and climate-resilient economy, highlighting public policy needs and aiming to maximize benefits and minimize hardships for workers and their communities in this transformation. The definition has broadened to include not only workers' rights but a broader definition of social justice that reflects intersectionality and decolonization, global justice and climate justice, as well as a deep, participatory democracy in society and workplaces and a rethinking of the processes of resource production, allocation, and distribution and of the relationships between human communities and with the environment.

32. Joey Escherisch and Clark A. Miller, *The Weight of Light: A Collection of Solar Futures* (Tempe: Arizona State University Press, 2019).

33. Samuel Holleran, trans. Samuel Seble, "Frenar La Distopía: Diseño Especulativo, Solarpunk y Herramientas Visuales Para Proponer Futuros Positivos," *Ecología Política* 57 (2019): 56–61.

34. Alexandra Köves, Judit Gáspár, and Réka Matolay, trans. Yago Mellado, "Future & Co.: Una Obra De Teatro-Acción Para Entender El Negocio Responsable y Sostenible," *Ecología Política* 57 (2019): 32–37.

35. Simon Fairlie, "End of the Month, End of the World," *The Land* 25 (2019), https://www.thelandmagazine.org.uk/articles/end-month-end-world.

CHAPTER 2

In Defense of Hope

Margaret Killjoy

Let's talk about hope for a moment, because recently hope feels like the only thing that matters. It's easy to let it slip away from us.

I haven't lived through events like this pandemic before, and I'm no prophet, but I assume the world will not return to how it was before. I assume the old status quo is gone. A new one will take its place.

I hope the new status quo will be better. I hope it will be built of resilient, interwoven communities. I hope it will be kinder. I hope the horrors of capitalism that have been laid bare will live on only in history books. I hope the horrors of policing and judicial solutions to crisis stay plain for everyone to see and become dark historical footnotes. I hope we remember mutual aid. I hope that in the new status quo we remember we can just . . . take care of each other.

That's what I hope. I think it's a long shot, but I think it's possible. I'll work my hardest to make it happen, and I hope you will too. If I didn't think it were possible, if I didn't have hope, I don't know what I would do.

———

For a while, when I was coming up in politics, it was popular to talk shit on hope. There were roughly two different lines of reasoning against hope. First was this idea that hope was inherently passive. That hope was about thinking that someone or something else would save you, that hope was about abandoning your agency and relying on something external—like hoping that "the masses" would have a revolution, or that the election would turn out how you want, or that scientists would cure any given disease.

Fundamentally, this critique advocated that we take more active control over our lives. It was to remind us that *we* are the ones we've been waiting for. Since it's true that no one is coming to save us, since we actually have to solve problems ourselves, I'm sympathetic to this critique.

The other argument against hope came from a more nihilistic position. The idea was that trying to create a better world was not necessary in order to fight against the horrors of the existent one. By letting go of hope, by accepting that we are doomed no matter which path we choose, we can finally be free. We might not win, but fuck it, we'll go down swinging because it's a better way to live, a better way to die.

Both of these arguments appealed to me more at a time when the storm of rising fascism and rising temperatures still sat on the horizon. I don't want to paint a rosy picture of the world at the beginning of this century, because it has always been full of horrors, but I think it's reasonable to say that for myself and for most of the people likely to read this, things are worse now.

Nationalism is more entrenched in more countries. Climate change is no longer on the horizon; it is here. And, of course, there's the COVID-19 pandemic. It's impossible, no matter how hard I might try on any given day, to forget the toll of this pandemic.

The world is worse now than it was then. What do I turn to? I turn to hope.

The opposite of hope is not "seizing my own agency" or "grim determination." The opposite of hope is despair. Despair, at a time like this, will literally kill us. Our mental and physical health are under attack right now, and morale is half that battle. We need hope.

The first argument against hope is simply a semantic one. Writers and theorists need to define terms in order to get their point across. They either latch onto and redefine existing terminology or they make up new terms. I think conflating what could be understood as "passive hope" with "hope" more broadly was likely a mistake.

One might say: "If you're hungry, you don't hope you get food. You get off your ass and find food." I'd argue that getting off your ass to find food is still an action predicated on hope. If I am hungry, I am hoping that when I search for food, I will succeed. If I had no hope of success, I would not get off my ass to find food. I would despair. If I am taking control of my life as best I am able, I hope I will succeed. This is an active form of hope.

Yet I'm not going to come out swinging too hard against passive hope, either. As much as I believe that we need to develop our sense of agency as individuals, we still live within communities and broader society. There are some things that I am more or less passively hoping will happen. I hope scientists discover a vaccine that is effective against COVID-19 and soon. I hope that fewer people die than might. I hope the people I love survive. I don't have agency in most of those things, or if I do it's a negligible amount. My role in this is to avoid getting sick if I can, to avoid getting other people sick if I can, and to bolster people's spirits when I can, whether through the work I produce or just through talking to loved ones on the phone. My role is to minimize my impact on an overburdened health system and to offer hope to people where I can.

The other stuff? Vaccines and fewer deaths? That's what I hope happens. It's a passive hope.

I'm okay with that.

Hoping that those things will happen can bolster my own sense of agency. If I am part of a team, I hope that my teammates are able to accomplish their tasks, because it takes all of us together to succeed. I am counting on, hoping for, the rest of my team's success so that my own actions matter.

As for the other critique of hope, the nihilist approach, the grim determination approach . . . there are use cases for that. Sometimes anger will suffice where hope has failed. Yet let's say I am hungry, and I have no hope of finding food. I will not go out and forage anyway out of grim determination. I will despair. A better use case for this grim determination approach might be, let's say, an impossible fight against an all-powerful enemy. By abandoning any hope of victory or even survival, I'm less likely to anxiously minimize every risk I take. I'm less likely to let fear destroy my ability to live. I'm more likely to act freely and make the best of the time I have. There's beauty, there's poetry, in the freedom one can find in hopelessness. Yet I've found even my grim determination works best when I feel as though I have a chance.

I imagine this as a board game, or a strategy game, against a player who is incalculably better equipped and experienced. Despair alone would lead me to forfeit. Anger alone might lead me to play unintelligently and simply lash out, trying to hurt my enemy as much as possible in a move destined to end the game early with my defeat.

I live my best life when I play to win, whether or not I succeed.

I assume I will not die as I intend to: really fucking old, having lived most of my life in an anarchist society, surrounded by friends and family. That's still my goal. That's what I'm fighting for. I live my best life by working toward that goal as though it were possible. Because it is possible. It's just not likely. Give me a sliver of hope with my grim determination.

Without hope, to be honest, I'd probably just get drunk and play video games, not live some wild and beautiful and short life of revolutionary crime.

———

We're *not* playing against an opponent who is incalculably better equipped and experienced. We're far, far more powerful than we give ourselves credit for. There are more of us than we'd ever imagined, and more are joining us every day.

———

Lately I've been taking stock of what gives me hope, and I refer back to my list whenever something happens in the world that strips hope away from me. I recommend this. Your list might not look like mine, and that's fine. In times like these, there are people who are going to step forward claiming to have all the answers, or that they know all the questions to ask. Those people are either lying or wrong, and either way they're trying to sell you something. Make your own list. Have your own goals.

Right now, I find hope in the mutual aid networks that are suddenly everywhere. I find hope in the prison riots in Italy, and I find hope in the judges in the United States who are letting more and more people out of jails and prisons. I find hope in how many former centrists or even capitalists are abandoning the profit motive to feed people, house people, and keep as many people safe as they can. I find hope in the rent strikers, the mortgage strikers, and even in the landlords who told tenants they didn't have to pay rent during the height of the pandemic. I find hope in the scientists who are refusing to let their findings help only a single nation. I find hope in the engineers who are breaking patent laws to create life-saving equipment. I find hope in the patent holders who are suspending their intellectual property claims en masse to let their inventions be used to save lives. I find hope in the General Electric employees who are demanding that their industrial production be moved over to the creation of ventilators. I find hope in the science fiction magazine in China that is sending me N95 masks to distribute to local frontline workers.

I find hope in the people who are finding ways to take care of one another from afar. I find hope in the people who are risking their mental health in order to preserve their own and other people's physical health. Choosing isolation is not a simple thing for anyone, but it's harder on some people than others.

Basically, I find hope in everyone who is doing what they do best—whether through criminal or legal means—to break apart the status quo as fast as possible in order to save lives.

It's happening everywhere. I never thought I'd live to see the day when so much of the world comes together to try to save each other.

So . . . it's us. I find hope in us.

Note

This piece originally appeared on Margaret Killjoy's blog *Birds Before the Storm* (http://www.birdsbeforethestorm.net/) in April 2020.

CHAPTER 3

Feeding Imagination

Giulia Lepori and Michał Krawczyk

This writing is grounded in Italy, in Sicily, in the Valley of Sagana. It is rooted in the land of the permaculture site[1] of the Center for Development of Consciousness—Thar dö Ling, established in relationship with the family of permaculture designers Simona Trecarichi and Danilo Colomela.[2] Over six months, we entered the intimacy of their lives to undertake our ethnographic fieldwork within the environmental humanities. From spring to autumn 2019, we were nourished for our doctoral research areas for the purposes of writing an ecocritical autoethnography on the imaginaries of water, plants, food, and waste based on stories from the field (Giulia) and making two ethnographic films on permacultural forms of dwelling (Michał).

We share one resolution: to narrate cultures of regeneration that are ecological and place-based. In fact, the current epoch of the Anthropocene is a timely opportunity to reconsider human life on Earth through narrations that communicate the more-than-human[3] interweaving of life making. In particular, the doom-and-gloom narratives that characterize the Anthropocene should be balanced with stories about things turning out to be okay.[4] What if, as Rob Hopkins writes, we had a sense that "the mere telling of them can create a degree of inevitability about their becoming a reality, and a sense that speaking them out loud is also of great benefit to our own mind, a powerful antidote to despondency and trauma"?[5] Thus, not only do we talk about people who focus on creative solutions and approaches to the Earth's state of degradation, but we also attempt to develop innovative methods of research that directly explore and participate in creative endeavors. As proposed by Katherine Gibson, Deborah B. Rose, and Ruth Fincher, "Research for the Anthropocene must and will harness the creativity of human potential to reduce harm and promote a flourishing biosphere."[6] As environmental humanists working with words and moving images, we practice and suggest the path of imagination, by crafting imaginative patterns from within the everyday human experience of life.

The imagination that we want to grow is fed by stories of relationships. What are the images that sprout within a permaculture site? Imagine we are made of living system within living system, crossed by webs of relationships that shape us as much as we shape them. To Simona and Danilo, their site is the system where energy flows and is produced, a place to observe and interact with life flourishing and decaying, to experiment and be experimented upon in the dynamic quest to embed ecological consciousness.

The following interviews with Simona Trecarichi and Danilo Colomela[7] are a testimony of applied imagination in the permaculture site of Thar dö Ling: listening, observing, interacting with land, understanding the expressiveness of nonhuman beings and more-than-human elements: imagining the possibilities of regenerative collaborations.

Notes for the reader: Engage with the words by envisioning the relationships at play. Feel the different microclimates as you enter the food forest to sit under a pine tree. Visualize the donkeys grazing in the rocky paths among terraces of olive trees. Follow them and let them be. Bend down to inspect their feces, smell them. It is digested grass. Insert your hand in the compost pile: Can you feel the heat? Can you see the trees growing from that soil?

———

These days, when someone seeks ecological literacy, they might start with composting. Managing food scraps, feeding worms, creating soil. Nevertheless, composting is not one-way travel toward an end goal. It is a collaborative exploration that is ever returning: the decomposition of life that is birth. Where did the food come from? Who are the beings that feed us? How is life digested by life to make more life possible? What is our relationship with death? Do we care for the soil?

"There's a general recipe, but as you go into the role that each ingredient plays, you can substitute the various ingredients with those that are easier to get hold of. The advice: the closer the material to your place, the better.

"The bokashi is a hot compost. It needs three main components: manure (we used that of the donkeys), straw or any carbon material, and clayish soil. A third in volume for each part. Then there are smaller quantities of other ingredients that are needed to activate the fermentation, which happens in the process of transformation: either beer yeast or sourdough, as a starter of organisms that begin to transform the organic matter, and sugar or honey (we used some honey that was slightly fermented) to give the organisms some initial food to begin their reproduction, so that their population grows and

Fig. 3.1. Dondolo and Giorgiana grazing in the Valley of Sagana

is then able to digest the whole mass, which needs to be at least one cubic meter.

"During the first days, the temperature reaches sixty degrees—it can even go beyond, although this peak is not advised because it can kill the very life that created it. Thus, turning the pile is necessary not only to better mix the ingredients but also to maintain a constant temperature.

"The other interesting ingredients are ash, which brings in the mineral component from the alkaline earth metals that remain in the wooden ash, and crumbled charcoal. The charcoal, a substance with many cavities, provides a house for microorganisms. Thus, when the compost matures and is then transported and spread on the land, they can continue to reproduce from those nuclei. As an alternative ingredient, because we didn't have charcoal, we used triturated cork panels (a residue of the house's construction site), which have a similar function to charcoal, being very porous. We also need soil from the forest, the forest's litter, with the function of capturing the microorganisms that belong to the place where a person lives and will start the compost pile. A bucket is enough. These microorganisms are moved in a pile where life is truly thriving. So the ones that will reproduce are those that were already adapted to that climate. Thus, when the bokashi will be used to transplant trees or shrubs, or in the garden, there will already be families of microorganisms that belong to the place and are therefore more suitable and will do their work better. Regarding the fibrous part, we have all the cooked herbs that we distilled, so they are included as components of cellulose fiber.

"In the bokashi recipe, we cannot forget about water, which must be added in the right quantity, because if there is too little, life doesn't happen and grow. The microorganisms need fluid in order to reproduce and carry out their activities. It shouldn't be too much, either, otherwise the pile gets clogged and there is no oxygen entering, which triggers anaerobic processes. In our case, to make the pile humid we added the water that comes out of the phytodepurator, which is also rich in life.

"Making a bokashi requires notable physical exercise because in the beginning it needs to be turned every day, to be moved to a different spot, and if the pile is two or three cubic meters . . . it's a great exercise for the arms and pectorals. It can be included in the people care. You do something useful for yourself, for other beings, and for life's own survival.

"The idea of having a soil rich in organic substance is very fascinating. The beauty of these compositions is that with common things you can make truly powerful things. The power of the bokashi in this sense is the regeneration of life in the soil, because to grow plants we need to care for the soil, and here we can draw on one of the other ethics of permaculture, which is earth care. If you want to grow good food, you need to be attentive to the soil that is the matrix through which plants develop. Thus, this making together, inserting microorganisms, feeding them, giving them a home, is really caring for life, which [is a cycle in which] you will be given back for your nutrition."

Then, how do we gift life back as animals? Human and nonhuman? We all feed on other beings and must excrete the transformation that happened within our biotic systems. That is food at different levels. The odor of waste disappears as we see feces with new eyes. Waste is not imagined,[8] there is only constant renewal.

"From the beginning of our project we've had to face the problem of keeping the grass short, for we live in a fire-prone area. After the encounter with permaculture, we learned that there were different ways

Fig. 3.2. Danilo Colomela turning the compost pile

to satisfy this need, particularly through the introduction of herbivore animals. So we started thinking about what kind of animal we could have in this system.

"We wrote a long list, from small animals like chickens, geese, ducks, to donkeys, sheep, goats, and so on. For each we did a functional analysis of the elements, pointing out the characteristics, needs, and products. The donkey seemed most apt to our situation: originally coming from rocky deserts, and this place is like that, as it is an uneven land and, in some parts, very steep.

"The donkey's principal function would have been weeding, but there was another one that we were aware of, which was that of increasing and favoring the organic substance in the soil. In fact, the donkeys eat the grass, then they give it back to the soil transformed and enriched with enzymes and bacteria, hence acting as catalysts for the activity and vitality of the soil.

"When Dondolo and Giorgiana [the donkeys] arrived, we thought about subdividing the available land into different zones, still contained within those that in a permacultural project are zones three and four—here, the olive grove and the future food forest. Initially the grazing areas were very rich, strongly vegetated, with abundant food. We also considered the number of donkeys, two in this case, proportional to the size of the land and the type of pasture. Indeed, we thought they would have to sustain themselves with what they could find in situ. This was possible for the first four years, precisely thanks to the presence of those zones with thick vegetation.

"After the fourth year, we observed that they cut those virgin zones and that the plants' capacity for regrowth was not balanced compared to the amount that was eaten. Thus, the plants and the soil couldn't keep pace with what the donkeys were eating, so in what we call phase two, we decided to extend the grazing zones. This year, we have entered what we like to call phase three. We fenced an area adjacent to the stable, creating a little paddock where we decided to leave the donkeys for some time.

"What changed for us is that we have had to buy big quantities of straw. This year we bought a hundred straw bales. We estimated that they would be enough for the whole year. Despite the external input of the straw,[9] there is balance, as the paddock also means that we have a very useful product, the donkeys' poo, concentrated in one area. When they graze, they excrete wherever. Obviously, this results in it being spread all over the land.

"Now, as they spend more time in the stable's proximity, we have a great quantity of poo all together, which we clearly need to—I dislike saying 'dispose of' because it's not the exact term—transform and reinsert in the system. At this stage, the concentrated donkeys' poo becomes the propulsive element for the fertility of zones one and two, which are those closer to the house, which we will be more densely cultivated with edible plants.

"Our project is to create grazing systems spread all over the land. The food forest will be one of those. In the food forest's design, we are also considering vegetal species suitable for forage.

"Since the beginning, after Dondolo and Giorgiana's first year, we have observed an increase in biodiversity. For example, I clearly remember the mushrooms, which appeared on the [feces]. It was an incredible happening, because they were in a place where we had never seen them and where mushrooms probably wouldn't have grown. Additionally, we started observing the appearance of plants never seen before, like St. John's wort. And wild oregano, which was already present, increased. This was because the donkeys' activities decreased those predominant plant species, like disa (*Ampelodesmos mauritanicus*),[10] which were overshadowing and preventing other plants' growth. In this way, other species could make their way in the land."

Deforestation is a complex, large-scale, and high-impact global matter. So is reforestation. What if more stories of creation were fostered? How many humans around the world are reforesting? Actively making life in more-than-human companionship? Are we aware of the magic of plants? Food forests are edible stories for humans, nonhumans, and elements to live by.

"A food forest is a woody area that offers many products, obviously starting from food. But it also gives forage, wood, medicinal plants, food for the bees and other insects, and so on. Normally we don't think that we could get our food from the woods. Indeed, a food forest, a forest that feeds, makes us think that we can gradually change our eating habits. After all, what is its peculiarity? It's a designed forest, where there is a plan that regards the plant species that live there.

"In general, it's designed according to seven or eight layers: big trees, medium trees, shrubs, herbaceous plants, covering plants, the crops that give roots, and vines. There are those who add an eighth layer, fungi. Besides, in the general design of permaculture, the food forest is usually situated in zone four, not that close to the house. The

Fig. 3.3. Chestnut sapling growing among the pine trees

beautiful thing about it is that it is a forest, thus a stable system. A zone where there's a lot of energy input in the initial projecting and planting, but once it gets started, it goes by itself. It is indeed a perennial and permanent ecosystem, which gifts us with products, where one eventually goes to harvest and does little management.

"In our system, we decided to insert the food forest element where we identified the fourth zone, in the property's margins. We chose a nucleus area, where we had found some existing pine trees taller than ten meters, which allowed a naturally different microclimate from the rest of the land, as in much cooler. They're mature trees, allowing us to plant those kinds of trees that need more coolness, rather than the exposed southern slope of the future food forest.

"Besides the pine trees, what did we find? Essentially a massive quantity of disa, thorny and rush broom, Italian buckthorn, and a bit of heather. Plus, a natural nursery of oaks and holly oaks, which tend to continually sprout, because of the Eurasian jays' work as acorn diggers. So the future food forest is already full of these saplings.

"Our design is just at the beginning. We're at the level of the tall trees, which require more time to grow. And they also occupy more space, which is why they need to be localized, so they're not that close to one another. And we are thinking about which trees to add. Some we already decided on and planted, like the chestnuts and hazelnuts, and we also put some cover plants like the wild strawberries, which are doing well.

"We like to take our time to observe and gather information that we haven't got yet. Especially since there are many plant species that can potentially be inserted in such system. As a parallel thought, when I conceive of the food forest, I also visualize myself in the future entering this place, and I imagine what I could be picking. So I like the idea of picking medicinal plants that could help me with health problems, therefore the species choice revolves around these thoughts too. I imagine that I pick edible flowers, associated with plants that are also melliferous.

"The plants depend also on the zone that we dedicate to the food forest. The future food forest will be spread over two slopes, one on the north side, another on the south. Thus, if the chestnuts and hazelnuts are in the northern slope, in the southern one we will tend toward carob trees, almond trees, those that prefer it dry and hot. Planting the hazelnuts and chestnuts within the pine grove allowed them to survive, as they're in a familiar microclimate. As for us, we used less water, having less irrigation in summer, because naturally the area has a higher level of humidity.

"This makes us reflect on the fact that a wooded system offers what are called ecosystemic services: it has incredible functions. It creates a thriving system for all the beings that populate its environment, as it is a varied environment, richer, with more water, a lot of organic substance, which develops in height, therefore there is more physical space and refuges. Thus, there are very favorable life conditions.

"We spoke about plants—let us not forget that the web of life is made of animals too. So we should favor, and keep in mind, the presence of wild animals. We are thinking of building nesting boxes of different types to offer little birds the possibility of a nest. In general, these birds make nests in the trees' hollows, but we understand that these trees won't have hollows from the beginning, hence the action of building little diversified boxes. The great tit, the tomtit, the tree creeper, they are all different animals that occupy different niches within the forest; therefore, by offering a refuge they will necessarily look after broods and they will look for food. And where? In their surroundings, hence they'll go to the olive grove, in the garden, and will live their life, which means they will eat insects, some of which could have caused problems for other crops. A thicker web of life reduces the problematic peaks of the so-called parasites.

"Thus, a food forest is a stable source of food and refuge for wildlife too. For example, at the level of shrubs, there could be hawthorns with small fruits, of which humans only need few. So there will be a surplus of small fruits that will be nutrition for other beings, and shelter, where they will be able to easily reproduce."

Now, imagine how you usually hear about the state of the world. If you do not resonate with that image, imagine redesigning it. You are already in the making of it. How do you feel?

Notes

1. Permaculture is a creative design process to establish "consciously designed landscapes which mimic patterns and relationships found in nature" (David Holmgren, *Permaculture: Principles and Pathways beyond Sustainability* [Holmgren Design Services, 2002], xix). It is based on whole systems thinking informed by

ethics and design principles, which can be applied to all aspects of human habitation. For the list of principles and the ethics, see permacultureprinciples.com.

2. Simona Trecarichi and Danilo Colomela, "Thar dö Ling," http://centrothardoling .it/.

3. "The phrase 'more-than-human' was introduced in 1996 by David Abram in *The Spell of the Sensuous*. Abram used it as a way to overcome the nature-culture bifurcation, suggesting that the human world should be considered a subset of the more-than-human world" (Serenella Iovino and Serpil Oppermann, eds., *Material Ecocriticism* [Bloomington: Indiana University Press, 2014], 16). To be sure, the expression does not satisfy the richness of all the living and nonliving collectives that create the world as it creates them; it remains a phrase that begins with the human to expand to *others*. However, we value it (and utilize it) for its work of acknowledgment, which illuminates the nonexceptionalism of humans.

4. Rob Hopkins, *From What Is to What If: Unleashing the Power of Imagination to Create the Future We Want* (White River Junction, VT: Chelsea Green Publishing, 2019), 1.

5. Hopkins, *From What Is*, 119.

6. Katherine Gibson, Deborah B. Rose, and Ruth Fincher, eds., *Manifesto for Living in the Anthropocene* (Goleta, CA: Punctum Books, 2015).

7. We define these interviews as informal performative interviews because they were gathered on the specific site that related to their topic without the use of questionnaires. Instead, they were anticipated by a collaborative mental mapping where Simona, Danilo, the designers, and we, the interviewers, offered our insights on the topic of the talk. They involved walking or sitting under trees, in front of the pond, or near the donkeys and the bees. The three interviews that follow are edited extracts translated from the Italian. Our questions are set as main text; Simona and Danilo's responses are set as block quotes. The interviews were performed toward the end of our six-month stay, so as to give us the time to feel familiar with and embody the discourses and the practices that created the topics.

8. For the permacultural concept of waste, please listen to Formidable Vegetable's song "No Such Thing as Waste," https://music.formidablevegetable.com.au/track /no-such-thing-as-waste.

9. The straw bales came from the same organic wheat that made the pasta eaten at Thar dö Ling (from Cooperativa Agricola Valdibella).

10. The *disa* is a pioneer plant that thrives in soils with little organic matter, which used to cover much of the land of Thar dö Ling.

CHAPTER 4

A Collective Gardening Shed of Concepts for Planting Solarpunk Futures

Christoph D. D. Rupprecht

Futures worth living don't imagine themselves. The futures whose seeds we plant today will be shaped in part by the tools we use to plant them. What if we had a collective gardening shed of the imaginary, a place where we gather a diverse mix of concepts as tools for our worldbuilding? An imagined place of gathering, where we can learn and teach, experiment and iterate, tinker and break apart and reassemble, each in our own ways and times? With each concept new (and old) doors open, new (re-)discoveries await, new journeys begin. Allow me here to share my personal, nonexhaustive, eclectic mix of concepts: the ones I think might spark curiosity, inspiration, or reflection when stumbled upon in such a gardening shed, in the form of brief notes, including directions for the adventurous.

Multispecies/More-Than-Human
The more we learn about what it means to be human, the more the boundaries of the human begin to blur. People, animals, plants, fungi, bacteria—living is an ongoing exchange in a dense web of entanglements, where agency is shared and distributed.[1] "Human nature is an interspecies relationship,"[2] and "becoming is always becoming with" someone.[3] What kind of entanglements between living beings lie at the heart of our stories? What relationships are cut, what relationships are we willing to fight for? What happens if we think of solarpunk futures from multispecies, more-than-human perspectives?

Degrowth
Many solarpunk stories tell of a time after, tales of coping and reinventing our lives that imply something grim happened. How did we get there? What if the crisis is real but the catastrophe is avoidable—because we can make

solarpunk happen, here and now? What if we could downscale production and consumption, increasing (more-than-)human well-being and enhancing ecological conditions and equity on the planet? The degrowth movement strives to imagine economics and politics not obsessed with growth and profit, a world where the river returns to its bed after a devastating flood to make room for regeneration.[4]

Radical Imaginary

For Cornelius Castoriadis, the collective meanings, norms, language(s), tools used by a society form its social imaginary.[5] In contrast, the radical imaginary is the capacity to see in a thing what it is not—to see it as other than it is. If being able to imagine a better future is key to building it, how can we as solarpunks learn to see the world, people, and maybe even ourselves as we are not? Could our stories create moments of shared radical imagination, reaching out beyond the moment and the place? In what ways could we teach these skills?

Sufficiency

Enough is as good as a feast. What if, instead of thinking in terms of planetary boundaries and ecological limits, we reclaimed the autonomy to decide when we have enough? In sufficiency lies the potential for freedom: self-limitation on our own terms defeats the artificial scarcity created by a never-ending quest for producing, consuming, owning more.[6] Competition ceases its stranglehold over the social, and everything beyond enough is there to be shared, gifted, left untaken, or paid forward. What if moving silently and planting things is enough to be happy?[7]

Solidarity

At times when we are pitched against each other, be it as individuals in neoliberal competition for meaningful work or as othered groups across strategic lines drawn to divide us, resistance in solidarity becomes a radical, punk-as-hell act.[8] Solarpunk can join a broad alliance of critical, hopeful futurisms to find intersectional and interspecies ways to practice solidarity in everyday life. Moving silently allows us to look and consider where and how we tread. Do we help others to flourish, knowing their joy is ours too? How can we dismantle the myriad exploitative ways we often unwittingly and unwillingly rely on and build new, fair, and equitable networks of mutual support for solidary solarpunk futures?

Biocultural Diversity

Solarpunk embraces and celebrates diversity. As people shape and are shaped by their more-than-human surroundings, so are cultural, biological, and linguistic diversity entangled in ways where the whole is more than the sum of its parts. For us who appreciate the whole spectrum of human experiences, biocultural diversity promises myriad journeys through the ways of being with the world. What solarpunk stories might only be told in a particular language? How can we forge solarpunk ties across cultures, celebrating our differences as rich treasures of wonder?

Feminist Care

We're solarpunks because the only other options are denial or despair. We wouldn't be solarpunk if we didn't care—even when it hurts. Much of solarpunk's power lies in looking beyond the technology to ask if it was imagined, designed, produced, used, repurposed, or abandoned in care-full ways. Feminist care enriches our stories, asking with Joan Tronto what care work takes place: caring about, taking care of, caregiving, care receiving?[9] And when we weave new worlds, let's keep María Puig de la Bellacasa's words in mind: "For interdependent beings in more than human entanglements, there has to be some form of care going on somewhere in the substrate of their world for living to be possible."[10]

Cybernetics

Imagine your boat is floating down a river splitting in two a bit farther downstream, with one arm leading toward a steep waterfall. You can hardly stop the river, so good steering will prove vital. Defined by Ross Ashby as the art of steersmanship, cybernetics offers nontotalitarian approaches to management for those who reject the illusion that total control of nature is possible (let alone desirable) but would still rather avoid a potentially deadly fall.[11] We need adapting and self-regulating systems that rely on operational autonomy instead of hierarchies: to rethink the way we organize work and collaboration, to coordinate across communities while preserving their freedom, and to strive for multispecies over anthropocentric sustainability.

Agroecology

Who feeds solarpunk futures? Very likely not industrial monocultures reliant on chemical fertilizers, ecologically devastating pesticides, pathogen-breeding plantations, and ruthless exploitation of human and more-than-human labor.

Vertical farms fit well into accelerationist visions of endless skyscrapers but provide neither fertile ground for biocultural diversity nor meaningful ways of engaging with the landscape. In contrast, agroecology aims to learn the intricate dance of coexistence, a true science in search of an agriculture based on multispecies sustainability. Emphasis is placed on crop rotation, polycultures, agroforestry systems, cover crops, and animal integration.[12] Freedom from external inputs gains a political dimension, and place-based knowledge and its transmission are centered. Feeding the world holds countless tales for solarpunk to taste.

Landscape (Co-)stewardship

Care for and solidarity with life can grow beyond the scale of our gardens. Reinventing our lifestyles only works if we rethink our place in the landscape: How can our cities and fields become good neighbors to forests and rivers, providing homes for all life and not just people? What would our lives look like if we sought meaning from collectively tending living networks and let ourselves be tended, our work celebrating, not alienating us from, the fruits of our labor?[13] What talents do we humans have that can contribute in multispecies landscapes? As solarpunks we can aspire to learn from plants and their photosynthesis, the mycelium networks, the beaver engineers, and many others to envision and (re-)discover the arts of landscape stewardship.

Post-Development

The classic path of development is a steep slope up a mountain of exploited people and ecosystems. Once on top, the air proves too thin to find true happiness. The myth of sustainable development feeds off the lies of decoupling and green growth. Yet many have begun to reject the mantra that there is no alternative—indeed, there must be many post-development paths for diverse societies to build better lives.[14] Solarpunk similarly rejects accelerationism and fatalist dystopias in search for yet-to-be-found tracks. Would a solarpunk world not resemble the Zapatista call for a world in which many worlds fit, a so-called pluriverse?[15]

Conviviality

If the futures whose seeds we plant today will be shaped by the tools we use to plant them, how should we choose which tools to pick as characters in our stories? Ivan Illich used the word *conviviality* to describe a society in which modern tools are used by everyone without relying on specialists who control the tools.[16] For Illich, industrialization risks depriving us of the autonomy to produce by ourselves and to share what we need outside of markets, because it turns our needs into commodities we end up depending on. In contrast, convivial tools can be used and adapted easily for purposes we choose on our own, and thereby such tools foster freedom, autonomy, and creativity. For solarpunks, this means we need to think deeply about how our futures engage with technology. How would solar-powered cars compare to bicycles? Can we reclaim powerful tools in information technology, healthcare, and energy production to make them convivial? What about geo-engineering? Or are there cases when a tool must be shunned on principle?

Informality

Regulation and rules may not seem like the stuff of thrilling stories. But how we decide to balance the formal against the informal weaves the deep fabric of our societies.[17] Who gets away with dumping toxic waste while others are punished for feeding the homeless? How can the invaluable aid of informal support networks reach those less firmly rooted in their community? In times of precarious work and forced mobility, how can urban community gardens reach out and share beyond rigid membership systems? What form would our social institutions, security, and insurance take if we looked at enabling over discipline, benefit of the doubt over obsession with who gets what? How do we negotiate fundamental questions of individual freedoms and collective welfare, from food safety practices in small-scale production (e.g., raw milk) to vaccination and homeschooling? Thought experiments around informality in solarpunk worlds can help us chart the paths we seek to travel or avoid.

Commoning

When resources are taken care of by a community or network, a commons is born. Community, resources, and the rules around them must be thought together, as commons are not things and best thought of as *commoning*, a verb.[18] Becoming involved means to join a participatory culture, where we jointly sketch what living together as a community should look like. Commoning is an antidote to the poison of total privatization and perceived scarcity: abundance emerges from a wealth created by sharing. In turn, sharing allows us to limit what we need and step more lightly upon the Earth; it remedies the need to compete in hoarding goods and power. For solarpunk futures where we make do yet flourish, commoning will be central. So what if we thought of landscapes as existing commons, waiting for people to learn the rules and join the stewardship collective? Because, in the end, commoning is more often than not a multispecies, more-than-human endeavor—and with multispecies commoning we return to the beginning of this short tour of our collective garden shed of concepts to plant solarpunk futures.[19]

Notes

I would like to thank my colleagues, the members of the Solarpunk and *General Intellect Unit* podcast Discord servers, and the many more-than-humans for their generosity. This work was supported by the FEAST Project (14200116), Research Institute for Humanity and Nature, and JSPS KAKENHI grant numbers 18K18602, 20K15552.

1. Piers Locke and Ursula Muenster, "Multispecies Ethnography," *Oxford Bibliographies—Anthropology*, last modified November 30, 2015, https://doi.org/10.1093/OBO/9780199766567-0130.
2. Anna Tsing, "Unruly Edges: Mushrooms as Companion Species: For Donna Haraway," *Environmental Humanities* 1, no. 1 (2012): 141.
3. Donna J. Haraway, *When Species Meet* (Minneapolis: University of Minnesota Press, 2013), 244.
4. Giacomo D'Alisa et al., *Degrowth: A Vocabulary for a New Era* (London: Routledge, 2014).
5. Cornelius Castoriadis, *The Imaginary Institution of Society* (Cambridge, MA: MIT Press, 1987).
6. Giorgos Kallis, *Limits: Why Malthus Was Wrong and Why Environmentalists Should Care* (Palo Alto, CA: Stanford University Press, 2019).
7. Andrew Dana Hudson, "On the Political Dimensions of Solarpunk," Medium, March 19, 2017, https://medium.com/solarpunks/on-the-political-dimensions-of-solarpunk-c5a7b4bf8df4.
8. David Graeber, *Bullshit Jobs: A Theory* (London: Penguin UK, 2018).
9. Joan C. Tronto, *Moral Boundaries: A Political Argument for an Ethic of Care* (Hove, UK: Psychology Press, 1993).
10. María Puig de la Bellacasa, *Matters of Care: Speculative Ethics in More Than Human Worlds* (Minneapolis: University of Minnesota Press, 2017).
11. Kyle Thompson and Shane Kilkelly, *General Intellect Unit*, http://generalintellectunit.net.
12. Miguel A. Altieri, *Agroecology: The Science of Sustainable Agriculture,* 2nd ed. (Boca Raton, FL: CRC Press, 1995).
13. N. McClintock, "Why Farm the City? Theorizing Urban Agriculture through a Lens of Metabolic Rift," *Cambridge Journal of Regions, Economy and Society* 3, no. 2 (2010): 191–207.
14. Ashish Kothari et al., eds., *Pluriverse: A Post-Development Dictionary* (New Delhi: Tulika Books, 2019).
15. Arturo Escobar, *Designs for the Pluriverse: Radical Interdependence, Autonomy, and the Making of Worlds* (Durham, NC: Duke University Press, 2018).
16. Ivan Illich, *Tools for Conviviality* (New York: Harper & Row, 1973).
17. Barbara A. Misztal, *Informality Social Theory and Contemporary Practice* (London: Routledge, 2000).
18. David Bollier and Silke Helfrich, *Patterns of Commoning* (Commons Strategy Group and Off the Common Press, 2015).
19. Cleo Woelfle-Erskine, "Beavers as Commoners? Invitations to River Restoration Work in a Beavery Mode," *Community Development Journal* 54, no. 1 (January 2019): 100–18.

independence

INTRODUCTION TO PART 2

Building toward Autonomy: Ways of Reclaiming the Present and the Future

Brontë Christopher Wieland

For those in the so-called United States, the term *independence* is loaded with patriotic connotation that either celebrates or ignores the genocide of the Indigenous peoples of the continent and that understands independence solely as the product of war. Community-focused leftists may also take umbrage at the term, insisting that it's a product of individualism incompatible with their politics. But the concept of independence of individuals has also been used to grant important protections to more-than-human beings by invoking a counterpart of human rights called the rights of nature. The way we see it, individual and community are not ends of a spectrum but complementary pieces of a healthy ecology. And one cannot be independent without the independence of the other. We see this understanding of the interplay of community and individual represented in fiction by the Odonians of Ursula K. Le Guin's *The Dispossessed* (1974) and the Garuda of China Miéville's Bas-Lag novels, and we also see how that balance begets an independence unlike the dangerously jingoistic "independence" of colonial nation-states. As solarpunks, we seek to design and manifest a different independence that recognizes the necessity of *interdependence* of individuals and communities in myriad combinations.

A solarpunk sense of independence necessitates a careful examination of globalized capitalist systems, through which a history of forced dependence becomes clear. As colonists and slavers discovered at the shores of what is currently known as the Americas, a community that can feed, clothe, house, and defend itself can resist outside domination. In order for those at the top of the capitalist hierarchy to establish a ubiquitous and resilient system of power and control, leaders need a critical mass of human reliance. By destroying Indigenous food systems (see the US government's calculated extermination

61

of the bison of the Great Plains),[1] dismantling and banning communally held lands (see the Zapatista uprising of the Mexican revolution),[2] and by destabilizing, illegitimating, and toppling sovereign (often noncapitalist) systems of governance (see the coup against Queen Liliʻuokalani in 1893),[3] colonial capitalist governments worked to subsume all modes of living under one model, creating individual and communal dependence on their power.

Accordingly, solarpunks' work toward independence is, largely and necessarily, work to reclaim power from centralized and commodified sources. This includes reclaiming electricity from a state-controlled and discriminatory grid system; reclaiming online spaces and social media from corporate data-mining projects through things like end-to-end encryption and federated networking protocols; reclaiming empty homes from developers and landlords; reclaiming labor and wages from corporate standards by forming democratic or consensus-based worker cooperatives; reclaiming time from attempts to monetize and commodify it; reclaiming healthcare infrastructure from insurance-based models that profit from human suffering; reclaiming aesthetic pursuits; reclaiming relationships to energy that aren't strictly extractive and consumptive; and so much more. This work is crucial to dismantling the profit-based practices and systems of false scarcity that drive the exploitation of human peoples, more-than-human communities, and natural resources and that have resulted in climate change as we now know it. In this chapter, the term *independence* connotes a community's capacity to provide for itself based on the resources locally available to it while also leaving room for the sharing of excess wealth to help other communities compensate for that which they have less access to. While we discuss independence, we must keep in mind that it goes hand in hand with mutually beneficial interdependence.

In part 2, we discuss energy independence through local and individual management of renewable energies, as opposed to reliance on centralized power plants with unilateral control over who gets energy and when, and a careful examination of our current access to twenty-four-hour electricity, but that is only one area where a community might create its own independence. At the core of a solarpunk conceptualization of independence is the practice and construction of autonomy as an intentionally liberatory practice. Our contributors to this part explore this independence through technical, technological, material, aesthetic, and logistical lenses. They urge us to interrogate the impact of our material needs (from the discussion of the necessity of mining in Gabriel Aliaga's piece to the demands of virtual infrastructure in Kris De Decker's piece) and to imagine ways of meeting those needs that center independence and interdependence. To complement their ideas and to seed future approaches to this idea of independence, our writing in this part focuses on working toward food sovereignty (by increasing a community's agency in terms of food production), on efforts to build dual power frameworks on various scales, and on the abolition of the police and the prison-industrial complex.

A note before covering each of these topics in depth: as mentioned above, these paths toward independence often involve reclaiming bits and pieces of autonomy and knowledge from the past. This requires retrospection and learning about how we lived independently in the past. This study should not be a process of fetishizing the past but rather of admitting that many ways of knowing and being were intentionally disrupted to create globalized reliance on a capitalist system. We can turn to the past to learn that our present situation was never inevitable and was instead carefully constructed via genocide and exploitation. We can learn from the past that human civilization has not been an unbroken chain of violent survival at any cost, but that we have a storied history of cooperation and care.[4] In our pursuit of lessons from the past, though, we must be mindful of how, in stolen and colonized lands like the so-called United States and Canada, the past has been both weaponized and diluted to further erase and subsume Indigenous realities. We notice many "moves to alleviate the impacts of colonization . . . which problematically attempt to reconcile settler guilt and complicity, and rescue settler futurity" among environmental movements, identified by Eve Tuck and K. Wayne Yang as "settler moves to innocence."[5] Environmental initiatives led by settlers are often guilty of all six moves to innocence that Tuck and Yang explore, but we want to highlight the danger of two in particular, which solarpunk must be explicitly conscious of while attempting to build independence.

The first is "conscientization," the development of a lens or ideology critical of colonization that nonetheless rationalizes and excuses continued occupation of Indigenous land by settlers. This move to innocence perpetuates that idea that by simply recognizing our colonial legacy, we have already done the work of decolonizing (reducing decolonization to a metaphor). It allows our ideas "to stand in for the more uncomfortable task of relinquishing stolen land."[6] We, as settlers, could upend the so-called United States' systems of oppression and institute a perfectly equal society today, but it would still be a settler project on occupied land without the work of literal, physical decolonization, meaning ceding back all stolen land. The second move to innocence is what Tuck and Yang call "re-occupation and urban homesteading." The hypothetical perfectly equal society mentioned above is also an example of reoccupation. Settlers' self-enfranchisement through the redistribution of wealth in the so-called United States obfuscates that the source of this wealth remains stolen

Indigenous land. But this is just an abstract (yet illustrative) example of reoccupation and urban homesteading. What isn't abstract is the numerous (often
white) environmentalists pushing for a new wave of homesteading, rural or
urban. Many environmentalists talk about getting off the grid, starting farms
or communes, living self-sufficiently, and thereby solving the problems of
capitalist-driven climate change all at once. While this example of individualism and independence seems positive, it undermines the necessary work that
environmentalists *must* do, which is to address and not perpetuate colonial
systems. Lifestyle homesteading maintains the colonial hierarchy, leaves control of resources in settler hands, and prioritizes settler comfort and futurity.

We do not offer any holistic solutions for the problems inherent in settler
conscientization and homesteading, as we believe answers cannot be resolved
with any sweeping speeches or actions. Instead, we hope that solarpunks and
other readers will keep these issues in mind while engaging with these essays
and enacting any of their ideas, and we urge all readers to support local and
(inter)national Indigenous-led decolonial initiatives. Not just the easy and
metaphorical stuff, like lip service land acknowledgments, but also actions
like the literal relinquishing to local Indigenous peoples of lands "owned" by
settlers, through whichever means they deem most feasible.

Any moves toward independence that settlers take without confronting
our colonial legacy are intrinsically hierarchical, benefiting directly from genocide and displacement, and any resulting community would more appropriately
be deemed parasitic than independent.

Food Sovereignty
Part of the forced move from the localized food systems of the past to our
present large-scale, long-distance food systems was a cultural shift in what,
exactly, qualifies as food. Because of the ease of access large chain retail gro-
cers have offered to large swaths of the world's population, and because of
rigorous marketing, they have in many ways monopolized the very concept
of food. The only legitimate food is that which comes from a store, from a
company, from any abstracted source other than the Earth. Produce that isn't
"pretty" isn't marketable, and dirty produce deters buyers.[7] Some companies,
like Imperfect Foods, have even tried to capitalize on "ugly" foods as an aesthetic retaliation to this type of marketing by taking advantage of popular
dialogues on food waste. But as Michael J. DeLuca describes in his essay on
foraging in part 4, food is all around us. Many of us have just not learned to
see it, or have been kept from such knowledge.

This inability to see the food around us and how to access it is part of a broader phenomenon, which some have called "plant blindness," that also impacts the way we interact with plants as part of our environment and may be contributing to the fact that "in 2011 plants made up 57% of the federal endangered species list in the US [while receiving] less than 4% of federal endangered species funding."[8] By prioritizing the knowledge of local flora and how they relate to their human and nonhuman environments, solarpunks can begin to build the foundations of new local food systems. However, foraging,[9] by itself and on an individual scale, is a supplement to one's access to food (and other materials) and is not universally accessible. For a more thorough independence of this type, we need to consider scale.

At the 1996 World Food Summit, the international organization La Vía Campesina coined the term "food sovereignty" to help illustrate their political vision. They describe it as "the right of peoples to healthy and culturally appropriate food produced through sustainable methods and their right to define their own food and agriculture systems," and they emphasize the need for small-scale, sustainable farming and local production and consumption as a way to protect both communities and their environments. The group, still active and vocal, also "sees Agroecology as a key form of resistance to an economic system that puts profit before life," considers seeds "an irreplaceable pillar of food production," and "struggles against attempts by corporations to control our common heritage."[10] Vía Campesina highlights the social and economic danger to local growers posed by patent-protected seeds, and rightfully so. In the so-called United States in 2013, 93 percent of planted soybean acreage, 85 percent of corn acreage, and 82 percent of cotton acreage used herbicide-tolerant seeds owned by companies like Monsanto, Pioneer/DuPont, and Synergenta. Instead of a system with such astounding corporate control, Vía Campesina proposes an agricultural model toward comprehensive food sovereignty globally that solarpunks have drawn great inspiration from.[11]

With community control over food systems comes a resilience and autonomy not found in current global agricultural systems, which are largely managed by massive corporate entities with strict control over production, reproduction, and distribution of foods. Amid the COVID-19 crisis that began in 2020, we have seen massive disruption of global supply chains and witnessed the effects on our food systems in particular. Because of centralized control of both produce and knowledge, rather than simple supply issues, the so-called United States experienced shortages in flour and yeast, the absence of canned goods on shelves, price hikes on staples like fruit and eggs, and a moment of reawakening regarding the safety and effectiveness of the animal agriculture industry—particularly in meat-packing plants.[12] As solarpunks wrote in Bangladesh's *Dhaka Tribune* during the pandemic, "Sustainability just happens to work on a model that also brings independence from the systems designed for, or at least capable, of oppression. So, the broken supply chains, and shortages to follow, are not only making self-sufficiency more acutely attractive: they also open up a path towards greater freedom."[13]

While mutual aid groups sprung up around the world, focused on feeding their neighbors and keeping each other healthy, and mitigated some of the harm from the failure of the supply chain, COVID-19 still disproportionately affected people living in food deserts.[14] Note that the presence of food deserts in the so-called United States is intrinsically tied to its colonial legacy. Approximately 25 percent of Native Americans are food insecure, and the Navajo Nation, which experienced the highest COVID-19 infection rate in the country, had, in 2015, only ten grocery stores operating in the 27,000-square-mile reservation.[15]

Diversifying the food supply chain by localizing agriculture would go a long way toward building both urban and rural communities' resilience and independence during similar disasters, local or global.[16] Many solarpunks take as inspiration for such a system the *organopónicos* of Cuba. After the collapse of the Soviet Union, and in the face of the continued US blockade, Cuba's food systems were thrown into turmoil. In the preceding decades, approximately 50 percent of Cuba's food had been imported, and without access to Soviet oil, domestic industrial agriculture became increasingly untenable.[17] Organopónicos arose in response. Gustav Cederlöf describes organopónicos as "urban farms in which raised beds are filled with organic material to allow farming in areas with poor soil quality," and they have been cultivated in "back gardens, parking lots, rooftops, demolition sites, patios, garbage dumps, and unused urban lots."[18] Some have estimated that, in the first years of the new millennium, almost "90 percent of the fresh produce consumed in Havana [was] produced in and around the city."[19]

Solarpunks have already started building toward local versions of organopónicos through individual and community garden efforts, starting their own urban farms, and practicing guerrilla gardening (grafting or planting edible plants—fruit trees in particular—in public places for free and public consumption). Based on the success of such efforts, it's easy to imagine a world in which cities, instead of leaving lots vacant and open for development for years at a time and instead of continually evicting and criminalizing the houseless, have invested in food forests and housing with farmable green spaces. Rather than life-antagonistic and profit-driven cities that prioritize corporate interests and turbocapitalist growth, we imagine *living cities* where food and housing are trivially easy to access, where urban farms are encouraged and widespread, and where green space is valued for more than how much concrete can be poured on top of it. Such a community, able to meet even 50 percent of its own nutritional needs, would be well on its way to a solarpunk sense of independence.

Building Dual Power

Dual power is a pillar of solarpunk independence, and the structures we explored toward building food sovereignty can lay the foundation for how we think about dual power in other realms. Dual power is the manifestation of the imaginative and transformative heart of solarpunk: it takes a sustained act of hope and imagination to envision and then create entirely new systems that upend our understanding of the impossible. In a country where unemployment is a perpetual issue, housing is increasingly inaccessible, social services are gutted, local representatives show little accountability to those they ostensibly represent, and the federal and state governments refuse to offer a consistent and universal safety net amid a global pandemic, efforts to build dual power are the natural conclusion of the DIY ethos of punks and solarpunks. As the structures and infrastructures of the ruling class repeatedly fail the exploited classes, it becomes increasingly clear that the circuitous road to reform isn't the only option.

Enter dual power. Like the punks who see that their social environments are stifling rather than empowering and resolve to make something new, people working toward dual power seek "[to build] institutions of popular power from below to challenge and replace the governing institutions of capitalist society."[20] Instead of pouring energy and resources into working within systems that are, by design and as a matter of practicality, resistant to change and hoping for a positive outcome, the guiding idea behind dual power is to operate entirely outside of uncooperative systems by outlining a community's unmet needs, making a plan to meet those needs, and building the community-managed structures and institutions that will empower the community to realize those needs. The organopónicos discussed above are a direct implementation of this, and they're not the only or first project to focus on meeting a community's needs independent of a centralized state.

In fact, one of the most comprehensive projects for community autonomy took place in the 1970s in a predominantly Hispanic section of New York City's Lower East Side, known to residents as Loisaida. Faced with a local unemployment rate of nearly 20 percent and an average annual income of $1,852, residents of Loisaida took matters into their own hands. Dan Chodorkoff, who cofounded the Institute for Social Ecology alongside the late Murray Bookchin and who was involved with CHARAS, a group of local activists that was foundational in the development of Loisada's experiments, writes:

> Guided by the principle of local self-reliance, Loisaida's communities built their own systems of community-controlled schools, health care, law enforcement and governance; food production, housing, planning and land use; energy production and conservation, waste treatment and neighborhood economies. The members of the movement emphasized the interrelationship of their struggles and understood their communities as ecosystems, inherently non-hierarchical and mutualistic. They urged people to view their crises as symptoms of a deeper social and cultural malaise, stressing that natural systems find unity in diversity.[21]

This project represented a complete renegotiation of what a community's role in the physical, social, agricultural, economic, and political environment could be in densely populated urban areas. Loisaida also represents a synthesis of almost every core tenet of solarpunk that took shape decades before the term was coined.

On the flip side, the Ejército Zapatista de Liberación Nacional (EZLN), or the Zapatista Army of National Liberation, colloquially known in English as "the Zapatistas" and operating primarily in the Chiapas region of Mexico, demonstrates how these ideas can be applied on a large scale in rural areas. Since 1994, Zapatistas have controlled an increasingly large area of the state of Chiapas, governed them autonomously through community councils, greatly advancing women's rights, and provided comprehensive alternatives to state-sanctioned education, healthcare, and communication, all while refusing funds from the Mexican government.[22]

The Black Panther Party also sought to actively build and maintain independence through their Survival Programs, which included the famous breakfast program as well as plans to provide medical services, transportation, and much more to their communities.[23] These numerous examples make it clear that building dual power is a viable and effective route toward any type of independence. As solarpunk progresses, it will have to imagine and reimagine all the myriad modes of independence that a community must find, and it will, as all its counterinstitutional predecessors have, face enormous outside pressure from the systems it seeks to supplant.

Of course, communities will naturally have their individual strengths and weaknesses. Depending on the locality, one thing may be produced or provided in abundance, and something else may be lacking. If solarpunks focus on building independence with an understanding of their community as a discrete entity, any individual weakness or scarcity becomes exploitable by the hegemonic powers the community is resisting. And this is one area in which a well-developed sense of interdependence as an aspect of independence becomes necessary. Much in the way that a community, when viewed as a closed system, is interdependent within itself and becomes its own ecosystem, with each aspect in some way benefiting from and bringing benefit to the other aspects of the community, so do communities benefit from interdependent and reciprocal relationships.

Solarpunk intentionally views the systems around us from this ecological lens and sees independence and interdependence as manifestation of symbiosis, through which the whole becomes more than the sum of the individual parts. In the process of cultivating independence, we don't just step away from oppressors, we uplift everyone in ways that capitalist systems never can. Healthy foods become more readily available, interpersonal relationships are cultivated, communities become safer, labor becomes a matter of sustaining those around us rather than a coercive obligation, and everyone is the better for it.

Abolition of police and prisons (and other structures supporting them) is perhaps the culminating action of a movement toward dual power. It represents the complete separation of a community from outside, top-down power structures by implementing bottom-up social infrastructure that prioritizes life and wellness for individuals and collectives.

Independence from the Prison-Industrial Complex

This is an extremely brief introduction to the diverse and robust currents of abolitionist thought and their movements in the US and an attempt to situate and solidify the absolute and unwavering necessity of solarpunks' solidarity with them. We are only students of the many teachers who have put forth and made whole the frameworks of abolition, and we cannot possibly cover all the crucial angles of this conversation. We do our best to cite generously from those radical teachers who have influenced our thinking here, but even so, there is much that hasn't made it into these pages. We encourage anyone reading this section to *begin* with the sources introduced here, but we recognize that this is a cursory beginning at best.

The first and inevitable question we must address is this: How is abolition environmental? What does it have to do with a solarpunk ethic?

While the ties between the prison-industrial complex and an environmental movement spawned from the subcultures of science fiction and fantasy may seem difficult to trace, consider the ways throughout the book that we, rooted primarily in the ideas of Indigenous scholar-activists and role models, argue for the expansion of personhood from human beings to encompass nonhuman and more-than-human entities from individual animals to local systems to, perhaps, all the unknowable systems of the planet as a whole: from an individual river to the entire water cycle, the stones that make up a mountain as individuals and collectives, and the smallest bacterium that we enter into symbiosis with. Any attempt to extend personhood beyond the strictly human confines imposed by colonial capitalist thinking is inherently flawed if it doesn't, at its foundations, advocate for the full personhood of each human being first. And, as Ruth Wilson Gilmore suggests, what allows us to keep humans in cages if not thorough dehumanization and the revocation of personhood? Gilmore further argues that "in the contemporary world, racism is the ordinary means through which dehumanization achieves ideological normality, while, at the same time, the practice of dehumanizing people produces racial categories."[24] With this understanding and the understanding that the "prison is not a building 'over there' but a set of relationships that undermine rather than stabilize lives everywhere," it becomes obvious to us that environmentalism cannot be separated from abolitionist and anti-racist work without transforming it into another framework for oppression.[25]

We must also recognize the reality that prisons, and by implication the police forces that fill them, are inherently exploitative of the human body above all else. As a solarpunk worldview understands humans as an interdependent part of our surroundings, any abuse of humanity is also an abuse of all corresponding environments, physical, social, and otherwise. Tuck and Yang, in their essay "Decolonization Is Not a Metaphor," identify enslavement and imprisonment as functioning in two dimensions. These institutions function via the "removal from land and the creation of property (land and bodies)." Abolition, then, needs to consider both dimensions and work for "the repatriation of land and the abolition of property (land and bodies). Abolition means self-possession but not object-possession, repatriation but not reparation."[26] In this way, dominion over land and dominion over bodies are inextricably connected, and solarpunk as an environmental movement cannot exist without taking on the work of abolition.

We also believe that solarpunk aligns naturally with abolition because of solarpunk's emphasis on community and its punk-born love for taking direct and tangible action. We dedicate an entire chapter of this book to community, and in the process of developing it we realized that, while functioning as its own pillar of solarpunk thought, community itself is at the core of the other ideas that Adam Flynn identified as additional pillars: generativity, ingenuity, and independence. In response to the frequent, often bad-faith, question asked of abolitionists, "Won't abolishing the police leave our communities subject to greater violence?" Mariame Kaba says,

> We are not abandoning our communities to violence. We don't want to just close police departments. We want to make them obsolete.
> We should redirect the billions that now go to police departments toward providing health care, housing, education and good jobs. If we did this, there would be less need for the police in the first place.[27]

What she's getting at is perhaps best elucidated by one of abolition's most vocal and accomplished thinkers, Angela Y. Davis. Davis identifies the prison as "an institution that consolidates the state's inability and refusal to address the most pressing social problems of this era."[28] As world leaders continually refuse to take radical action on a global scale, climate change will increasingly reveal itself as not an environmental issue but a social issue rooted in environmental exploitation. As climate change accelerates, so will mass incarceration. It is therefore impossible to respond positively and with hope to climate change, to transform in the face of climate change, without accordingly changing our acceptance of widespread and brutal incarceration.

Much like cultural resistance to the structures that perpetuate and profit from climate change must move us to decisive action, so must our opposition to the prison-industrial complex. With a concern for the well-being of human and nonhuman beings and a penchant for taking action alongside artistic expression of beliefs at the core of the solarpunk ethic, we find that solarpunks make for natural accomplices for abolitionists and that, indeed, solarpunk is lip service at best without a meaningful support of abolitionist, anti-racist, and decolonial endeavors.

Finding Interdependence

The following chapters—addressing resource extraction, travel, relationships to technology and power, and the principles that can guide solarpunks toward an independence-minded design aesthetic—have in common a vision of the present and future rooted in the material impact we have on everything around us. They suggest routes toward building greater and more life-affirming systems. We encourage readers to engage with these pieces while reflecting on the discussion of independence and interdependence above, as we believe understanding the issues of food sovereignty, colonization, dual power, and abolition are crucial to constructing different and transformative modes of independence.

To start the conversation, Gabriel Aliaga points out the invisibility of mining when solarpunks discuss the future. The "solar" of solarpunk doesn't just mean solar panels, but many solarpunk stories and practitioners have them. Aliaga reminds us of our "mineral footprint," which is just as disruptive as our carbon footprint. As an industry insider and geologist, Aliaga explains that turning to solar panels and electric cars will increase mining even as the US works to shut down mining within its borders, which means these extractive processes will happen in systemically oppressed countries instead. Rather than switching to sustainable technology, which will initially require more mining, Aliaga asks the reader to consider how to change our ideas around technological consumption.

Following Aliaga, Navarre Bartz offers design guidelines to help makers and creators consider the "cradle to cradle" life span of their designs. In other words, how can creators consider the entire life span of a piece of technology, include what happens once it is used beyond repair. When paired together, these essays question our reliance on new technology and ask: If we can design better, how might this roll back our dependence on mining?

Kris De Decker's detailed essay on the construction of the *Low-tech Magazine* website demonstrates how Aliaga's and Bartz's ideas can be utilized in an everyday setting. Decker's essay explains why the internet uses such large amounts of energy and offers solutions that he and his design team have already put into place to build a successful and informative website. While this essay offers the beginning steps to building a solar-powered website, Decker also offers further articles and a link to their open-source project code.

Craig Stevenson's piece about solarpunk travel options ends the part with a more meditative and brainstorming response. He reminds us that travel can open positive pathways for cooperative understanding and cultural awareness that isn't always possible without being face-to-face. Stevenson proposes multiple ways to travel that, if approached with a solarpunk sensibility, would support the living world rather than harm it while undermining colonial tourism practices rather than supporting colonization. With Aliaga, Bartz, and Decker in mind, this essay gives the reader a jumping-off point to imagine how all these practices could come together to create a just and sustainable travel alternative.

Notes

1. Roxanne Dunbar-Ortiz, *An Indigenous People's History of the United States* (Boston: Beacon Press, 2014), 188.
2. John Womack, *Zapata and the Mexican Revolution* (New York: Vintage, 1970).
3. Liliuokalani, Queen of Hawaii, *Hawaii's Story by Hawaii's Queen* (Boston: Lee and Shepard, 1898).
4. David Graeber and David Wengrow, "How to Change the Course of Human History," *Eurozine*, March 2, 2018, https://www.eurozine.com/change-course-human-history/.
5. Eve Tuck and K. Wayne Yang, "Decolonization Is Not a Metaphor," *Decolonization: Indigeneity, Education & Society* 1, no. 1 (2012): 1.
6. Tuck and Yang, "Decolonization," 19.
7. Lauren Grewal et al., "The Self-Perception Connection: Why Consumers Devalue Unattractive Produce," *Journal of Marketing* 83, no. 1 (2018): 89–107.
8. Christine Ro, "Why 'Plant Blindness' Matters—and What You Can Do about It," *BBC*, April 28, 2019, https://www.bbc.com/future/article/20190425-plant-blindness-what-we-lose-with-nature-deficit-disorder/.
9. In particular, we recommend learning how to use the so-called invasive plants that grow in your area. (A full discussion of the use of the term "invasive" to describe plants introduced by colonizers is outside the scope of this section, but we believe it is well worth investigating.)
10. "International Peasant's Voice," *La Vía Campesina*, accessed June 30, 2019, https://viacampesina.org/en/international-peasants-voice/.
11. "International Peasant's Voice."
12. Katherine Kam, "How COVID Is Affecting U.S. Food Supply Chain," *WebMD*, June 18, 2020, https://www.webmd.com/lung/news/20200618/how-covid-is-affecting-us-food-supply-chain/.
13. Carin Ism, Marcela Sabino, and Julien Leyre, "The Call of Solarpunk Piercing through This Silent Spring," *Dhaka Tribune*, June 8, 2020, https://www.dhakatribune.com/feature/2020/06/08/the-call-of-solarpunk-piercing-through-this-silent-spring/.
14. "Collective Care Is Our Best Weapon against COVID-19," Mutual Aid Disaster Relief, accessed April 13, 2019, https://mutualaiddisasterrelief.org/collective-care/; Nathaniel Meyersohn, "Groceries Were Hard to Find for Millions. Now It's Getting Even Worse," *CNN*, June 9, 2020, https://www.cnn.com/2020/06/09/business/food-deserts-coronavirus-grocery-stores/index.html.
15. "Food Deserts, Food Insecurity and Poverty in Native Communities," First Nations Development Institute, https://www.firstnations.org/wp-content/uploads/publication-attachments/8%20Fact%20Sheet%20Food%20Deserts%2C%20Food%20Insecurity%20and%20Poverty%20in%20Native%20Communities%20FNDI.pdf; Hollie Silverman et al., "Navajo Nation Surpasses New York State for the Highest Covid-19 Infection Rate in the US," *CNN*, May 18, 2020, https://www.cnn

.com/2020/05/18/us/navajo-nation-infection-rate-trnd/index.html; Alysa Landry, "What Is a Food Desert? Do You Live in One? 23.5 Million in This Country Do," *Indian Country Today*, April 28, 2015, https://indiancountrytoday.com/archive /what-is-a-food-desert-do-you-live-in-one-23–5-million-in-this-country-do-eCu Qcy2SyOK6EQozR3IsDw.

16.   Marielle Dubbeling, René van Veenhuizen, and Jess Halliday, "Urban Agriculture as a Climate Change and Disaster Risk Reduction Strategy," *Urban Agriculture: Another Way to Feed Cities* 20 (2019): 32–39.

17.   Jason Mark, "Growing It Alone," *Earth Island Journal* (Spring 2007), https://www .earthisland.org/journal/index.php/magazine/entry/growing_it_alone/.

18.   Gustav Cederlöf, "Low-Carbon Food Supply: The Ecological Geography of Cuban Urban Agriculture and Agroecological Theory," *Agriculture and Human Values* 33 (2016): 775.

19.   Nelson Companioni et al., "The Growth of Urban Agriculture," in *Sustainable Agriculture and Resistance: Transforming Food Production in Cuba,* ed. Fernando Funes (Oakland, CA: Food First, 2002), 235.

20.   "Symbiosis: A New North American Grassroots Political Network," *ROAR Magazine*, March 1, 2019, https://roarmag.org/2019/03/01/symbiosis-movement-congress -announcement/.

21.   ROAR Collective, "Dual Power Then and Now: From the Iroquois to Cooperation Jackson," *ROAR Magazine* 9 (2019), https://roarmag.org/magazine/dual-power -then-and-now-from-the-iroquois-to-cooperation-jackson/.

22.   Zapatista Army of National Liberation, "Sixth Declaration of the Selva Lacandona," *Enlace Zapatista*, June 30, 2005, http://enlacezapatista.ezln.org.mx/2005/06/30 /sixth-declaration-of-the-selva-lacandona/; "Words of the EZLN," *Enlace Zapatista*, June 2, 2016, http://enlacezapatista.ezln.org.mx/2016/01/02/words-of-the-ezln -on-the-22nd-anniversary-of-the-beginning-of-the-war-against-oblivion/; Kurt Hackbarth and Colin Mooers, "The Zapatista Revolution Is Not Over," *The Nation*, September 9, 2019, https://www.thenation.com/article/archive/zapatista-chiapas -caracoles/.

23.   Ruth Gebrevesus, " 'One of the Biggest, Baddest Things We Did': Black Panthers' Free Breakfasts, 50 Years on," *The Guardian*, October 18, 2019, https://www .theguardian.com/us-news/2019/oct/17/black-panther-party-oakland-free-break fast-50th-anniversary.

24.   Ruth Wilson Gilmore, *Golden Gulag* (Berkeley: University of California Press, 2007), 243.

25.   Gilmore, *Golden Gulag*, 243.

26.   Tuck and Yang, "Decolonization," 30.

27.   Mariame Kaba, "Yes, We Mean Literally Abolish the Police," *New York Times*, June 12, 2020, https://www.nytimes.com/2020/06/12/opinion/sunday/floyd-abolish -defund-police.html.

28.   Angela Y. Davis, *Freedom Is a Constant Struggle* (Chicago: Haymarket Books, 2016).

CHAPTER 5

Your Mineral Footprint

Gabriel Aliaga

If you can't grow it, you have to mine it.

The above phrase is something you are likely to run into if you ever visit a mine or quarry. It's an important reason why people work in the mining industry. Mining is often associated with issues of labor, wealth inequality, geopolitics, and the environment, but these are not isolated problems associated solely with mining.

Solarpunk wants green spaces and may desire zero fossil fuel consumption, but does solarpunk envision a future where there is zero mining? What materials are needed for that future, and where do they come from? If everything is powered by renewable energy, how do we build the necessary infrastructure to harness that energy?

What I would like to talk about is the mineral footprint of our society, similar to the carbon footprint. Everything that did not originate from a plant or something living must be extracted from rocks. That's all there is to it. When we need galvanized nails for an outdoor project, we go to the hardware store. But acquiring such a small item requires a tremendous effort to extract the iron and zinc from naturally forming rocks in the ground. There is an entire industry of mining and metallurgical processing dedicated to converting a rock into a product with the right properties. If you have lived in a major city for most of your life, chances are you have never seen any of this industry in person.

The mineral footprint does not consider the energy and greenhouse emission involved in the extraction of minerals but the tons of rock you extract to live your life. The Minerals Education Coalition estimates that each person in the United States requires 40,633 pounds of new minerals every year.[1] For example, twelve pounds of copper will have to be mined to fulfill your demands across all the buildings, electronics, plumbing, and transportation you will encounter and use for the year. Copper mines can be economically feasible with ore grades as low as 0.5 percent—that is, a ton of rock with 0.5 percent of its mass being copper. To fulfill your twelve pounds of copper, about a ton of copper ore will have to be mined every year. To meet the demands of 300

million people? Or seven billion? You can begin to imagine what the mining industry does to meet those demands, and why new mines are needed to replace
exhausted ones every year.

I'm surprised when people pooh-pooh the sight of an oil refinery or a
mine, as though they have also never visited a gas station or purchased a light
bulb. To face and acknowledge your mineral footprint is a first step toward
building respect for your material wealth. The cost of replacing your cell phone
with the latest model is not just the number of dollars, it's the number of tons
of rock removed from the Earth and processed in several facilities to isolate the
copper, gold, silica, and rare earth metals, not to mention any plastic derived
from petroleum.

Land disturbance is the cost of replacing your cell phone. Open-pit mines
are often protested by the public, since it typically means an entire mountain-
side is removed just to extract the smaller ore body. Copper mines tend to be
open pits, and there are geologic and economic reasons for this. Imagine a
volcanic eruption occurring underground, such that all the gas, water, sulfur,
and assortment of metals—including copper, lead, zinc, and molybdenum—
are trapped in rocks instead of released into the atmosphere. That is a copper
porphyry deposit. The scale of these deposits is so massive that the economics
dictate an open-pit mine to extract the copper. I personally wish to see an end
to open-pit mining because I believe, with a change in culture and mindset, we
can instead extract metals from underground mines at a higher cost but with
reduced land disturbance. But I also think some context is important.

When I look out the window of a commercial airline flying over Nevada,
where I currently live and work as a geologist, the mines are easy to spot: giant
holes in the ground so that people can build new power lines, computers, cell
phones, cars, and the airplane I'm currently sitting in. But the rest of the land
is largely untouched by mining. Nevada is a high desert, and the towns are
small and sparse. However, the desert is not barren but rich with plants and
animals that have very little interaction with people; for the most part, they
are undisturbed. The airplane flies past the mountains of Nevada, past Utah
and Colorado, and is now over Nebraska, and all I see is an endless blanket of
farms until the horizon. *All* of the land here is disturbed in contrast with the
little pockets of land used to extract minerals. The farms exist to meet the demands of people, and the mines exist to meet the demands of a society that uses
technology. Regulation to stop farming does not mean people will eat less, nor
does regulation to stop mining mean people will buy fewer computers or cars.

The United States has been on a trajectory of banning mining. And while
we decrease the metal production in the country, I don't think we do enough

to decrease the consumption and demand for those metals. And so the mines move across seas and extract from developing countries, and we continue to purchase and ship that material back to us. We have foreign mining and exploration companies negotiating with economically challenged governments, which often leads to exploitation of those workers and communities. We see the poor treatment of Indigenous workers and weak environmental protection. In contrast, mines in the US have rigorous requirements under the Mine Safety and Health Administration (MSHA), and it takes over a decade for a new mine to open after a deposit has been discovered because of the time required to process permits and environmental assessments. Eliminating these regulations is not the answer; we must reduce our consumption. I keep hearing the economy must grow, grow, grow, but that requires more and more mining.

I challenge the reader to think carefully about what materials they consume today and what materials they require in their future. Really, I wish Americans would slow their consumption. I wish I didn't see so many car commercials for the latest model every single year. The progress toward all-electric vehicles *increases* the demand for mining, as more sophisticated materials are required to assemble these machines. Copper and electricity are best friends. Anything that runs on electricity will probably use copper wiring and components. A traditional gasoline vehicle typically requires about fifty pounds of copper, whereas an electric vehicle requires over 180 pounds of copper, as well as additional nickel, cobalt, lithium—whatever the rapid advancement of technology demands.[2]

Tossing out old technology isn't just adding to landfills, it also adds to the demand for mining. Because when you throw out your old computer, you are planning on replacing it with a new one, correct? People love new technology in all its forms: medical, entertainment, transportation, etc. But the rapid advancement of technology has a mutual growth relationship with mining, and it highlights a question: How important is technological innovation?

Pick an element from the periodic table of elements, one with a name you don't recognize. That element may have unique properties that are integral to tapping a renewable source of energy, but we just don't know it yet. Aluminum was once a rare metal, valuable enough to make into jewelry. But new technology in the 1880s allowed for cheap extraction of aluminum from bauxite ore, dirt that is rich in aluminum clay minerals. It was after the invention of this processing technology that aluminum became the principal material for canning food, replacing tin. And today we mine more than 160 million metric tons of bauxite to meet the global demand for countless products and new technologies.[3]

How important is new technology? If we envision a solarpunk future that is high-tech and in harmony with the ecosystem, I still struggle to understand where all that material and technology will come from without any environmental impact from mining.

You might say that recycling is the answer. And, indeed, recycling is my dream. A world that runs 100 percent on renewable energy and recycled materials will likely make my exploration geologist job obsolete, but that is a price I will pay without hesitation. Jobs come and go, and my geological interests will find a new home. But still, even if we recycle everything we have already produced, do we have enough cobalt for the next wave of electric cars? Do we have enough neodymium for all the cell phones of the future? And if we don't have enough neodymium for every person from every country to have a cell phone, what then?

The current imbalance of resources today is also important to consider. There is already an unequal distribution of resources simply because of geology. Ore deposits formed millions of years ago by unique and sometimes catastrophic conditions, independent of where humans live today. My point is that the US might be able to meet its metal needs by recycling everything it has produced in its history, but what about developing countries? What about places that still need power lines or water lines? Perhaps a mining-free future requires dismantling some of our infrastructure and material wealth so countries that don't have them can build the basic amenities. Are you willing to give up some of your materials?

Notes

1. "Mining and Mineral Statistics," Minerals Education Coalition, accessed June 30, 2020, https://mineralseducationcoalition.org/mining-mineral-statistics.
2. Nicholas LePan, "How Much Copper Is in an Electric Vehicle?" *Visual Capitalist*, November 13, 2018, https://www.visualcapitalist.com/how-much-copper-is-in-an-electric-vehicle/.
3. "Industry Statistics," Aluminum Association, accessed June 30, 2020, https://www.aluminum.org/statistics.

CHAPTER 6

Solarpunk Design Guidelines

Navarre Bartz

Solarpunk first came to my attention in 2015 through my interest in maker culture and steampunk. While steampunk has its share of baggage, the fascination with understandable technology is its most admirable trait. A series of pipes or gears can be difficult to design or maintain, but since the parts of the machine are visible to the naked eye, the machine is understandable even if you aren't a specialist. This speaks to an unmet need in our increasingly specialized and proprietarian society.

As technology has become more complex and electronics have miniaturized, even those of us who have degrees in engineering find many of these devices baffling. That said, not everything in life needs to be completely understandable to everyone. Specialization has its advantages, but it's inexcusable for companies or institutions to use complexity to hide corruption or maximize profits at the expense of people and the environment. Even when a repair would be simple, there are often artificial constraints like digital rights management (DRM) that must be circumvented to complete the repair. In most cases, this will void the manufacturer warranty for the item. Intellectual property has strayed from its original intent to protect small, independent inventors into a tool for big companies to maintain their hold over the market.

For me, solarpunk is about making an equitable future for everyone that best integrates natural and technological systems. As a maker and a solarpunk, I've been thinking a lot about how we can design objects and systems for that solarpunk future. Solarpunk doesn't advocate for either extreme of primitivism or techno-optimism, instead employing appropriate technology centered on improving life and the world around us. It is a minimalist approach to technology.

Minimalists focus on identifying the things that are truly important to them and intentionally adding only those things to their lives. It's not about giving things up but about being intentional in what we include. When it comes to designing our solarpunk future, we should keep this in mind. Just because we've always designed our devices, our cities, or even our social structures a certain way doesn't mean that we need to keep doing it that way. There's often a lot of vestigial matter in the built environment because we've been unintentional in our design approach.[1]

So when it comes to designing things, let's think about what really matters to the project and avoid adding things for the sake of having a longer feature list. When developing a new product or service, entrepreneurs talk about developing a minimum viable product (MVP). This MVP is designed to test the core functionality of a design to enable rapid iteration and not spend time on superfluous features. Feature creep should be examined with skepticism.

The pencil is a great example of solarpunk technology. Its function is to mark paper. The pencil's shape helps it fit in a person's hand to achieve that primary purpose, and while the eraser is a secondary function, it directly improves that experience. If you're like me, the erasers of your pencils get a lot of use. Not having an eraser can make writing or drawing a huge pain, so always having one at hand is excellent. That basic form provides a template for a variety of ways to put marks on the page, like more accessible grips or different types of graphite hardness for drawing.

A more recent example of good solarpunk design is the Pebble smartwatch. While a smartphone works without a smartwatch, the Pebble can help slow the torrent of notifications to a more manageable flow. By selecting which applications can send notifications to the watch and setting the phone to silent, I find my digital life to be much more tolerable. Anything I need to know immediately I have come through, and anything that can wait will be there when I turn on my phone. Think of it as digital triage. I haven't used any other smartwatches, but the Pebble's black-and-white e-paper display that works in broad daylight keeps things simple. There are apps that can enhance the watch's functionality, but given its limited processing power, they never get overwhelming. All this leads to a device that helps my mind be a little clearer throughout the day in exchange for a weekly battery charge.

To help me reframe how I design my own projects, I've developed a few questions to guide the process. Please take from them what you can, and let me know how they can be improved.

1. Would you let kids play with that?

When you design something, would you feel good handing it to a child? If not, is there a specific reason for that? It's one thing if you are making a saw and think it would be better handled with adult supervision because it is designed to cut things. It's quite another to hand a child a toy that contains lead-based paint because that gave it the color you wanted. Toxics are just one example, but if you're including something in your design you wouldn't want a kid to get their hands on, you'd better have a good reason. Hint: Making the product cheaper or easier to manufacture is not a good reason.

2. Did you make it circular?

William McDonough and Michael Braungart spill a lot of recyclable ink in *Cradle to Cradle* (2002), reiterating the importance of not being "less bad" when designing a product or system but making it "more good."[2] This means that you're actively ensuring that the production, use, and disposal of your design is a positive for the environment around us. For example, if you were making a bicycle tire, you would want to make sure not only that the bicycle tire is safe for the end user but that in every step of the process workers and the environment aren't exposed to toxic chemicals. Another aspect is designing objects with longevity. The tire should be designed to last as long as possible with robust components and a clear way to make repairs with nonproprietary materials.

In nature, there is no waste, only a flow of material from one use to the next. This eco-effectiveness is the central tenet of the circular economy. The eco-efficient approach of being less of a drain on the world around us just isn't enough. For our tire, this means that when it reaches a stage where it can't be repaired, it can be recycled into its constituent components. How can you make sure that the end of your design's life leaves behind a starting point for the others in our ecosystem?

3. Could you accomplish this task with less?

Solarpunk design neither eschews technology nor unquestioningly accepts it. Solarpunk takes the middle road of technological minimalism, using the appropriate technology for the job and not getting hung up on endlessly adding features or developing a product for its own sake.

For example, while data collection and monitoring are valuable for some applications, the explosion of "smart" devices in the home and city is concerning. Appropriate technology matches the task and the technology, instead of slapping an internet-connected microcontroller on every piece of equipment to maximize the collection of data. Many things in a city or a home can be accomplished more effectively with up-front investment in systems and passive designs that require little upkeep and no invasion of privacy to make our lives better.[3]

4. Are you focused on the object or the person?

As a young engineer, I assumed that if an object were properly engineered, it would get the job done, and that would be good enough, right? Now that

I'm older, and hopefully wiser, I've found that "form follows function" isn't the whole story when it comes to design. We can become overly focused on technology for its own sake or the parameter we've been assigned to optimize. The most common egregious example of this is engineering to minimize cost. Look no further than the Ford Pinto exploding-gas-tank debacle to see how optimizing a design for cost over other factors is a life-and-death decision.[4]

We need to look at the whole picture of how a product or system will be used in order to provide the best outcome for the person using it. Sometimes form is as important as function because it impacts how a thing is used. How does a person feel when they use the object? Will it enhance their natural abilities or frustrate them?

5. Are you taking a systems approach?

For a solarpunk designer, design starts with how the materials are sourced and ends with the product reentering either biological or technical nutrient cycles. Making sure workers are treated fairly and are not exposed to dangerous chemicals is as critical as how long it takes something to break down in the environment.

A simple example is a park here in Charlottesville, Virginia, that's between two neighborhoods. Because a large, busy road separates the park from one of those neighborhoods, parents won't bring their kids here because it isn't safe to cross that street. A more holistic systems approach to design would have included safe routes for people to get to the park from both neighborhoods and not just the greenery and facilities of the park.

Another aspect to consider is what societal systems are being reinforced or challenged by the design choices made. Does a product require a centralized production model with proprietary knowledge, or can it be made in a more distributed way? How can local manufacturing be encouraged while fostering international collaboration? The production of personal protective equipment (PPE) to respond to the COVID-19 crisis, where people from around the world have worked together on designs that can easily be made at the local level, is an excellent example of thinking globally but acting locally with our designs.

As we transition from our current society to a solarpunk future, a solarpunk designer will make the best choices they can and be honest about what compromises were made and why. I hope you find these guidelines helpful in making those determinations. If you take nothing else from this, I encourage you to put people first in your own work so that we can make a solarpunk future a reality.

Notes

1. Matthew Thomas, "When Good Interfaces Go Crufty," *The Web Blog of Matthew Thomas*, November 9, 2002, http://mpt.mirror.theinfo.org/stories/story Reader$374.
2. William McDonough and Michael Braungart, *Cradle to Cradle: Remaking the Way We Make Things* (New York: North Point Press, 2002).
3. Amy Fleming, "The Case for . . . Making Low-Tech 'Dumb' Cities Instead of 'Smart' Ones," *The Guardian*, January 15, 2020, https://www.theguardian.com/cities/2020/jan/15/the-case-for-making-low-tech-dumb-cities-instead-of-smart-ones.
4. Max Bazerman and Ann Tenbrunsel, "Ethical Breakdowns," *Harvard Business Review*, April 2011, https://hbr.org/2011/04/ethical-breakdowns.

CHAPTER 7

How to Build a Solar-Powered Website

Kris De Decker

Low-tech Magazine challenges the belief in technological progress for progress's sake and highlights the potential of past knowledge and technologies for designing a sustainable society. The website was launched in 2007 and has attracted a large following over the years. Many of the published stories deal with forgotten technologies that aim to inspire sustainable energy practices, such as heat-generating windmills, compressed-air energy storage systems, and human-powered tools. Because a web redesign was long overdue—and because we try to practice what we preach—we decided to build a new low-tech website that meets our needs and abides by our principles.

To reduce energy use, we opted for a back-to-basics web design, using a static site instead of a database-driven content management system. We further apply default typefaces, dithered images, offline reading options, and other tricks to lower energy use far below that of the average website. In addition, the low resource requirements and open design help to keep the blog accessible for visitors with older computers or less reliable internet connections.

Because the website uses so little energy, it can be run on a minicomputer with the processing power of a mobile phone. It needs 0.5 to 2 watts of power, which is supplied by a small off-grid solar photovoltaic (PV) system on the balcony of my home. Typical for off-the-grid renewable power systems, energy storage is limited. This means that the website will go offline during longer periods of cloudy weather.

Why a Low-Tech Website?

We were told that the internet would dematerialize society and decrease energy use. Contrary to this projection, it has become a large and rapidly growing consumer of energy itself. According to the latest estimates, the entire network already consumes 10 percent of global electricity production, with data traffic doubling roughly every two years. In order to offset the negative consequences associated with high energy consumption, renewable energy has been proposed as a means to lower emissions from powering data centers. For example, Greenpeace's yearly ClickClean report ranks major internet companies based on their use of renewable power sources.

However, running data centers on renewable power sources is not enough to address the growing energy use of the internet. To start with, the internet already uses three times more energy than all wind and solar power sources worldwide can provide. Furthermore, manufacturing, and regularly replacing, renewable power plants also requires energy, meaning that if data traffic keeps growing, so will the use of fossil fuels. Finally, solar and wind power are not always available, which means that an internet running on renewable power sources would require infrastructure for energy storage and transmission that is also dependent on fossil fuels for its manufacture and replacement. Powering websites with renewable energy is not a bad idea. However, the trend toward growing energy use must also be addressed.

Websites Are Getting "Larger"

The growing energy use of the internet is associated with two trends. First, content is becoming increasingly resource-intensive. This has a lot to do with the growing importance of video, but a similar trend can be observed among websites. The size of the average web page (defined as the average page size of the 500,000 most popular websites) increased from 0.45 megabytes (MB) in 2010 to 1.7 MB in June 2018. For mobile websites, the average page weight rose tenfold, from 0.15 MB in 2011 to 1.6 MB in 2018. Using different measurement methods, other sources report average page sizes of up to 2.9 MB in 2018.[1]

The growth in data traffic surpasses the advances in energy efficiency (the energy required to transfer 1 MB of data over the internet), resulting in more and more energy use. Over and above this, "heavier" or "larger" websites not only increase energy use in the network infrastructure but also shorten the life span of computers—larger websites require more powerful computers to access them. This means that more computers need to be manufactured, which is a very energy-intensive process.

Always Online

A second reason for growing internet energy consumption is that we spend more and more time online. Before the arrival of portable computing devices and wireless network access, we were only connected to the network when we had access to a desktop computer in the office, at home, or in the library. We now live in a world in which no matter where we are, we are always online, including, at times, via more than one device simultaneously.

Always-on internet access is accompanied by a cloud computing model—allowing more energy-efficient user devices at the expense of increased energy use in data centers. Increasingly, activities that could easily happen offline—such as writing a document, filling in a spreadsheet, or storing data—now require continuous network access. This does not combine well with renewable energy sources such as wind and solar power, which are not always available.

Addressing Both Issues

Our new web design addresses both these issues. Thanks to a low-tech web design, we managed to decrease the average page size of the blog by at least a factor of five compared to the old design—all while making the website visually more attractive. Second, our new website runs 100 percent on solar power, not just in words but in reality: it has its own energy storage and will go offline during longer periods of cloudy weather.

The internet is not an autonomous being. Its growing energy use is the consequence of actual decisions made by software developers, web designers, marketing departments, publishers, and internet users. With a lightweight, off-grid solar-powered website, we want to show that other decisions can be made. Below are some of the design decisions we made to reduce energy use.

Static Site Generator

One of the fundamental choices we made was to build a static website. Most of today's websites use server-side programming languages that generate the website on the fly by querying a database. This means that every time someone visits a web page, the page is generated on demand. On the other hand, a static website is generated once and exists as a simple set of documents on the server's hard disk. It's always there—not just when someone visits the page. Static websites are thus based on file storage, whereas dynamic websites depend on recurrent computation. Static websites consequently require less processing power and thus less energy.

Dithered Images

The main challenge was to reduce page size without making the website less attractive. Because images take up most of the bandwidth, it would be easy to obtain very small page sizes and lower energy use by eliminating images, reducing their number, or making them much smaller. However, visuals are an important part of *Low-tech Magazine*'s appeal, and the website would not be the same without them.

Instead, we chose to apply an obsolete image compression technique called dithering. The number of colors in an image, combined with its file format and resolution, contributes to the size of an image. Thus, instead of using full-color high-resolution images, we chose to convert all images to black-and-white, with four levels of gray in between. These black-and-white images are then colored according to the pertaining content category via the browser's native image manipulation capacities. Compressed through this dithering plug-in, images featured in the articles add much less load to the content: compared to the old website, the images are roughly ten times less resource-intensive.

Default Typeface/No Logo

All resources loaded, including typefaces and logos, are an additional request to the server, requiring storage space and energy use. Therefore, our new website does not load a custom typeface and removes the font-family declaration, meaning that visitors will see the default typeface of their browser. Only one weight (regular) of a font is used, demonstrating that content hierarchy can be communicated without loading multiple typefaces and weights.

We use a similar approach for the logo. In fact, *Low-tech Magazine* never had a real logo, just a banner image of a spear held as a low-tech weapon against prevailing high-tech claims. Instead of a designed logotype, which would require the production and distribution of custom typefaces and imagery, *Low-tech Magazine*'s new identity consists of a single typographic move: to use the left-facing arrow in place of the hyphen in the blog's name: LOW<TECH MAGAZINE. This pared-down identity drew inspiration from the past as well as the banner image of the previous design.

No Third-Party Tracking, No Advertising Services, No Cookies

Web analysis software such as Google Analytics records what happens on a website—which pages are most viewed, where visitors come from, and so on. These services are popular because few people host their own website. However, exchanging this data between the server and the webmaster's computer generates extra data traffic and thus energy use.

With a self-hosted server, we can make and view these measurements on the same machine: every web server generates logs of what happens on the computer. These (anonymous) logs are only viewed by us and are not used to profile visitors.

Why Does It Go Offline?

Quite a few web hosting companies claim that their servers are running on renewable energy. However, even when they actually generate solar power on-site and do not merely "offset" fossil fuel power use by planting trees or the like, their websites are always online. This means that either they have a giant battery storage system on-site (which makes their power system unsustainable) or they are relying on grid power when there is a shortage of solar power (which means that they do not really run on 100 percent solar power).

In contrast, this website runs on an off-the-grid solar power system with its own energy storage and will go offline during longer periods of cloudy weather. Less than 100 percent reliability is essential for the sustainability of an off-the-grid solar system, because above a certain threshold the fossil fuel energy used for producing and replacing the batteries is higher than the fossil fuel energy saved by the solar panels. Apart from sustainability (and costs), my home has limited space for installing solar panels and batteries. Keeping the server online no matter what—the standard business model of web hosting companies—simply requires too many batteries.

How Often Is It Offline?

Over a period of roughly one year (351 days, from December 12, 2018, to November 28, 2019), the server was up for 95.26 percent of the time. This means that we were offline for 399 hours (which corresponds to 16.64 days). These numbers don't tell the whole story, though. During the first ten months of this period, the server was online for 98.2 percent of the time. This means that it was offline for only 152 hours (6.4 days)—and this includes the winter months. However, uptime from October 1 to November 30 plummeted to 80.17 percent. This was caused by a software upgrade of the Linux kernel, which increased the average power use of the server from 1.19 to 1.49 watts, and consequently brought the website down for at least a few hours every night.

The data above refers to a setup consisting of a 50 watt (W) solar panel with an energy storage capacity that is equivalent to that of an 86.4 watt-hour (Wh) lead-acid battery. In December 2019, we started running the system on different sizes of solar panels and batteries. The uptime of these configurations is not yet known. At the moment, the solar website is powered by a 30 W panel and a 168 Wh lead-acid battery.

When Is the Best Time to Visit?

The accessibility of this website depends on the weather in Barcelona, Spain, where the solar-powered web server is located. Because it is solar-powered, the website is most often online during the summer. To help visitors "plan" their visits to *Low-tech Magazine*, we provide them with several pointers. A battery meter provides crucial information because it may tell the visitor that the blog is about to go down—or that it's safe to read it. The design features a background color that indicates the capacity of the solar-charged battery that powers the website server. A decreasing height indicates that night has fallen or that the weather is bad.

In addition to the battery level, other information about the website server is visible with a statistics dashboard. This includes contextual information of the server's location: time, current sky conditions, upcoming forecast, and the duration since the server last shut down due to insufficient power. To access *Low-tech Magazine* no matter the weather, we have several offline reading options available. For example, we offer a printed version of the website, which takes the form of two volumes with a total of 1,328 pages and 427 images.

Electricity Use and System Efficiency

Let's have a look at the electricity used by our web server (the "operational" energy use). We have measurements from the server and from the solar charge controller. Comparing both values reveals the inefficiencies in the system. Over a period of roughly one year (from December 3, 2018, to November 24, 2019), the electricity use of our server was 9.53 kilowatt-hours (kWh). We measured significant losses in the solar PV system due to voltage conversions and charge/discharge losses in the battery. The solar charge controller showed a yearly electricity use of 18.10 kWh, meaning that system efficiency was roughly 50 percent.

During the period under study, the solar-powered website received 865,000 unique visitors. Including all energy losses in the solar setup, electricity use per unique visitor is then 0.021 watt-hour. One kilowatt-hour of solar-generated electricity can thus serve almost 50,000 unique visitors, and one watt-hour can serve roughly fifty unique visitors. This is all renewable energy and as such there are no direct associated carbon emissions.

Compromise between Sustainability and Uptime

When researchers examine the energy use of data centers, which host the content that is accessible on the internet, they never take into account the energy that is required to build and maintain the infrastructure that powers those data centers. There is no such omission with a self-hosted website powered by an off-the-grid solar PV installation. The solar panel, the battery, and the solar charge controller are as essential as the server itself. Consequently, energy use for the mining of the resources and the manufacture of these components—the embodied energy—must also be taken into account.

Unfortunately, most of this energy comes from fossil fuels, either in the form of diesel (mining the raw materials and transporting the components) or in the form of electricity generated mainly by fossil fuel power plants (most manufacturing processes). The embodied energy of our configuration is mainly determined by the size of the battery and the solar panel. At the same time, the size of the battery and solar panel determine how often the website will be online (the uptime). Consequently, the sizing of the battery and solar panel is a compromise between uptime and sustainability.

Embodied Energy and Carbon Emissions

The carbon emissions associated with hosting the solar-powered *Low-tech Magazine* during the first year (50 W panel, 86.4 Wh battery) correspond to 9 kg—as much as an average European car driving a distance of 50 kilometers. A 50 W solar panel with a battery of 440 Wh—large enough to get through several days of bad weather—increase the yearly carbon emissions to 15 kg. A tiny 5 W solar panel with a tiny 15 Wh battery—which keeps the site online only while the sun shines—has a carbon footprint of 3 kg per year. Uptime and embodied energy are also determined by the local weather conditions, so the results we present here are only valid for our location.

Possible Improvements

There are many ways in which the sustainability of our solar-powered website could be improved while maintaining our present uptime. We already made some changes that have resulted in a lower operational energy use of the server. For example, we discovered that more than half of total data traffic on our server (6.63 of 11.16 TB) was caused by a single broken RSS implementation that pulled our feed every couple of minutes. Fixing this as well as some other changes lowered the power use of the server (excluding energy losses) from 1.14 watts to about 0.95 watts. The gain may seem small, but a difference in power use of 0.19 watts adds up to 4.56 watt-hours over the course of twenty-four hours, which means that the website can stay online for more than 2.5 hours longer. System efficiency—only 50 percent during the first year—could also be improved.

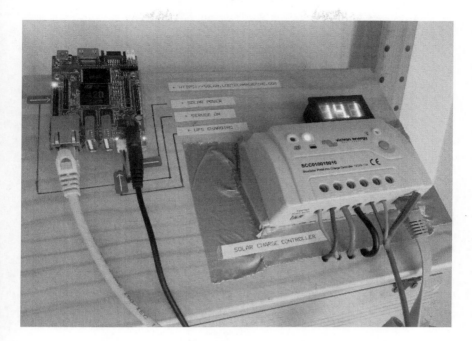

Fig. 7.1. The server and the solar charge controller

Another way to lower the embodied energy is to switch renewable energy sources. Solar PV power has high embodied energy compared to alternatives such as wind, water, or human power. These power sources could be harvested with little more than a generator and a voltage regulator—as the rest of the power plant could be built out of wood. Furthermore, a water-powered website wouldn't require high-tech energy storage. If you're in a cold climate, you could even operate a website on the heat of a woodstove, using a thermoelectric generator. However, unless we start powering the website by hand or foot, we're pretty much stuck with solar power.

Let's Scale Things Up!

A final way to improve the sustainability of our system would be to scale it up: run more websites on a server and run more (and larger) servers on a solar PV system. This setup would have much lower embodied energy than an oversized system for each website alone. If we were to fill the author's balcony with solar panels and start a solar-powered web-hosting company, the embodied energy per unique visitor would decrease significantly. We would need only one server for multiple websites, and only one solar charge controller for multiple solar panels. Voltage conversion would be more energy efficient, and both solar and battery power could be shared by all websites, which brings economies of scale.

Of course, this is the very concept of the data center, and although we have no ambition to start such a business, others could take this idea forward: toward a data center that is run just as efficiently as any other data center today but is powered by renewables and goes offline when the weather is bad.

More Information

The website: https://solar.lowtechmagazine.com

Web design and development: Marie Otsuka, Roel Roscam Abbing, Lauren Traugott-Campbell

The project is open source. We have released the source code for "solar," the Pelican theme we developed, here: https://github.com/lowtechmag/solar.

We wrote three articles with more in-depth technical information:

Abbing, Roel Roscam. "How to Build a Low-tech Website: Software and Hardware." *Homebrewserver.club*, September 8, 2018, https://homebrewserver.club/low-tech-website-howto.html. This article focuses on the back-end.
"How to Build a Low-tech Website: Design Techniques and Process." *Github*, October 30, 2018, https://github.com/lowtechmag/solar/wiki/Solar-Web-Design. This article focuses on the front-end.
De Decker, Kris, Roel Roscam Abbing, and Marie Otsuka. "How Sustainable Is a Solar Powered Website?" *Low-tech Magazine*, January 8, 2020, https://solar.lowtechmagazine.com/2020/01/how-sustainable-is-a-solar-powered-website.html. This article focuses on the sizing of the solar PV system and the optimal balance between uptime and sustainability.

Notes

An earlier version of this essay appeared in *Low-tech Magazine*.

1.   "Report: Page Weight," HTTP Archive, httparchive.org/reports/page-weight.

CHAPTER 8

Solarpunks See the World: Traversing the World without Destroying It

Craig Stevenson

Travel broadens the mind. Being able to meet people who live in different societies gives us a greater perspective on our own. Seeing the world and all the beautiful and unique places it contains, both natural and historical, gives us greater spiritual enrichment. Visiting new people and places can change our worldview in profound ways.

Air travel, currently the most common method of long-distance travel, is almost unparalleled in the environmental damage it inflicts. The fuel consumption of taking a single flight can wipe out years of ecological living. There is also the cultural damage caused by a tourism industry. Yet the idea that we may have to end air travel to change our relationship with the planet, losing all the opportunities it provides, makes me incredibly sad.

So how can we imagine a sustainable world that still allows for globe-spanning travel? How can we still have the joys of seeing long-distance friends? How can we still venture to new places and see new sights?

Perhaps the first hurdle is purely in our expectation of how we travel: we must sacrifice the expediency of the high-speed travel we do today. However, that wouldn't be an entirely bad thing.

Right now, jet travel has become more unpleasant for those who can't afford luxury. The drive to constantly maximize profits from air travel has seen those who can't pay for extra space and comfort crammed like sardines into tiny, uncomfortable chairs for long periods of time. For those without the extra capital, the journey is something to be endured before the real fun of travel can be enjoyed. This can be extra hard on disabled people, where the lack of space and restriction of movement can exacerbate chronic conditions. If we are to travel long distances, then an emphasis on a better level of comfort for all will be necessary. With that, the journey really can become just as important as the destination.

In today's work-centric world, our time away is measured in days and at most one or two weeks. This leads to the necessity of super-fast travel to make the most of this time. But with more time for leisure and exploration, we could focus on more long-term travel—slower, yes, but far more comfortable, sustainable, and enjoyable.

Trains

Trains are a wonderful way to travel. Currently, in the United Kingdom, I can travel between any major city by train, and traveling the 332 miles from London to Edinburgh takes about four hours. I can also travel internationally using the Eurostar. I can go from London to Paris, Brussels, or Amsterdam in about two to four hours. The UK's rail infrastructure isn't in the best shape by any means after years of neglect, underfunding, and being gifted over to corporate monopolies; it focuses purely on city hubs, letting infrastructure age and crumble and leaving low population branch lines to suffer. But with abundant funding and careful planning, a rail system can wonderfully transform an area's transportation.

The United States has had many proposals for a high-speed rail network that have never come to fruition, in no small part due to the automotive industry's lobbying power. This could be an amazing leap, being able to travel cheaply and comfortably across such a vast nation in about a day.

Trains would also be relatively easy to make eco-friendly. There is already a fully solar-powered train in Byron Bay, Australia, and because most trains are already electric powered, outfitting the infrastructure with clean energy supplies would be easy.

Imagine it: It's time to see your family or friends who live across the country, so you get a ticket for the cross-national train and, suitcase in hand, turn up at the station one afternoon. You glide through, so glad you don't have to deal with security and baggage handling and long boarding times like those awful old airports used to have. You walk through the platform to the sleeper car, where you find your allotted cabin. As the train pulls away, you finish stowing your luggage under the bunk. You first try the entertainment car; they have live music, but you find you don't like the band, so you opt to spend time up on the observation deck in a comfy chair instead. You have options to pass your time. You look out the big, clear windows as the sun sets on the beautiful scenery, noting how it changes so drastically as you speed across the nation.

After sunset, you go to the dining car for a good meal. You turn in for the night. Next morning you shower and enjoy a light breakfast from the continental buffet. As the train pulls into your station, you grab your suitcase and step off refreshed and ready to see your loved ones.

The question has crossed my mind: Could we make a cross-Atlantic train? It would certainly solve the big issue of travel across oceans at speed. However, it would be a massive undertaking. The English Channel tunnel between England and France was an engineering marvel, and it is only a fraction of the size needed for a track between continents. However, it would solve a lot of the major problems of boat travel.

Boats

Travel by boat is complicated on the ecological front. While it doesn't have the immediate impact of air travel, it has its own problems. Powering and managing cruise liners, which are essentially floating cities nowadays, is an ecological nightmare—not to mention the drastic effect their noise pollution has on marine life. The waste generated at sea by cruise ships is suspected to be a major cause of coral bleaching.[1] When you add the compounded effects of commercial shipping into the calculation, the damage of our current methods of seafaring becomes all the more egregious. If we are to have ecologically sound, long-distance boat travel and infrastructure, we are going to need to rethink it from the ground up.

Let us start with the base advantage of size. If you remove some of the more extraneous items from cruise ships, say, in-ship shopping malls, and re-place them with something useful, say, hydroponic food farms, you can begin to neutralize their resource demands, maybe even make them a self-contained community ecosystem. Then there needs to be a way to have the propulsion system run fully off self-contained renewable energy and reduce noise pollu-tion. It could be a hybrid system that uses traditional wind sails in favorable conditions and adds electric motors when needed. There is also something to be said for simply reducing the size of ocean transport. At smaller scales, wind power becomes far more effective, and the impact on the environment is naturally less.

Planes and Dirigibles

Dirigibles are largely seen as steampunk territory, a bygone technology whose era passed before it could reach its fullest potential, but a solarpunk frame-work and application could potentially bring back this romanticized form of transportation. Current designs for dirigible airships already use about 80 percent less fuel than jet engines, and in good conditions they could travel between the UK and the US in about two days.[2] If the propulsion system could be replaced with a noncombustion system, say an electric system, this would become a near-perfect air-travel method. It would still be faster than boat travel but great when you need to get about between landlocked areas. If a solar array could be attached at the top of the ship, then theoretically it could stay aloft for months at a time. Another proposal for maximizing space and weight in a dirigible is having no onboard engine and instead having it towed by a small boat via a tether. Sometimes we need to take a few steps back to go forward, and bringing back airships would be a perfect example of that. Learning to rethink our views of progress and technology can open up doors we previously closed. The revitalization of airships is a perfect example of what can be done with applying imagination to existing methods.

Traveling without Destroying Cultures

There is so much to be gained—spiritually, culturally, experientially, personally—from mass travel and long-distance travel. We can know friends with lives and experiences so different from ours. We can see the beauty in the world that would be closed off to us without long-distance travel methods. But there are many problems with the current structures of the tourism industry. Too often the homes and lives of the locals of big destinations are made invisible, wiped out, or displaced to make room for carefully curated resorts offering bland, carbon-copy experiences. The same strip-mall aesthetic dropped into a new location, walled off from the real lives and struggles of the communities around it.

This form of tourism is deeply rooted in colonialism. It devours Indigenous communities and their resources for the benefit of a select few from a wealthier and more dominant group. For travel to be solarpunk, we can't just change the technology. We must also examine why we are traveling and who it impacts. To travel responsibly is to gain new experiences, to meet new people, to gain a greater understanding of other cultures and not to simply go for the weather while imposing a system of exploitation on the communities and ecosystems we are visiting. No resorts, no uprooting and taking land to build an artificial playground for ourselves. It's traveling with the understanding that we are guests in other people's communities. There must not just be an element of equal reciprocation, although that is highly important, but also a sense of respect and a spirit of friendship to the places traveled.

Notes

1. Lauren Kent, "A Cruise Ship Spills Thousands of Liters of Waste in the Great Barrier Reef, Harming Coral Already in Troubled Water," *CNN*, October 23, 2018, https://www.cnn.com/2018/10/23/health/cruise-ship-spills-waste-in-great-barrier-reef-trnd.
2. "British Company Gives the Airship a Makeover," *The Manufacturer*, May 9, 2011, https://www.themanufacturer.com/articles/british-company-gives-the-airship-a-makeover/.

PART 3

COMMUNITY

"All Organizing Is Science Fiction": On Dreaming a Solarpunk Community

Phoebe Wagner

Since its inception, solarpunk has worked to redefine community. As Adam Flynn writes in his manifesto: "Solarpunk is about finding ways to make life more wonderful for us right now, and more importantly for the generations that follow us—i.e., extending human life at the species level, rather than individually."[1] Flynn's idea about the combination of contemporary issues with far-future concerns points to one of the more freeing aspects of solarpunk as a genre and ideology. It can focus on the present just as easily as it can imagine a post-apocalypse future. That tension between the present and the future allows for solarpunks to work in their communities now in hopes that the children or grandchildren of that community might experience the hopeful futures we've written down or imagined.

adrienne maree brown speaks to this timely tension between present and future by combining activism and speculative fiction: "I believe that all organizing is science fiction—that we are shaping the future we long for and have not yet experienced. I believe that we are in an imagination battle, and almost everything about how we orient toward our bodies is shaped by fearful imaginations."[2] As solarpunk creators, we've long connected with the idea of an "imagination battle," as solarpunks continue to imagine new futures in the shadow of and in opposition to environmental collapse, then working to create those futures. The longing and imagining must occur first before we can begin to visualize and act on the path to create those changes. We can't build a world without police until we imagine what that might look like—particularly when in the US state and federal governments have worked hard to make sure we can *only* visualize a world with the police. In the same way, governments and large corporations have attempted to make sure we can't imagine the nonhuman as alive in any sense we might consider "human" because how could extractive industries continue their destruction once we recognize the trees, mountains, rivers, minerals, flora, and fauna as kin we are responsible to? If all beings are equalized, how could police continue to dehumanize their human victims? Once we imagine and create stories or protests or reforms around these "unimaginable" ideas like abolition, kinship, anticapitalism, decolonization, suddenly other options with realistic possibilities appear.

Kin and Community

Certainly different cultures and groups have already engaged with a wider definition of community to include the rest of the living world, but the casual destruction of biological life in the US and by US imperialism across the world demonstrates the need for a new definition. Community cannot be restricted to simply you and your blood relatives, you and your religious group, you and your neighbors. We must understand that, intentionally or not, we are in community with our "pets," the bugs that live in our homes, the trees, the mushrooms sprouting after rain, and so on. To be clear, this idea goes far beyond campaigning for animal rights (though that might be a way someone chooses to engage with this larger community). Like much of what we've discussed with solarpunk, the first step is to change our thought patterns by bringing intentionality to the table.

In expanding our idea of community, we can also empower current social justice struggles that often organize around the word *community*. With a restrictive concept of community, it can be easy to interpret the assertion of a community as an act of isolation, as building a wall. This much was made obvious by the widespread and immediate ubiquity of "All Lives Matter" as a response to the Black Lives Matter movement. What underlies a response of "all lives matter," in addition to racism and white supremacy, is an understanding of community as an exclusive, rather than an inclusive, force. That a member of one community cannot be a member of another community, and that what one community has cannot be shared by any other. Instead, we argue for an enmeshed and interdependent sense of community that allows us to understand the world around us as intersecting subsets of a whole. Under this model, it becomes clear that issues in one community have a tangible impact on all related communities.

One aspect that constricts our idea of community in the so-called United States is a capitalist-driven false scarcity. Additionally, the institutionalization of monogamous marriage, the nuclear family, and the consequent delegitimization of other types of relating dictate what a "normal" community looks like.

But what does redefining community look like practically? How does expanding our community actively change what we do in our daily lives? One place we may start is with the demolition of the so-called United States' belief in human dominion over nonhuman and more-than-human beings. The unchallengeable dominion of human beings over the "natural world" is so deeply rooted in "Western" thought as to be traced to the earliest Chain of Being, which ordered "man" above animals, plants, and minerals. In other words, the separation of human and nonhuman is so integral to "Western" ideas of modernity, progress, and philosophy, from Plato to Francis Bacon and beyond, that to reimagine these relationships takes a serious act of will. Further action toward building inclusive communities means dismantling any system founded on these ideas, from white supremacy to big agriculture.

As solarpunk creators, one way we can work to weaken this ideology is to consider the language we use and write with. In "Learning the Grammar of Animacy," Robin Wall Kimmerer states, "[In] scientific language our terminology is used to define the boundaries of our knowing. What lies beyond our grasp remains unnamed."[3] Such a description might sound simple, harmless. Science is about "discovery," so of course there are boundaries that need to be crossed. But what happens when those boundaries point to knowledge that has been dismissed, such as the Anishinaabe worldview? What happens when those boundaries mean scientists must acknowledge that the animals they have experimented on for decades are in fact kin? That cutting down a tree means so much harm to a forest that it must outweigh the profit of the big-business lumber company? Science was and continues to be another arm of colonial capitalism that serves to commit atrocities in the name of modernity and profit—particularly through scientific language.

We are trapped by the English language when it comes to imagining community as anything but human/nonhuman or animate/inanimate. It might seem simple to modify English to match shifting cultural values, as we have done with the increased usage of nonbinary pronouns and neopronouns, but Nick Estes's description of animate language shows the depth such understanding must reach:

> Many Lakotayapi nouns, like "Mni Sose," indicate not merely static, inanimate form, but also action. In this landscape, water is animated and has agency; it streams as liquid, forms clouds as gas, and even moves earth as solid ice—because it is alive and gives life. If He Sapa is the heart of the world, then Mni Sose is its aorta. This is a Lakota and Indigenous relationship to the physical world. What has been derided for centuries as

"primitive superstition" has only recently been "discovered" by Western scientists and academics as "valid" knowledge. *Nevertheless, knowledge alone has never ended imperialism.*[4]

Estes recognizes how this idea of animacy in some Indigenous languages is already becoming trendy among academics, therefore granting it legitimacy by "Western" standards. The key point is that understanding this idea is not enough—we must translate the knowledge off the page and into action. These ideas are powerful because our disconnect from an animate, alive world as instituted through the English language makes it that much easier to abuse those "objects" rather than view them as alive, as kin.

One step is to adopt this grammar of animacy into our ideas of community and our responsibility to that expanded community. Donna Haraway rethinks this issue of translating knowledge into anti-imperialism by expanding the idea of kin as more than blood relatives or neighbors. She writes: "*Kin* is a wild category that all sorts of people do their best to domesticate. Making kin as oddkin rather than, or at least in addition to, godkin and genealogical and biogenetic family troubles important matters, like to whom one is actually responsible."[5] If we become responsible for these kin, then cutting down a tree because the branches block a view of the lake is impossible. We are responsible to the tree and the biome the tree is part of, just as we are responsible to the next generation.

Haraway turns these ideas into a slogan for expanding how we define family outside of bringing new children into the world: " 'Make Kin Not Babies!' Making—and recognizing—kin is perhaps the hardest and most urgent part."[6] Recognizing is key here, as for many folks, it will be much easier to recognize the animal companions one shares the house with as kin than the houseless community in the park up the street. We *cannot* sacrifice recognizing one community while disappearing another.

In many ways, modernity has simply recreated the Chain of Being, placing capitalism at the top rather than a god. A white man with a job is more important than a houseless man living in the park. The COVID-19 pandemic has demonstrated to what degree this Chain of Being orders who lives and who dies, as federal and state governments continued to sacrifice lives in order to "reopen" the economy, thus causing hundreds of thousands of people not only to contract the disease but also to risk the lasting physical impact doctors are only just beginning to understand, in addition to massive hospital bills, income and job loss, evictions, and the death of those made most vulnerable due to systemic oppression: people of color, the poor, the elderly, and the disabled. We have also seen who gets money and who does not, whose survival is a priority and whose is an afterthought or even a nuisance.

When evoking Haraway's Make Kin!, it must not mean the community a person already belongs to. On a small scale, making kin with friends and animal companions feels attainable—but humans are responsible to a much larger community. Indeed, Haraway gets at the fantastical nature of what "making kin" really means: "All critters share a common 'flesh,' laterally, semiotically, and genealogically. Ancestors turn out to be very interesting strangers; kin are unfamiliar (outside what we thought was family or gens), uncanny, haunting, active."[7] Making kin isn't only about finding like-minded people or familiar more-than-human relationships. It is something much larger and stranger. It will be uncomfortable, but nothing about the climate crisis will be familiar or friendly.

Further, we must consider why we need to make kin. It might be easy to dismiss this idea of kin and animacy as science fiction, but we must remember what Nick Estes points out: the US government knows of this power and has acted against it.

> The US military understood this vital connection to place and other-than-humans in the 1860s when it annihilated the remaining 10 to 15 million buffalos in less than two decades. A century later another branch of the military, the US Army Corps of Engineers, constructed five earthen rolled dams on the main stem of the Missouri River, turning life-giving waters into life-taking waters.[8]

If the US government recognizes the power of these ideas—returning the aliveness to the nonhuman—then we can work toward changing our thought patterns and our speech patterns to acknowledge the aliveness of those around us. We can work to reclaim that understanding in our own ways and through our own cultural connections.

This change will require creativity, as Robin Wall Kimmerer acknowledges when she points out the limitations of English. The language, born out of the same ideology as the Chain of Being, automatically restricts what can be alive: "This is the grammar of animacy. . . . In English, we never refer to a member of our family, or indeed to any person, as *it*. That would be a profound act of disrespect. *It* robs a person of selfhood and kinship, reducing a person to a mere thing. So it is that in Potawatomi and most other indigenous languages, we use the same words to address the living world as we use for our family. Because they are our family."[9]

As we stated in the introduction to this book, there is not yet an English term that truly gives the nonhuman a status equal to personhood without placing the nonhuman in a binary position to the human. Timothy Morton points out this challenge by asking: Where is the ecological pronoun? "There is no pronoun entirely suitable to describe ecological beings. . . . If grammar lines up against speaking ecological beings at such a basic level, what hope is there?"[10] If we accept the living world as kin and work toward Haraway's "Make Kin Not Babies!" then we must find different ways of thinking, speaking, and interacting with the living world, even in our limited English language.[11] The English language is not only a capitalist force but a colonial one, as Nick Estes and Robin Wall Kimmerer (and numerous other Indigenous scholars) have pointed out. As we work toward symbiosis with kin, perhaps solarpunks can rely on our speculative fiction roots—a literary genre that never had trouble coming up with new words—as we learn and relearn ways of speaking and writing about the living world.

An initial step to understanding kin is to recognize the kin and community present in our own bodies. In the US, much of the cultural ideology and propaganda uses the idea of the individual to separate people. Too often, individual rights are invoked to oppress minorities, whether it's the individual right of a store owner to refuse service to a queer couple or the right to display a fascist flag. The problem of American individualism came to a head during the COVID pandemic as certain sections of the population that valued their individualism cared more about their personal comfort than helping the nation stay healthy by remaining at home or wearing masks. Popular news media began to investigate the problem with individualism, such as the *Atlantic*'s Meghan O'Rourke: "We also live in a country stubbornly hung up on a damaging idea of self-reliance, a nation pathologically invested in the idea that we should all 'just do it.' . . . We are so addicted to the concept of individual responsibility that we have a fragmented health-care system, a weak social safety net, and a culture of averting our eyes from other people's physical vulnerability."[12] Capitalist propaganda also fueled the pandemic fires of individual rights as the economy, once again, became more important than human life. This is a fundamental failure to understand the humans around us as intrinsically connected to ourselves, but it also offers a path toward breaking down this ideology through reimagining our individualism by making kin with the more-than-human in our own bodies.

Our bodies only survive due to the numerous other beings living inside us. As Anna Tsing and coauthors point out, new research demonstrates that human and nonhuman are so connected we could not survive without each other: "Twenty-first-century research on organisms ranging from bacteria to insects to mammals has shown that symbiosis is a near-requirement for life—even for *Homo sapiens*. . . . [Our] bodies contain more bacterial cells than human ones. Without bacteria, our immune systems do not develop properly."[13] This recognition undermines the popular myth of survival of the fittest that underlies much of US individualism and capitalism. Our concept of the "individual" falls apart when symbiosis is recognized. When we understand that our symbiosis with the microscopic life inside of us impacts everything from the functioning of our immune system to our mental health and beyond, the "pull yourself up by the bootstraps" narrative of capitalism becomes even more indefensible.[14] We can't possibly be the masters of our own destiny, as capitalist narratives would have us believe, if even our bodies are a collaboration.

But capitalism and symbiosis are fundamentally incompatible. Capitalism rationalizes hierarchy by propagating the myth that the right and most qualified person will always get the job, that the market will correct if it isn't serving those most deserving, that productivity is a moral signpost. Rather than beneficiaries of systems designed to enact and take advantage of systematic oppression, capitalism says those at the top of the hierarchy are the most individually virtuous. None of this can be true if the individual as we understand it has never existed. Tsing et al. summarize this issue: "For later thinkers, rationalization meant individualization, the creation of distinct and alienated individuals, human and nonhuman. The landscape-making practices that followed from these new figures imagined the world as a space filled with autonomous entities and separable kinds, ones that could be easily aligned with the capitalist fantasies of endless growth from alienated labor."[15] Indeed, this distinction between human and nonhuman serves the capitalist regime and isn't born from our scientific ways of knowing. Nick Estes puts it this way: "Indigenous ways of relating to human and other-than-human life exist in opposition to capitalism, which transforms both humans and nonhumans into labor and commodities to be bought and sold."[16] By shifting our worldview to symbiosis, starting with the nonhuman kin living in our own bodies, we enact direct resistance to individualism and capitalism.

While many of the pieces in this part, especially those by Octavia Cade and Susan Haris, discuss how we can rethink this relationship with nonhumans, the struggle to rethink multiple ideologies so prevalent in US culture still may seem daunting. Anna Tsing et al. offer some suggestions that feel very solarpunk, including writing and reading "stories that take us beyond the modern individual."[17] They also suggest the most important place we could start: "Slowing down to listen to the world—empirically and imaginatively at the same time—seems our only hope in a moment of crisis and urgency."[18]

Building Community: Mutual Aid, Protest, and Communal Living

While the COVID pandemic and the 2020 summer of protest is changing how we think of our human communities, we must realize that change is difficult, and as the energy around these historical moments shifts, the community must transform with it. Building community takes time, and investing that time can be difficult. adrienne maree brown in conversation with activist Cara Page poses these questions: "And can I let people into where my visioning happens? Can we be intimate at the level of our longings? What as a society can we truly long for? Can I truly say out loud?"[19] These questions point to the necessary trust and foundation a community must build before the dreaming and working at a communal level can occur. Especially because the word *community* lies at the heart of contemporary organizing and solarpunk thinking, we must always remember that community building takes time and is revolutionary work constrained by toxic, capitalist ideology that we must work through independently and together.

During the spring of 2020, we observed a small mutual aid network develop around an online chat group. The goal was to make sure that people had everything they needed to survive during the spring COVID lockdown, and people were encouraged to offer skills that they would be willing to share, such as teaching magic tricks or school lessons for kids. In other words, the mutual aid network went beyond just survival to fun, particularly as many entertainment options vanished with the lockdown. The only problem was—everyone wanted to give and nobody wanted to take. Taking is necessary for the flow of a mutual aid network because it makes that community stronger as everyone is participating in the give-and-take. There's no single patron handing out gifts, and it acknowledges that *everyone* needs aid, not just those that society has deemed impoverished.

Part of the lack of taking is how US society stigmatizes receiving—asking for assistance is a shameful act, whether it's from the government or a friend. Like many people found out for the first time as the pandemic caused over forty-two million people to file for unemployment by July 2020, asking for assistance is institutionally discouraged through inoperable website design, confusing or limited instructions, and information scarcity, in addition to other methods.[20] In summarizing the studies of gift economies, Lewis Hyde writes: "[Gift] economies tend to be marked by three related obligations: the obligation to give, the obligation to accept, and the obligation to reciprocate."[21] The "obligation" to give as an act of benevolence has been spread throughout the neoliberal parts of the US, whether it's the soon-to-be trillionaire Jeff Bezos donating the bare minimum or the ever-present holiday bell ringers. Yet the chain weakens around the obligation to accept. We've watched friends who are in need refuse gifts, and we've also refused gifts when in need, preferring instead to give. Being the giver puts one in a position of power that resides better within our cultural concepts of wealth and excess. It also satisfies the US ideal of pulling yourself up by the bootstraps—making a way without any handouts while remaining a good, generous person by giving to others.

This broken chain in gift-giving certainly doesn't appear in every community, but the pressure put on regulated gift-giving around special occasions or holidays suggests the insidious capitalist underpinnings around something that should be foundational to a healthy community. Accepting the gift is just as necessary as giving the gift. One must be able to admit the need or simply enjoy the moment rather than feeling indebted or ashamed or guilty, as our capitalist ideas around worth have instilled in us. When one gives into a community, sees that community grow, and then accepts the returned gift from that community, it tightens the community: "The gift leaves all boundary and circles into mystery. . . . But when the gift passes out of sight and then returns, we are enlivened."[22] Being enlivened comes from reciprocally giving and accepting, whether that's from a close friend or family member or a neighborhood. Giving and taking also keeps the community healthy as it ensures there isn't excess that could serve to weigh down the community. Receiving is a form of allocating surplus, meeting need, and dynamically redistributing wealth. In other words, this type of gift-giving is ephemeral rather than accumulative and market-based; we don't only give birthday and holiday gifts but give something that can be used rather than accumulated. The potluck or church dinner might be the most familiar example—regardless of what is brought, everyone eats and takes home leftovers until nothing remains. The gift is consumed, not accumulated for capital gain. This gift-giving is in direct resistance to capitalism, as Hyde points out: "To move away from capitalism is not to change the form of ownership from the few to the many, but to cease turning so much surplus into capital, that is, to treat most increase as a gift."[23] Mutual aid networks not only make sure that needs are met but also provide an outlet for the surplus, whether it's a monetary surplus or extra phone chargers.

This type of gift-giving network might sound like science fiction, but it's easy to work for change out of anger and frustration rather than joy. Resistance, even when based in prayer and ceremony like during the Dakota

Access Pipeline protests at Standing Rock, is exhausting. Not all activism must be born out of opposition. Instead, we can start by creating what we want. We echo adrienne maree brown's crucial question: "How would we organize and move our communities if we shifted to focus on what we long for and love rather than what we are negatively reacting to?"[24] The work toward satisfying this longing is where solarpunks could really step up in their communities. Because solarpunk emphasizes local thriving over unilateral changes, solarpunks can dedicate themselves to realizing and building the environment their community longs for.

That being said, solarpunk is not immune to its own biases, having primarily grown out of speculative fiction and environmentalism—both places that have struggled with predominantly white (and at times explicitly white supremacist), heteropatriarchal foundations and power structures. Therefore, it has been and remains important for solarpunks to know when to be quiet and listen rather than lead the way, when to yield our platforms and power to those with experiences we don't and can't have.

If a core concept of solarpunk is imagining these new worlds—such as how we might transform the climate crisis—then solarpunk creators are in a position to imagine and record the longings of their personal communities as part of the project to enact them. Let's take the police as an example. We *know* our communities would be better without the police. Yet, as calls to defund or disband police become more widely reported, one of the first questions is almost always centered on "community": How will we protect our communities? First, what does the word *protect* mean, and who is so far outside our communities that we must be "protected" from them by a group better equipped than many military forces? Obviously, numerous people in our communities are not protected by the police but actively brutalized by the police, including people of color, disabled people, women, and queer people. In other words, everyone except the neurotypical, cisgender, straight, white men, who largely represent the population of the police in the US.[25]

The question then becomes: What are they protecting? Obviously not our right to protest, as seen by the summer spent protesting in 2020. Our bodily safety? Not if you are anything but white and male. Our property? Again, questionable since the ACLU and other organizations have well documented the abuse of civil forfeitures laws: "Civil forfeiture allows police to seize—and then keep or sell—any property they allege is involved in a crime. Owners need not ever be arrested or convicted of a crime for their cash, cars, or even real estate to be taken away permanently by the government."[26] Prod at these questions, and they begin to fall apart, yet until recently it was difficult to even suggest starting a conversation about defunding the police, let alone abolishing them along with the rest of the prison-industrial complex.

Scholars David Correia and Tyler Wall associate the struggle with the police around the narrative the US government (as well as other governments) have constructed for the police. They think through this issue with the term *copspeak*:

> This is a book about the language of police and police reform, both of which come to us in a register we might call copspeak: a language that limits our ability to understand police as anything other than essential, anything other than the guarantor of civilization and the last line of defense against what police call savagery. When we see the world that copspeak describes to us—one forever threatened by disorder and chaos—we have no choice but to trust that police, even in Ferguson, can get better.[27]

If solarpunk is truly the genre of reimagining a different world with hope through action, then reimagining what communities could look like without police is necessary. We must remember that the police infrastructure has actively tried to make sure we can't imagine such a world. We must resist by envisioning and enacting.

This is why, as an example, calls to defund, disband, and abolish the police should be as foundational to a solarpunk as environmental justice. Just as solarpunk literature calls to first *imagine* a world with sustainable practices or nonhuman relations or transforming the climate crisis, so too we must *imagine* what the world without police looks like. In the US, we have been so culturally infected with the idea that the police must exist that it can be hard to realize that policing only "works" for white people because it is a system of oppression for people of color. Part of imagining a world that utilizes solarpunk ideals means imagining what no police looks like. Too often, speculative writers with environmental dystopias show a lawless world without police, thus becoming complicit with the cultural idea that the police do something to protect communities.

When imagining and dreaming as a community, a solarpunk should be concerned not just about environmental impact but about how to make life better for everyone. As creators, solarpunks can work to normalize certain ideas that might seem far-fetched, much like the recent protests have worked to normalize conversations around abolishing the police. For example, one way to take back community organization is through living spaces and normalizing the idea of communal living, which includes multispecies spaces, as pointed out by Christoph D. D. Rupprecht, Aoi Yoshida, and Lihua Cui in their piece "Multispecies Community Garden." While the pandemic has introduced the idea of social pods—groups that might not normally live together but agree to interact only with each other for some sort of benefit, such as kids' playdates—say the word *commune* and eyebrows will go up.[28] If not outright suspicion, the idea of communal living, which is all "commune" really means, still prompts questions of feasibility.

As people, particularly millennials, learn to live in nontraditional homes—whether it's a tiny home or a camper van—the possibility of communal living seems more likely. Renting an apartment is generally considered the most sustainable and flexible living situation, yet this usually requires a landlord, and depending on where one can afford to live, one might face conditions that are nearly unlivable or dangerous due to the militarization of the police. Living in an apartment also continues to separate humans from the rest of the community. Having a landlord means less room to modify the space to make it more sustainable and less autonomy of living conditions. Sharing close spaces with other people also works to change what kin or family might mean. It shifts the idea of family away from relatives, particularly a monogamous pair with children. As Haraway writes: "My purpose is to make 'kin' mean something other/more than entities tied by ancestry or genealogy."[29] The nuclear family has long been understood as capitalist and conservative propaganda, meant to disconnect families from extended agricultural communities as encouragement to move to the cities. Living communally disrupts this ideology while also potentially providing a safe living space that is supportive, sustainable, and cheaper, allowing more monetary surplus to flow into the community rather than to a landlord.

We hope this discussion of reimagining community through the examples of abolishing the police and communal living with kinship points to a necessary change in environmental thinking: the idea of the environmentalist as the rugged hiker versus community organizer and community host. Environmentalists, and solarpunks, can no longer lean on the myth of the lone transcendentalist, the Thoreau, the Muir. We must recognize that environmental problems and colonialism, racism, sexism, poverty, capitalism, individualism, the myth of progress—all of it—are entangled with one another, as Anna Tsing et al. would say. They write: "[Industrial production] bury once-vibrant rivers under urban concrete and obscure increasing inequalities beneath discourses of freedom and personal responsibility."[30] It's all connected, an insidious form of parasitism that feeds and oppresses through each entangled problem. Therefore, the environmentalist attending a climate protest should be also attending marches and occupy protests for Black Lives Matter, abolishing ICE, and anticolonial movements. There is no room, particularly among white environmentalists, to protest one injustice without protesting the others. Abolition of the police is just as much of a success for transforming the climate crisis as it is for ending violence in oppressed communities.

Practices of Community

A common theme in this part is the need to grow our idea of community through changing our thought patterns, our language, and our worldview. The following essays look at how we as humans might reexamine how we live and how we move through a space, particularly by searching for rather than ignoring what else occupies that space, from disability activism to architecture to street dogs. When the local community comes to mean more than just the couple across the street but also their plum tree and the cat that lives a few doors down and the baby bunnies living under your wheelbarrow and the Black Lives Matter protest on Main Street and the microbes in your partner's gut—the community expands.

Petra Kuppers begins this process of expansion through practicing fiction. In "Science Fiction and Disability: Engage!," she gives the reader a story to finish, an exercise that engages with characters that have disabilities the reader/writer may not have experience with or recognize. This empathetic and imaginative exercise not only engages with disability history but also encourages the reader/writer to consider the relationships in their own communities. Is everyone as lovingly supported as the characters Kuppers presents in her fictional community? Kuppers guides the reader/writer into some of the foundational aspects of solarpunk living: changing thought and action patterns, imagining new worlds and ways of community. And, perhaps most importantly, facing these struggles with excitement and hope through action. As Kuppers writes: "To continue this narrative is to take sides."

Octavia Cade and Susan Haris tackle similar topics in different localities: How do we change our thinking and relationship to the living world? Cade asks us to change how we look at cities, shifting from not just ecosystems but to coral-like substrate that can be built upon, thus incorporating walls and roof spaces as well. Cade sees solarpunk as a way to change how we look at urban areas: "People who are looking to use solarpunk as inspiration, then, need to look for multiple uses in their urban architecture and infrastructure." Indeed, throughout her essay, Cade presents solarpunk thinking in action as she addresses urban problems. Haris reconsiders the Indian street dog, reframing the dogs as kin rather than nuisance. Both essays encourage us to, as Tsing et al. put it, "[slow] down to listen to the world—empirically and imaginatively."[31] When, as Cade suggests, an empty building is no longer empty but a habitat and home for endangered black-billed gulls, then our worldview has changed. When street dogs become kin, then our understanding of community has changed. These essays provide specific examples that the reader can study, then apply to the kin around them.

Connor D. Louiselle ends the part with his thoughts on the solarpunk revolution as "fruitful." In "Solarpunk: The Fruitful Revolution," he questions the stories we tell ourselves and how these narratives shape our capitalist ideas around a hopeful future. In particular, he contrasts cyberpunk and solarpunk, using the reoccurrence of cyberpunk narratives, such as the popular video game *Cyberpunk 2077* (2020), as an example of how narratives can have a powerful effect on our communities at large. Rather than focus on the individual hero going in guns blazing, Louiselle repositions "hero" to be plural: a community full of heroes that all work toward an abundant world.

These pieces provide a more in-depth exploration of how certain people and communities are already rethinking capitalist modes of connection. First and foremost, these essays recognize that capitalism places value—both in terms of monetary value and productivity—on human and nonhuman, so we must reshape our thinking to unlink value and "personhood." We also must learn how to make community spaces accessible for both more-than-humans and nonhumans as well. Part of the solarpunk ethos arises out of questioning these narratives of value and imagining alternatives that support our communities.

Notes

1.   Adam Flynn, "Solarpunk: Notes toward a Manifesto," *Hieroglyph*, September 4, 2014, https://hieroglyph.asu.edu/2014/09/solarpunk-notes-toward-a-manifesto/.
2.   adrienne maree brown, "Introduction," in *Pleasure Activism: The Politics of Feeling Good* (Chico, CA: AK Press, 2019), Kindle.
3.   Robin Wall Kimmerer, "Learning the Grammar of Animacy," in *Braiding Sweetgrass: Indigenous Wisdom, Scientific Knowledge, and the Teaching of Plants* (Minneapolis: Milkweed Editions, 2013), 49.
4.   Nick Estes, "Prologue," in *Our History Is the Future: Standing Rock Versus the Dakota Access Pipeline, and the Long Tradition of Indigenous Resistance* (New York: Verso, 2019), Kindle. Italics added.
5.   Donna J. Haraway, *Staying with the Trouble: Making Kin in the Chthulucene* (Durham, NC: Duke University Press, 2016), 2.
6.   Haraway, *Staying with the Trouble*, 102.

7. Haraway, *Staying with the Trouble*, 103.

8. Estes, "Prologue."

9. Kimmerer, *Braiding Sweetgrass*, 55.

10. Timothy Morton, *Humankind: Solidarity with Nonhuman People* (New York: Verso, 2017), 3–4.

11. Haraway, *Staying with the Trouble*, 102.

12. Meghan O'Rourke, "The Shift Americans Must Make to Fight the Coronavirus," *The Atlantic*, March 12, 2020, https://www.theatlantic.com/ideas/archive/2020/03/we-need-isolate-ourselves-during-coronavirus-outbreak/607840/.

13. Anna L. Tsing et al., "Introduction: Bodies Tumbled into Bodies," in *Arts of Living on a Damaged Planet: Ghosts of the Anthropocene; Monsters of the Anthropocene* (Minneapolis: University of Minnesota Press, 2017), M5.

14. Scott F. Gilbert, "Holobiont by Birth: Multilineage Individuals as the Concretion of Cooperative Processes," in *Arts of Living on a Damaged Planet: Ghosts of the Anthropocene; Monsters of the Anthropocene*, eds. Anna L. Tsing et al. (Minneapolis: University of Minnesota Press, 2017), M79.

15. Tsing et al., "Introduction," M6.

16. Estes, "Prologue."

17. Tsing et al., "Introduction," M9.

18. Tsing et al., "Introduction," M8.

19. brown, *Pleasure Activism*, section one.

20. Dominic Rushe, "New US Unemployment Claims Reached 1.9m Last Week Despite Rate of Increase Slowing," *The Guardian*, June 4, 2020, https://www.theguardian.com/business/2020/jun/04/us-unemployment-claims-top-4xm-despite-rate-of-increase-slowing.

21. Lewis Hyde, *The Gift: Creativity and the Artist in the Modern World*, 2nd ed. (New York: Vintage, 2007), xxi.

22. Hyde, *The Gift*, 25.

23. Hyde, *The Gift*, 48.

24. brown, *Pleasure Activism*, section one.

25. Dan Keating and Kevin Uhrmacher, "In Urban Areas, Police Are Consistently Much Whiter than the People They Serve," *Washington Post*, June 4, 2020, https://www.washingtonpost.com/nation/2020/06/04/urban-areas-police-are-consistently-much-whiter-than-people-they-serve.

26. "Asset Forfeiture Abuse," ACLU, accessed April 14, 2019, https://www.aclu.org/issues/criminal-law-reform/reforming-police/asset-forfeiture-abuse.

27. David Correia and Tyler Wall, "Introduction," *Police: A Field Guide* (New York: Verso, 2018), Kindle.

28. Ryan Prior, "Creating a Pandemic Social Bubble: A How to Guide," *CNN*, April 30, 2020, https://www.cnn.com/2020/04/30/health/how-to-form-a-bubble-wellness/index.html.

29. Haraway, *Staying with the Trouble*, 102–3.

30. Tsing et al., "Introduction," M7.

31. Tsing et al., "Introduction," M8.

CHAPTER 9

Science Fiction and Disability: Engage!

Petra Kuppers

You are at a writing workshop on disability and science fiction. Here is your prompt: a short reading, 1,000 words to set up a scenario. Sit back and enjoy the ride, with some provisos: this is disability culture, and it witnesses the terror, oppression, and pain of discrimination and its effects. The prompt invites you to change the future—and act in the present. Free our people, now.

ADAPT in Space!

The lug nut was stuck. Ham tried to find better leverage. He reached across the corridor and rammed one end of his pike into the soft pleather. Now he tried again, and the lug came loose with ease, allowing the wheelchair wheel to detach from its axle. Ham sprinkled oil into the elderly screw housing, careful not to let any of the precious fluid lift off into the air. After reassembling it all, he patted Ravenna's shoulder. Ravenna engaged the electromagnet that kept her attached to an arbitrary "down" position in the corridor and pressed the joystick forward. She rolled.

"Yay! Thanks, Ham. I think we are good for now."

Ham smiled shyly, and carefully tucked away the tools with his living hand. He never spoke with his mouth, but the fingers of his one hand were delicate apparatuses, ready to be augmented flower stamen to insert and twist in the smallest spaces. All his shipmates appreciated his skill. They let him know with their eyes and caressing touches when he had saved them again from immobility.

Ravenna rolled down the corridor, then reengaged the magnet on a different level at the next juncture. At the end of the corridor lay the sustainment bay. The three other travelers had already assembled around the circular table.

When Ravenna slotted herself in she joined Clara, also a powerchair user. Behind her was Jamie, triple amputee who couldn't sit on her decimated butt cheeks and who instead leaned against a portable pole magnetically fixed to either relative ceiling or relative floor. Lastly, there was Colo, demurely folded up in their chair, a non-Earth student taking Anthropology 425 as part of an Outward Bound degree course. Colo's green skin and six major appendages had long ceased to be remarkable to Ravenna, who had grown up on *Star Trek: TNG* reruns in her bio-family's holopod. Colo had been the one to call this meeting, as was their weekly duty.

"Ham just fixed my stuck wheel. He's putting away his gear. Should be here soon."

Clara signaled her response, an appreciation for their mechanic, with swift fingers. Her tiny dark digits emerged from the pouch she used to keep her small body safe, since her thermal self-regulation was inadequate to the leaching cold right next to the vacuum.

Ham emerged. A smile creased his brown skin when he saw his comrades.

"All together! All together now!" Colo couldn't contain their excitement again.

"So what's the plan for the next docking?" Jaime asked, accompanying her speech with a quick slide of her fingers down Ham's living arm, to make sure he felt included in their discussion.

Ravenna had their new itinerary ready on her tablet.

"Here's what we discussed last week. Entry on Centauri 7, Jamie in full limb drag establishes visitor credentials, talks about a child to give up, and visits with Un-Perfect Camp 37. Scope. Map. Then she comes back and we prepare dark entry, once we figure out the guard holiday schedule for 37. Any comments, news, issues?"

They discussed the plan, one not dissimilar from many unsuccessful and a few successful raids. If the personnel of the holding camps were thin on the ground and inattentive, they had always been able to rescue some of the Un-Perfects. Some children, some grown but kept like babies in beds, voiceless, agencyless, rarely able to see themselves as part of any group.

Colo took notes, acted as scribe. They got way too excited by planned future actions and needed something to focus on to be fully present in these meetings. Colo's people had also warehoused their cripples, but not for as long and never as systematically as Earth's people, and they were still unused to the normality with which Earthlings and their seeds discarded precious fellow humanoid life in holding tanks. The proposed liberation would be Colo's third raid, so they were still an activist greenhorn.

Clara had much to say about fine-tuning the selection process. She wanted more U-P6s, the ones labeled "useless lives," a category that had reemerged from Nazi Germany's catalogs around year 2035, shortly after the complete privatization of old Earth.

"They are so hard to move, though, Clara. I want to rescue them, but we could get out three or four U-Ps for each U-P6 we liberate." Ravenna wanted to be reasonable, but she couldn't figure out how to bring this argument home to Clara.

Clara signed back, "The other U-Ps usually have language, can sing to one another from one bed to the next. The 6s have nothing there, and so much to give us."

She was right, of course. Each category 6 had been able to modulate new speech and communication protocols, had been able to enrich the neuro-net of practices immensely, more than any U-Ps that had been able to adapt to their jailor's communication styles.

Ham pushed his good hand onto the table, fingers wide. They all watched the open palm and the waving digits. Each fingertip wove a song, a color, a flower opening—one for Ravenna, one for Clara, one for Jaime, one for Colo.

Late that night, Ravenna dreamed of the rescue. She witnessed herself rolling past locked doors, dark and light eyes looking out at her, pleading arms, fingers, mouths open and stretched tongues. Tears streamed down her face as she passed them by, careful not to roll over outstretched hands reaching through bars. She remembered her own liberation, a regular U-P, hoisted aboard a tricked-out electric chair, the rescue she had so long heard about in myths and fables passed from cell to cell at night, as little boys, girls, and others tried to soothe themselves to sleep.

Her re-education had begun in Ham's arms and in Clara's eyes, and culminated when they gifted her with her own specially manufactured bay at the oval table.

She had been given a choice: rehome on one of the sanctuary planets or join the resistance, fight the normals, and liberate their people one by one. The choice had not been a hard one.

A tenday later, Ravenna stood outside Camp 37, her graphite wheels whisper-quiet on the glass-like obsidian pavement, even in the near-Earth gravity of the small planet. Inside, Jaime had already disengaged a relatively weakly secured guard routine, had bypassed codes and electric locks with an hour's work once the guards were either out for a night in the local bars or asleep. Security was lax, as the objects of imprisonment were not valuable commodities—their lone value lay in insurance claims, not in any labor capacity.

A click. The lock in front of Ravenna disengaged, and the door swung inward.

Here ends this story fragment. To continue this narrative is to take sides, to engage, to identify, beyond the secure parameters of the potential suspense and narrative drive of a fully formed story. Interdependence is one core value of disability culture observations—and so this chapter practices user-focused, interactive, interdependent, and open forms as a way of marrying formal elements of storytelling to ways of knowing (or productive unknowing) disability. Tell your own story, maybe another fragment, maybe an ending, maybe a new beginning. Write with a partner, if that feels more supportive, or tell the story orally if you prefer.

Go on your own story journey now. As you enter the inner worlds of Ravenna, Jamie, Clara, Ham, and Colo, see their emerging skinshapes as invitations. Who would you like to be, or who would you like to meet? What are their thoughts, being part of this rescue mission, the break into the facility to "free their people"? Why are they in the fight? What is their backstory, their motivation, and their breaking point?

"Free our people" is one of the rallying calls of grassroots disability rights movements and organizations like the real ADAPT, a US-based group that uses actions like sit-ins in Senate offices as tools to draw attention to the plights of warehoused disabled people. Here is their mission statement: "ADAPT is a national grass-roots community that organizes disability rights activists to engage in nonviolent direct action, including civil disobedience, to assure the civil and human rights of people with disabilities to live in freedom."[1]

In this "ADAPT in Space" future story, who is behind bars, who awaits our team on the other side of the slowly swinging gate? Use your own imagination to flesh out the scene: Will there be a love interest? If so, of which gender/sexuality arrangement? Will there be racialized and class narratives of who is behind bars, who without, who cares for whom, who are the prison guards? What kind of U-P6 people will the team find in the camp? What are the differences between U-P6s and U-Ps in your mind? What will their options be for liberating them, for establishing contact, for communication consent? What happens when they have to leave some U-Ps behind, appendages full with U-P6s? What will go on inside your chosen hero when one of the U-Ps shouts out a heart-wrenching plea for freedom—or maybe, if they are to be left behind, for death? Would you assist them?

Many of the ethical and moral dilemmas and deep-seated ideas of "lives not worth living" come to the fore in our communal and different narrations of disability. Issues that arise include:

- complex issues of valuing people with communication differences and with cognitive differences
- pain and isolation
- mental distress associated with and not associated with mental health differences
- matters specific to acquired disability or veteran status
- effects of racialization and colonialism on denigrated humanity
- effect of being undervalued on one's own sense of self, and much more

As you unspool your own story, see where the understories are, the basements or hidden corridors that link parts of stories together. Transections and intersections, travels and encounters, are the driving forces of much creative writing, so allow yourself moments of surprise in the telling of what is happening on the other side of the gate and in the retreat to the starship.

Follow one character as they try to connect with a freshly freed prisoner. What concepts of freedom and responsibility make sense to someone who has been incarcerated their entire life? What survival strategies might they have, honed in a place with rationed food, set times of observations, little and highly codified markets of affection, warmth, and commodity? How can these strategies adapt to life in a free-er disability culture community, rattling about in space? Does hierarchy, traumatic stress, or fear affect newly freed people as they integrate with the shipmates? How do people find ways to be together, to survive and thrive? Are any of their tools and strategies particular to disability status, or does the team adapt tactics from other social justice movements? Think of something very practical like "the human mic" as a way to amplify quiet voices between cells (an instrument much used in the Occupy movement of the early 2000s, where lack of electricity created a way of amplifying a speaker's voices through a human-made echo). Or think of the tactic of pill hoarding, preparing a (final) exit path for desperate folks in the folds of mattresses or under loose tiles, or maybe just as a way of reminding oneself of the possibility of (even complicated) ways of establishing and fantasizing control.

Maybe you'll find yourself encountering aliens. Engage nonrealist forms of embodiment and enmindment (i.e., ways of being that are not known in the world we live in) and touch them to the lives of people whose bodies and minds were or are denigrated, seen as tragic or lost. How can you shape new worlds, with new openings for difference?

These are some questions to get you going, resources for engaging with important disability culture questions. You can spin on Jaime's or Ravenna's story while taking a bath or having a meal. You could talk with someone about it, maybe even slip into their voices. Or you could analyze a TV show with disabled characters. Do you see Ham anywhere when you turn on the TV or read a book? Or Clara? Why would Jaime be a likely figure in mainstream cinematic representation of "positive images" of disabled people? How do the people here relate to highly visible disability representations in science fiction, such as actor Dominique Pinon as John Vriess, the motorized-wheelchair-using mechanic in *Alien: Resurrection* (1997), or Professor Xavier in the *X-Men* franchise?

Think about the interiority of the people you are fantasizing stories around. In the fragment here, Ravenna is the emotional center, and we get just a few glimpses into some of the other characters based on Ravenna's past interactions and observations. How would this story look if Ham were the narrator? What sensations might be foregrounded, which might be less important? Or Colo? Or an as-yet-unknown character, either a rescuer or an escapee, or both, like Ravenna? In conclusion: this story has no conclusion. It is open; it points the way to new narratives; it offers incompletion as a linking strategy.

Disability authors have begun to reclaim disability from the often stereotypical and one-dimensional uses in mainstream texts. Collections like *Accessing the Future: A Disability-Themed Anthology of Speculative Fiction* (2015) and some of the stories in *Sunvault: Stories of Solarpunk and Eco-Speculation* (2017) address these openings for thinking disability differently in genre literature.[2] Genre narratives help to get disability unstuck: unstuck from eugenic stories of who could be left to die (for instance, in COVID-19 times), whose contribution is negligible enough to institutionalize them in nursing homes (just like so many in US prisons) or to keep building inaccessible homes that do not allow people to age well in place. To many people, current ways of engaging disability are "normal"—speculative writing allows readers to posit different values, to image a different spatial and emotional engagement with one another. That's why the speculative is such an important part of solarpunk: imaging and feeling a different world.

Activists of all kinds are embracing again the value of storytelling as a way of generating and sharing knowledges, as a form of analysis in its own right. *Octavia's Brood: Science Fiction Stories from Social Justice Movements* (2015) is an example of this kind of inquiry.[3] Evoking Octavia Butler, an African American science fiction writer and a form of fictional sociologist, the two editors, Walidah Imarisha and adrienne maree brown, worked with activists in multiple fields to explore the use of genre narrative as a way to communicate the need for and the opportunities of change.

"ADAPT in Space" sees itself in that heritage, embracing the capacities of all humans to tell stories, and to rehearse actions and reactions in them. Storytelling is an activist tool, a way of making change. Participatory artistic practices can allow us to feel things, to feel things differently, and to invent new appreciations for the diversity of humanity and beyond. The storytelling roundtable is prepared, your adapted and comfortable seat is waiting. No open fire in the space station, but everything else goes.

Notes

An earlier, altered version of this essay appeared in the *Routledge Handbook of Disability Arts, Culture, and Media Studies* (Routledge, 2019).

1. "Welcome to ADAPT," ADAPT, https://nationaladapt.org/.
2. Djibril Al-Ayad and Kathryn Allan, eds., *Accessing the Future: A Disability-Themed Anthology of Speculative Fiction* (The Future Fire, 2015); Phoebe Wagner and Brontë Christopher Wieland, eds., *Sunvault: Stories of Solarpunk and Eco-Speculation* (Nashville, TN: Upper Rubber Boot Books, 2017).
3. Walidah Imarisha and adrienne maree brown, eds, *Octavia's Brood: Science Fiction Stories from Social Justice Movements* (Chico, CA: AK Press, 2015).

CHAPTER 10

The Urban Reef: Breaking Down Barriers between Green Spaces in Urban Environments

Octavia Cade

We think of cities as places of opportunity. Too often, however, we also think of them as places of opportunity cost, as if the advantages of museums and nightlife are somehow offset by car parks and concrete. Far too frequently, this is a reflection of reality—and it is futile to refute the fact that cities overtake existing ecosystems and destroy what they are built over.

Yet this perspective ignores the ability of cities to develop ecosystems of their own, and in a way that is more than suburbs or corporations or school districts. This approach necessitates, however, the reinterpretation of the *entire* city as potential ecosystem, and not just allocated portions of it. Areas such as parks, reserves, and green belts are often perceived as separate from the more typically urban environments of the city, and urban experiences of the natural are often limited by the boundaries of these separated spaces. People who live in apartment blocks, for instance, may not have gardens of their own and may have to rely on city parks and similar green spaces for leisure activities. This may inspire loyalty to, and affection for, established green spaces within an urban environment, but it also encourages the lingering perception of other areas of that city as being irredeemably nonnatural, and therefore incapable of significant ecological contribution.

Solarpunk has the potential to reimagine the idea of the city as a holistic ecosystem, one in which increased biodiversity and an emphasis on ecosystem services are fundamental concerns. This reimagination, however, requires a radical reinterpretation of infrastructure, one that perceives built structures as if they were coral reefs: substrates on which a managed and diverse ecology may be supported.

If infrastructure is perceived as a substrate, the available surface area of any city instantly increases, and the potential for ecological contribution increases as well. This potential may be exploited in a number of ways. The first of these is taken from the example of the coral reef. Such ecosystems are places of enormous biodiversity: consider Australia's Great Barrier Reef, for example. Apart from the coral species themselves, the Great Barrier Reef is home to numerous species of algae, mollusks, fish (including sharks and stingrays), frogs, birds, crocodiles, sea turtles, sea snakes, dugongs, dolphins, whales, and many other organisms. The coral itself is the structure that supports the marine ecology of the reef, both above and below sea level.

It is, admittedly, unlikely that any urban environment could mimic this level of biodiversity, but it should be remembered that increased diversity within an ecosystem increases the resilience of that system. This is something to which the city of New Orleans could testify, following the landfall of Hurricane Katrina in 2005. The historical and ongoing destruction of much of the wetlands around the city—a result of such factors as logging, erosion due to levy construction, and the impacts of oil and gas exploration—meant that the wetlands' ability to buffer the effects of the hurricane, and give an extra measure of protection to New Orleans, was severely compromised.

A diverse, healthy, and complex ecosystem does more than provide aesthetic pleasure and a setting for leisure activities. It is also a provider of ecosystem services. These services range from the ability of wetlands to withstand disturbance or to sequester carbon, for instance, to vegetation types (such as tussocks) that can retain water in drought-prone soils, to the fertilization of crops by insects and other pollinators. Should an ecosystem be stripped of its services, as is often the case in urban environments, substitutes have to be made.

Green roofs and green walls are one potential means of this. Urban construction ensures a large amount of available surface area, or substrate, and the ability to adapt architecture to the reef parallel has the potential to provide significant ecosystem services. Roof space alone, within a city, is substantial. Often solar panels can be used to generate energy for the building, but the addition of a rooftop garden offers both ecological and financial benefits. Such a garden reduces the heat island effect so often associated with cities, helps to insulate the building and regulate temperature (leading to energy savings), and reduces stormwater runoff. Green roofs can also provide food, if intensively farmed, or flowers that support insect and birdlife. Beehives can be placed there. Green walls—also known as vertical gardens—have similar advantages, and the use of trellising or espaliered plants may increase the surface area available for colonization.

These techniques are used frequently around the world today. Clearly building green walls on a skyscraper is more challenging than building green walls on a bungalow, but the technology to do so is readily available. Patrick Blanc's construction of a vertical garden on a five-story car park building in Avignon, France, is an example.[1] A car park building is not something that is generally associated with surpassing loveliness. They are ecological and architectural blights, and typically they have only a single purpose: to provide temporary storage for cars. Instead, the building itself, when perceived as a substrate, can be used to mitigate the damage of what it contains, as yet another ecosystem service of vegetation is the filtration of pollutants and the provision of cleaner air.

Solarpunk, as a genre, places a high value on environmental health and sustainability. In an increasingly developed world, such things do not occur by accident. They are not a result of passive observation or indifference; they require management, thought, and the understanding that ecosystems, even in cities, exist *here* and not *over there*, in a distant park or along a riverbank. Usefully, solarpunk also places a high priority on community values, on bringing disparate people together for common goals. This view of community is something that must be applied beyond people, and even beyond other organisms. A city is a collection of disparate *structures*. These structures are linked economically and socially. They must also be linked ecologically. However, large-scale integration rests upon the holistic perception of the city as an ecosystem in its entirety, rather than in its parts. The Great Barrier Reef contains hundreds of islands, but this does not undermine its identity as a whole. Similarly, the urban environment may contain a multitude of single structures. It is still a city—and it is still an ecosystem.

Perceiving the city as an ecosystem results, as well, in consideration for the idea of the ecological niche. Within a natural environment, organisms compete to successfully exploit every possible living space within that environment. The classic example here was popularized by Charles Darwin in his description of the finches of the Galapagos: the birds' beaks differ in size and shape depending on the type of food the finches eat, and this allows different species with different diets to coexist in a limited space where seed eaters do not compete directly with fruit eaters or insect eaters. If urban spaces are regimented into natural and nonnatural spaces however, and those nonnatural spaces have, like a car park, a ruthlessly singular purpose, then the ability of organisms to exploit the architectural representation of that purpose is limited. Lichen, needing little water and less soil, may colonize the concrete substrate. Sparrows may nest in odd corners. Rats might scurry about inside, foraging for scraps that people have dropped—but this is an impoverished environment, and one that is incapable of supporting any real diversity in its inhabiting organisms. The place is largely sterile.

The goal of solarpunk, arguably, is to avoid sterility. Both in human communities and in ecosystems, the single perspective, the single purpose, is anathema to healthy function. Solarpunk, then, is well placed to address the crucial need for multiplicity, both of purpose and of perspective. People who are looking to use solarpunk as inspiration, then, need to look for multiple uses in their urban architecture and infrastructure. Actively perceiving the city as a reef, as a provider of substrate, encourages the deliberate construction of ecological niches for the purpose of diversity and healthy ecosystem, and it is this—the active provision of niches associated with structure—that links the urban reef together.

The possibilities of such niche environments can be surprising. They can also, sometimes, be invisible. If urban structure allows for ecologies to spread upward along the sides of skyscrapers and multistory car parks, it also includes the potential introduction of *subterranean* ecologies, and this is something that infrastructure can encourage. For example, in 2019, in the city of Wellington, New Zealand, scientists discovered that fish—specifically eels, whitebait, and banded kōkopu—were colonizing stormwater systems, living in pipes beneath the city.[2] Some of these stormwater systems included streams that had been covered over as part of the city construction, and while the freshwater systems of those streams, prior to construction, had ecologies that disappeared from the city as the streams disappeared from sight, the observed colonization indicates that such ecologies are not entirely lost.

Admittedly, this has significant consequences for water management. Storm systems beneath a city are frequently managed differently from stream systems (especially aboveground stream systems), and the Wellington example indicates that a change in perception is required. As with other reef organisms, fish are vulnerable to changes in their environment, and challenges resulting from, for example, pollution of the stormwater system will have to be met. Furthermore, different types of construction can affect these liminal environments. Water pipes that are particularly smooth (as is often the case when the pipes are new) have decreased friction and encourage faster water movement, making it more difficult for fish to navigate the waterways—especially when they need to swim against the current. Observation of the Wellington fish also indicates that, even underground, eels take advantage of hiding spaces as they would under riverbanks, and that tree roots and broken pipes provide habitats for them within the stormwater systems.

Given this example, the solarpunk city can envisage underground water systems colonized by indigenous fauna and can actively aid that colonization by providing dual-use infrastructure, which meets the needs of both human and nonhuman inhabitants. Pipes that have a rougher internal texture, with built-in sheltered places and deeper sections to cater to larger fish, are more likely to encourage these subterranean ecologies. Education campaigns on the importance of keeping pollution out of these waterways, combined with rigorous water testing to ensure the health of the underground stream systems, can therefore increase biodiversity in the urban environment.

Another example of this opportunistic type of urban colonization can be seen in the city of Christchurch, New Zealand. Following a severe earthquake in 2011, much of the city center was left in ruins, and parts of it were rendered uninhabitable—at least by humans. In late 2019, however, in the crumbling and derelict remains of an office block, a colony of tarāpuka, or black-billed gulls, was reported as living and nesting at the site.[3] These gulls are the most threatened gulls in the world, and so a thriving colony of 300 individuals is a promising sign. The habitat of the black-billed gull is primarily found in the vicinity of braided river systems—particularly on islands within these systems, which gives them some protection from predators. A fenced-off derelict building, with flooded foundations, seems to have provided a similar opportunity.

It is illegal, in New Zealand, to harass protected birds or to disturb them during nesting season, but the building's owner has plans to decrease the future viability of this new nesting site during subsequent migrations. Constructing nets over the remains of the building to limit access to nest sites in future breeding seasons, for instance, is one option being explored. In response, an online petition calling for the safeguarding of the new nesting site was established.

There are a number of factors to consider here. The reef analogy has proved an apt one—the biodiversity of this particular site has arguably increased, due to the introduction of a new species to that site. The existing (urban) structure is acting as substrate, providing a very literal support in order to sustain the new habitat. The birds are undoubtedly threatened both by development and by their preexisting vulnerabilities (a small population and declining natural habitat). And, as is often the case in the natural environment, ecological disturbance has allowed for a new colonization, just as the increasing warmth of ocean waters has allowed the colonization of the Great Barrier Reef by the crown-of-thorns starfish. Alternately, however, there is a valid economic—and engineering—claim. Reserving the site for the black-billed gulls removes the possibility of rebuilding the office block, and structures destroyed by earthquakes may be both unstable and unsafe.

It is here that the solarpunk ethos of community-building and ecological prioritization may be useful in brokering mutually satisfying solutions. Under a capitalist system it may be considered unreasonable to expect a single individual or company to absorb the financial loss that donating such a site to conservation efforts may cause. It could be possible, however, for that economic loss to be offset by compensation from government or community groups, or for subsequent rebuilding efforts to create a structure usable by gulls and humans alike. This may require some imaginative architecture and consultation with ecologists, but it can also prove an effective long-term solution that might garner significant public support.

In ecology, opportunity is everything. If urban dwellers can come to see the ecological possibilities inherent in the very walls and roofs where they live, in the derelict zones and the invisible infrastructure of urban environments, they can exploit it—and encourage other organisms to exploit it—more effectively.

If solarpunk's aim is to encourage a positive future by depicting the potential intersection of community, ecology, and technology, then that vision, applied to the city, is a roadmap for urban planning and architecture. Cities are not going away. The world is becoming more urban, not less, and so the focus on urban ecology is a growing priority. That can most effectively occur when the city itself is seen as a vast and interconnected ecosystem, full of ecological niches that can be both exploited and valued by the city's human inhabitants.

Just as the cities of the world are not going away, however, they are not going to be replaced. There will be no mass migration from New York or Lagos while each city is torn down wholesale and reconstructed along sustainable lines. Nor should there be: not only is such an outcome unrealistic in the extreme, it is also profoundly wasteful. Solarpunk prioritizes sustainability, and that includes the efficient use of current resources. A city may not be leveled to create, from scratch, an idealized urban community—but a single dwelling in that city might be, if it is beyond repair. A mass project to replace all the stormwater pipes within a city, regardless of their age and condition, is likewise not feasible, but when such pipes come to the end of their lives and must be replaced, they can be replaced with pipes designed to encourage the organisms capable of living within them.

Until then, small things can be done. Portable shelters can be placed in existing pipes. Suburban lawns can be replaced with native wildflowers and other plants that encourage pollinators, water conservation, and food production. Apiaries can be established on the tops of public buildings. Community groups can crowdsource the monitoring of plant and animal populations. Subsidies for solar panels can be made available; green walls and green roofs can be developed to provide valuable ecosystem services. These are not unachievable goals; they are things that are already taking place in many urban communities. What they are not, however, is linked.

These actions should not be cut off from each other. There is no reason that the cities of the future should be segmented into "natural" and "nonnatural" spaces. This limits the ability of *all* urban inhabitants to effectively exploit the very structure of their city. Imagine a reef that holds no seaweed or supports no fish. If such a reef did exist (and some are sadly becoming close to it), then it would be undergoing ecological collapse.

Such is the case with our cities. Green belts are not enough. They are useful tools, it's true, but they exploit often rigidly limited areas within urban boundaries, and the space that remains is a coral reef without fish.

There should be fish in cities. They should exist in more than just the aquarium. They should be in harbors and in pipes, in ponds and in rivers and along coastlines. They should be in canals. The waterways they travel through should be constructed to meet their needs as well as ours. The same should be true for many of the plants and animals that are currently found in cities; it is only by supporting biodiversity within the urban reef ecosystem that that ecosystem is strengthened.

It's the community-minded thing to do.

Notes

1.   Patrick Blanc,"5 Storey Car Parking above Les Halles, Avignon" (2005, Avignon, France).
2.   Kate Nicol-Williams, "Whitebait, Eels Found in Wellington's Stormwater System," *1 News*, April 6, 2019, https://www.tvnz.co.nz/one-news/new-zealand/whitebait -eels-found-in-wellingtons-stormwater-system.
3.   Charlie Gates, "Urban Bird Colony in Ruins of Former Office Block in Christ-church," *Stuff*, November 5, 2019, https://www.stuff.co.nz/the-press/news /117183089/urban-bird-colony-in-ruins-of-former-office-block-in-christchurch.

CHAPTER 11

The Commensal Canine

Susan Haris

In his celebrated essay "The Animal That Therefore I Am," Jacques Derrida points out that philosophers since Aristotle have denied animals language because they are not able to respond "with a response that could be precisely and rigorously distinguished from a reaction."[1] This marginalization is accentuated even more strongly in the Anthropocene, where the poetics of living determines the need to survive as the foremost character of life just as extinction is here the ultimate denial.

There is no univocal description of street dogs in the Anthropocene that will show them as heroic survivors against the onslaught of anthropogenic climate change or human exceptionalism. As animals that live in intimate articulations of relationships with humans, the lives of street dogs in the Anthropocene are influenced by human living. This asymmetry of power is such that the possibility of total animal liberation, so to speak, or a turn in human fortunes is predicated only on a dystopian future. For the moment, however, street dogs survive within human environs, their lives not completely shaped by human discourses or altered by human anxieties. They live commensally with us, forging a hard-won existence where they negotiate the perpetually changing landscapes of the Anthropocene alongside humans.

Indian street dogs are free-ranging animals that rely on waste and food from human settlements to successfully adapt and survive. A significant aspect of their existence is their legal status as street dogs. Under Indian law, street dogs can roam freely, need not have owners, and cannot be killed or dislocated. This legally sanctioned vagrancy allows Indian street dogs to exercise agency in their relations with humans. They enjoy freedom of movement, staying in self-demarcated territories existing in packs that may or may not comprise family members. In India they are highly visible fixtures of the city, imprinting on the architectural expanse, and an animal presence that is at the same time dependent on humans and relatively self-contained.

Canines are frequently cited as examples par excellence of interspecies friendships. Ethical relations, such as friendships, between species have acquired a new urgency in the Anthropocene because of the specter of radical extinction and apocalypse that loom over all life. In such a moral cosmos, as Zipporah Weisberg (2015) has argued, an animal ethics that is based on their suffering or capabilities or because they are "subjects-of-a-life" is inadequate. We should not strive to care for other species because of qualities they may possess or because they suffer. She argues instead for a phenomenological approach that strives to understand how animals perceive and experience the world around them. Such an intersubjective relationship between the human and the animal would recognize animal existence in its particularities, and it would supplement ethical injunctions by emphasizing embodiment as something that is shared between human and animal.[2]

In India, street dogs challenge our reductive assumption of being *the* sole species of cosmic importance in many ways. Unlike other urban nonhuman inhabitants such as pigeons, street dogs live completely conspicuous lives. They are not tiny, and they do not simply disappear from sight. They laze around and forage for food in human settlements that are marked out and divided up as territories among them. This criterion of visibility is crucial to recognizing certain multispecies possibilities in the Anthropocene.

Like other common nonhumans visible across India, such as the mynah or the common crow or even the cow, their visibility is not erratic or itinerant. They stick to their territories with tenacity by guarding and fending off dogs from other territories. Their visibility is most striking when they are injured and require medical help. Often, these wounds are caused by fights with other dogs or by passing vehicles, and in these cases the dog will continually lick the wound, sometimes aggravating a minor injury to one that needs decisive medical intervention. In such contexts, I argue that the Levinasian "face" of the suffering dog is thus offered to us for acknowledgment, and their canine visibility makes moral claims upon us by asserting the very alterity that usually remains marginal except in the case of an exigency.

This visibility-*as*-marginality is not only because of an ethical lack or a moral deficiency on the part of the human. The liminality of the street dog between a pet dog and a feral dog as a marginal but present figure is also sustained by the fact that street dogs easily traverse these different categories. Often, street dogs will prefer to remain outside the house except during inclement weather, will return to the streets once their wound has healed, or will prefer the company of other street dogs to a person who is affectionate and gives the dog food. The ethical response to the street dog is thus never complete or definite and is often highly context-dependent. For this reason, strategies for caring for street dogs vary widely. While legally street dogs cannot be relocated or dislocated from their territory, there is a concerted effort among NGOs and other welfare organizations to promote the adoption of street dogs over purebred dogs. The promise of transformation of a free-ranging dog into a domesticated dog only attests to the dog's adaptability. An adopted street dog's origins are patently obvious, which confers on it another layer of visibility.

Crucially, the territory that the street dogs occupy challenges the planetary perspective that we are encouraged to adopt in the Anthropocene where we think in terms of the planet and the universal impact of human-made change. The proximity of human lives to street dog lives complicates bestial imaginaries such as Jennifer R. Wolch's "zoopolis" that would redraw spatio-cultural geographies as more than just human because street dogs depend on human use of cities.[3] As modern urban humans navigate architectures of home, work space, and other social spaces, the street dog conflates shelter with territory and feeds on human food and waste. Street dogs in India stay within a particular loosely demarcated territory, but they often turn to shelter, both human and nonhuman architectures alike, whether it is a car or a banyan tree, a porch or a deep-dug hole.

Street dogs thus populate their diverse territories shaped by not only intraspecies and interspecies relations but also mutual perception, desire, and survival. One of the reasons for this adaptability is that their widely acknowledged ingenuity is closely connected to indigeneity. As "natives," or "locals," Indigenous populations are typically connected with locality, such as nature. As Francesca Merlan argues in her study of global and local Indigenous groups of people as a geocultural category, indigeneity implies dense links between group and locality by connoting belonging and origin.[4] While the cow has been appropriated and politicized in India for ideological purposes, the street dog has managed to evade such discourses—perhaps because of their tenuous autochthony, which allows them to be local without being privileged enough to lend to ideological propaganda.

The diversity of genetic profiles and crossbreeding makes street dogs unsuitable for a strategic essentialism that is often deployed to frame indigenous breeds and groups. Though dogs have superstitions and mythology associated with them, the street dog is a continually forming socially constructed category of free-ranging dogs that is open to both abandoned pet dogs and pedigree dogs. Thus, though the indigeneity of the street dog is played up with positive traits such as strength and loyalty for adoption, foreign breeds continue to be linked to status, wealth, and power for the average middle-class Indian, and hence preferred. In the popular imagination, however, there is not a huge distinction between the Indian stray dog and the Indian pariah dog, which is a landrace unique to the Indian subcontinent. The spiritual, political, and economic insignificance of the Indian street dog can be underscored by the fact that neither it nor the Indian pariah dog is recognized as a standard breed by any major kennel club or organization.

Nevertheless, in India, street dogs are recognized legally as ownerless dogs and cannot be killed or dislocated. Their vagrant, hybrid existence is thereby validated, and they are ubiquitous, especially in urban areas. Amid humans, their animal natures offer a curious contrast to the ever-increasing develop-ment narratives in India. They live in enclaves within larger territories popu-lated by people. As free-ranging dogs, Indian street dogs blur the boundaries of companionate species by living on the streets in specific territories and actively negotiating crises and catastrophes of location and place. These territories are marked out by animal hierarchies and availability of food, yet the street dog also gives the appearance of self-rule within them.

However, with increasing urbanization, street dogs do not face loss of land and home; instead, they combine and coalesce with the urban landscapes. This is not to suggest that they do not face mistreatment and cruelty at the hands of humans but that in the Anthropocene they are also part of the evolving urban mythologies of modern societies in India. Tentatively and precariously Indigenous, street dogs are not consigned to an unchanging, invariable tradi-tion of fixed location.

This is not to say that they live an unimperiled existence of free play. They are subject to the 2001 Animal Birth Control (ABC) rules requiring neutering and vaccination to manage their population. Before these laws were passed, street dogs could be electrocuted or poisoned. As carriers for the rabies virus, they also pose credible threats to humans, and dog bites are widely feared. Street dogs are therefore not animals with which we typically have a symbiotic relationship. In fact, street dogs do not meet the criteria for meeting our eco-nomic interests, social benefits, or aesthetic standards. They are also not char-ismatic megafauna like leopards or endangered beings like the Bengal tiger.

How then can we contextualize their existence in the Anthropocene? Animals have been described as living in the "eternal present" as opposed to humans, who continue to evolve because of our special culturally mediated re-lationships with time. Psychologists often point out that humans can interpret successive events and think in time to form causal connections and conceive of alternative pasts and futures. In the Anthropocene, though, the addition of the dimensions of geological time complicates such a neat division. Geological time not only renders humans insignificant in the planetary history of innumerable species but also equalizes by showing us how other species compose time and living in the Anthropocene as more than transitory or momentary. Is survival in the Anthropocene, then, provisory?

While theorists like Donna Haraway have made it clear through work on simians and cyborgs that the divisional hierarchy between human and animal is untenable, there remains an entrenched focus on the human as the principal actor of the Anthropocene. Cthulhucene, Haraway's renaming of the Anthropocene, aims to decenter the human in its unhuman formulation. The Cthulhucene is the age of deeply entangling human stories with the Earth such that we are part of the biotic and abiotic assemblages that comprise the human, nonhuman, other-than-human, etc. Such an active rewriting of history is hopeful at the present moment: by "staying with the trouble" with what is at stake now is thus the Cthulhucene story where "we are humus, not Homo, not anthropos; we are compost, not posthuman."[5]

Street dogs in India eke out a hard-earned existence by living *commensally* with human beings. Commensality is an important theme in religious and ritualistic contexts that focus on a common sociality based on what is holy, clean, customary, etc. Street dogs live in great proximity with humans harmlessly, but they also live alongside us in the other sense of the term, which refers to fellowship at the table; that is, to eat together at the same table. Commensality in this sense is both literal and metaphorical. The commensality of shared food generates a tactical association where the human and the dog consume the same food. Street dogs are often given human food such as cheap glucose biscuits, rice, or roti. But commensality refers also to the shared finitude and vulnerability even as the relations between humans and dogs vary through indices of power, class, culture, etc.

I propose that the contingency of the Anthropocene is such that it invites us to undercut human exceptionalism not only by recognizing nonhuman ways of inhabiting infinite phenomenal worlds but also by actively registering and foregrounding the permanent precariousness of the relationships forged between species such as between the street dog and the human.

Discussions of Jakob von Uexküll's useful concept of the *umwelt* tell us that animals do not merely carry out functions; instead, they are "always already engaged in meaningful encounters with and in the world and the objects and beings it encounters."[6] Yet, despite the barriers of language and species, the promise and possibility of multispecies ethnography lies in the forms of meaning that can be produced between species. Can meaning be generated between different species that is not human-determinative and privileged when existence for the animal is provisory?

Dogs feature prominently in Donna Haraway's *Companion Species Manifesto*

(2003).[7] Anyone who is friendly with dogs would immediately identify with Haraway's descriptions of canine play and freedom without discounting canine personalities and eccentricities. With street dogs, however, this dynamic is slightly different, as they fracture the satisfying and rewarding conviviality of our pet companions. Among street dogs, kinship is randomized as they are differently friendly and engage in varying degrees and styles of relationality with humans. Thus, in spite of their near total dependence on humans for sustenance, street dogs individuate in ways that go beyond immediate responses or characteristic personalities. That is, it cannot be oversimplified that some street dogs *are* friendly and some are *not*, or that relationships with street dogs are regulated *solely* by canine and human personalities. While the terrible phantasm of robots rising up in revolution against humans or cinematic fantasies of rebellious sentient apes rely on technology or imaginary processes akin to uplift, questions of sentience and species-being are secondary to a group as hybrid and varied as street dogs. In the radical present of the Anthropocene, street dogs resist narratives of collective subject-hood and domination and also, by extension, submission to the human.

In *Staying with the Trouble* (2016), Haraway exhorts us to "Make kin not babies!" to point out how kinship norms among humans perpetuate oppression by reproducing hierarchies along divisions of gender, labor, and race.[8] For Haraway capitalist structures are reproduced in traditional families that naturalize exclusions and hierarchies. Street dogs carelessly and unselfconsciously undo these hierarchies and social orders by mating across breeds, and thus they seem to combat the classificatory discourses of the Anthropocene and extinction.

There has been an increased emphasis on narrative and place in multispecies ethnography that shows us how the narratives of nonhumans such as animals, fungi, and plants should matter. Furthermore, this "nonhuman storying of places" makes animals constitutive of existence in the Anthropocene by figuring alternative ways of individuating, emplacing, and embodying that are not restricted to the human.[9] Even so, in urban environments that are so markedly human, this poses a dilemma. In urban spaces that are ostensibly considered human spaces of cultural and political life, it may be difficult to privilege multispecies communities where interactions with urban animals like pigeons or dogs are marked out as ordinary, mundane, and insignificant. If we are cohabiting a space with an animal, how can we make them a narratival subject contra humans without making their utilization and operation of the urban cosmos look artificial and unnatural?

The key to the problem lies in waste. The relation between street dogs and garbage is well documented. Street dogs in India rarely turn predator other than while chasing squirrels and birds, and instead they rely on garbage for food. This necessarily means that street dogs are more visible in urban areas near places where public waste is disposed. Indeed, street dogs are visible not only near garbage dumps and landfills but also frequently at hotels, restaurants, shopping centers, and homes, where they are given food that is left over and in excess.

Waste plays a crucial role in the urban economy and urban ordering apart from being a witness to and remainder of development and industrialization. Waste is what is determined as expendable by citizens and the state, and increasingly waste management is also associated with a clean, urban, green future. In addition, however, there are numerable informal economies of poor people, children, and animals who engage with waste. The superior knowledge of waste-pickers and ragpickers through their collection, sorting, and salvage procedures has been noted in studies of urban waste and infrastructures, and street dogs also possess a similar repertoire of expertise relating to garbage.

Street dogs are, of course, not part of the official economies of bureaucratic waste management. Even as modern state apparatuses in India such as municipal corporations attempt to regiment waste through better and bigger bins so that animals cannot forage through them, street dogs continue to skillfully improvise. Some dogs jump into the bins to access food, some wait till the bins are filled to the brim, and some simply knock the bins over. Their evolutionary ingenuity reminds us that consumption in the Anthropocene can never be attuned solely to human needs, expectations, projections, and machinations. The street dog forages tirelessly and regularly through garbage by using its brilliant nose to fish out delicious morsels. Thus, while street dogs may very well have alternative nonhuman Weltanschauungen that can alert us to other ontologies, they are also already workers in a multispecies workplace and are co-constitutive of urban ecologies through their participation.

Compare a street dog with the Japanese matsutake mushroom that Anna Tsing has extensively studied for its ability to grow in damaged ecosystems. The first living thing to grow in the "blasted landscape" of Hiroshima after it was destroyed by the atomic bomb in 1945 was the matsutake mushroom. For Tsing, the mushroom's growth in that devastated landscape lets us navigate the "ruin that has become our collective home."[10]

Compare now a street dog with apocalyptic narratives from Hollywood that feature a man and his dog looking back at the end of the world, such as the 2007 movie *I Am Legend*. In the film, which is set in 2009, US Army virologist Lt. Col. Robert Neville, played by Will Smith, works on infected rats alongside his only companion, Sam, a German shepherd who becomes infected and is ultimately killed by the end of the movie. In a morbid turn of events, Neville also sacrifices himself after having found the cure and having passed it along to a set of immune humans to protect them. The apocalypse dog shares his fate with the human, and hope is generated after their deaths *beyond* the movie. But in the "blasted landscape" in the movie, the apocalypse dog lives out its life.

The street dog is intimately bound up with modern urban human practices, and it is widely accepted that it is sturdier than the pedigree dogs and has a tougher stomach and stronger immune system. As opposed to the pet dog that lives in the comfort of the human shelter, the street dog has acquired some resilience through living already in the blasted landscape of today. In the "patchy Anthropocene," where "the uneven conditions of more-than-human livability in landscapes" are determined by industrial landscapes, what will the street dog do in the apocalypse?[11]

The beginning of an answer may lie in the fragile commensality that exists between the street dog and the human, which relies on a sharing of food, waste, home, and terrain. Commensality in the Anthropocene entails survival amid confrontation and crises in the shared blasted landscapes of the present. In the Anthropocene, this proximate visibility is also a transgressive one as it interrogates and even breaks down boundaries of culture and society, as the apocalypse dog that survives alongside the human demonstrates. Will the apocalypse be a cosmic meal-sharing experience where dog and human will finally break bread at the same utopian table? Because it is only through a distribution of living that accounts for the reality and the significance of the nonhuman in the present that we can begin to envision utopian multispecies landscapes and architectures.

Notes

1. Jacques Derrida and David Wills, "The Animal That Therefore I Am (More to Follow)," *Critical Inquiry* 28, no. 2 (2002): 400.
2. Zipporah Weisberg, " 'The Simple Magic of Life': Phenomenology, Ontology, and Animal Ethics," *Humanimalia: A Journal of Human/Animal Interface Studies* 7, no. 1 (2015): 86–105.
3. Jennifer R. Wolch and Jody Emel, *Animal Geographies: Place, Politics, and Identity in the Nature-Culture Borderlands* (New York: Verso, 1998).
4. Francesca Merlan, "Indigeneity: Global and Local," *Current Anthropology* 50, no. 3 (2009): 304.
5. Donna J. Haraway, *Staying with the Trouble: Making Kin in the Chthulucene* (Durham, NC: Duke University Press, 2016), 55.
6. Jacob von Uexküll, *A Foray into the Worlds of Animals and Humans with A Theory of*

Meaning, trans. Joseph D. O'Neil (Minneapolis: University of Minnesota Press, 2010), 170.

7.   Donna J. Haraway, *The Companion Species Manifesto: Dogs, People, and Significant Otherness* (Cambridge, MA: Prickly Paradigm Press, 2015).

8.   Haraway, *Staying with the Trouble*, 102.

9.   Thom Van Dooren and Deborah Bird Rose, "Storied-Places in a Multispecies City," *Humanimalia* 3, no. 2 (2012): 1.

10. Anna Lowenhaupt Tsing, *The Mushroom at the End of the World: On the Possibility of Life in Capitalist Ruins* (Princeton, NJ: Princeton University Press, 2017), 5.

11. Anna Lowenhaupt Tsing et al., "Patchy Anthropocene: Landscape Structure, Multispecies History, and the Retooling of Anthropology: An Introduction to Supplement 20," *Current Anthropology* 60, no. S20 (2019): 12.

CHAPTER 12

Solarpunk: The Fruitful Revolution

Connor D. Louiselle

The radical rebellions of speculative fiction seldom bring about a fruitful change for life and the natural world without first destroying it. It is admirable to fight for a fair and sustainable future. It is agreeable to dismantle capitalism's chokehold on our human communities and the nonhuman communities we feel called to protect. History is at a crossroads, and our new heading depends on the prevailing notions of our collective hearts and minds. Redefining our relationship with the natural world calls for bold revolutions in the next years. When we pursue a decidedly fruitful future (sustainable, fair, and just), we must wonder whether violent and destructive tactics for getting there are justified. Egalitarianism, a doctrine claiming all people deserve equal rights and opportunities, would claim they are not. Few writers of action movie screenplays would take advice from egalitarianism when writing plot points like the explosion of the Death Star in *Star Wars: A New Hope* (1977). When a moviegoer later draws the parallel between Darth Vader's Galactic Empire (a totalitarian dictatorship operating an exploitative capitalist society) and some real-world corporation in bed with the government, should they assemble squadrons of rebel fighters to blow the whole thing up in one triumphant moment? No. How could egalitarianism personified rally forces to change the world toward fairness without trying to blow up and guillotine the people standing in the way? Egalitarianism, unlike the heroics of Han Solo and Luke Skywalker, would have wanted every poor soul swept up into Death Star employment to live on and find better opportunities—to turn over a new leaf. If revolutions in the real world took inspiration from the rebel leaders of speculative fiction (and you'd better believe they're postured to), we would see perhaps more bloodied soil than reforested land in the decades ahead. In our collective empathy for nature and its rights, we must find a fruitful way to remove the profiteers of injustice. For most of history, telling stories about the future leaned on either idealism and the utopian or the end of the world as it was so that new heroes and ways of life could rise from its rubble. What if there was a variety of near-future tale that presented epic victories for the world and its life at large without relying on an apocalypse or terrorist bombing runs to secure them? To find such a thing, we should first define and investigate its cultural opposite.

In the dark, gritty branches of speculative storytelling, antiheroes rise to conquer corporations in just three acts of drama. We see it in action films, gripping novels, and immersive video games. Rebels storm the castle, and with enough explosions, duels, chases, and tear-jerking sacrifices, the capitalist and monarchist overlords come toppling down from their ivory towers. Cyberpunk fiction is a prime example. It is satisfying to endure a late-capitalist corporate dystopia from the armchair. From these grim imagined scenarios, audiences can join social rebellions with enough plans and power to usurp the oppressor. Those fictitious plans usually require ending many lives, but we don't think about that as viewers of entertainment media. We just want to feel a part of resistance forces with enough push to shove. Never mind the damage to structures, wildlife, and ecosystems lingering after the credits roll. These exaggerated victories light fires in the hearts and minds of people robbed of their real-life agency. They struggle under exploitative economies and parasitic political structures. A problem with cyberpunk tales like *Snowpiercer* (2013) and *Blade Runner* (1982) is that their brand of heroism may not apply to the actual world. How might the average person imitate the victories of *Blade Runner*'s Replicants without having to replicate their violent acts? How can life's lower 99 percent get radical reform without murderous retribution against our own Tyrell Corporation elites? Without echoing the domestic terrorist acts of right-wing extremists and supremacists during the 2021 storming of the United States Capitol?

If cyberpunk, steampunk, and other established branches of rise-and-fight fiction were a cookbook for the revolution, our heroes might get a life without parole instead of a victory ceremony scored by John Williams. We need class rebellions, and one inspired by cyberpunk narratives could indeed usher in a *less*-perverse iteration of late-stage capitalism. Cyberpunk narratives are too often Eurocentric, however—even when set in Neo Tokyo. The fact is, those raised by cyberpunk wolves are prone to dream of victories that mirror its tropes. A fate-chosen, cisgender white man (aided by his sometimes-diverse companions) will receive a trophy for having blown up some base that his enemy used against him. He protected himself and those like him from any further white-on-white crime. In his epic fight for victory, he may have ignored the call for climate justice and every unfair system that still suppresses his cast of comrades. His audience, however, tends to look like him, think like him, and have his privileges. Is Cyberpunk Man's triumph secretly regressive? To him and his primary audience, probably not.

And another thing, Cyberpunk Man: Wouldn't it serve us well to inspire our audience with stories that dealt with corporate apocalypses *before* capitalism ruins the world? Such a future is nigh—we must act *now*. In 2021, people want solutions that can be fruitful for ourselves and our planet. We crave new methods that won't needlessly harm our enemy—holders of natural rights to life—to achieve a fair world that will protect others from their misdeeds. Fortunately, a new movement primed to inspire such better outcomes sprouted in the early 2000s. It acknowledges the need to supplant capitalism, to redefine humanity's relationship with nature, to improve governments, and to put scalable ecocentric reforms into economic and moral mechanisms. Enter solarpunk: the fruitful revolution.

The solarpunk movement is best explained as cyberpunk's antithesis. Popular cyberpunk storytelling throughout the late twentieth century shifted the attitudes of many Americans away from capitalism. Films with cyberpunk sensibilities, such as *Blade Runner*, *Judge Dredd* (1995), and *The Matrix* (1999), depicted the societal cost of endless growth. For many fans, it was empowering to watch could-be-me antiheroes rise against unfettered corruption. There are other tropes essential to cyberpunk, like technology as a double-edged sword, but the heart of cyberpunk stories is where multinationals have run amok.

At the true dawn of the cyberpunk movement, the nihilism of the 1980s met the rapid advancement of technology in the United States and the world. People enjoyed cyberpunk films and books, then noticed their own role as bricks in the wall of the dystopias those authors warned against. Since the 1980s, fans have role-played as cyber-slick heroes like Neo, RoboCop, Judge Dredd, Motoko Kusanagi, Rick Deckard, and others. Some donned the costumes of these protagonists at comic conventions. Others worked to create their own cyberpunk films, video games, novels, and comics. Forty years on, the trend continues. In early 2020, Black Lives Matter protests erupted across the United States in the wake of George Floyd's murder by officers of the Minneapolis Police Department. Floyd's unjust death—suffocating under the knee of an unflinching police officer—demonstrated the systemic racism in US government. The tragedy inspired people to yet again rise up against the way things were. Floyd's murder was overt evidence of just how little the lives of citizens—especially nonwhite citizens—could matter to a late-capitalist, donor-dominated United States. Millions took to the streets, demanding immediate reform of police departments and agencies in the US that enable systemically racist behavior. One Black Lives Matter protester dressed up as

Batman (a cyberpunk antihero) in solidarity with those affected by white supremacy. This Black Lives Matter Batman walked through clouds of tear gas to make a statement. Tear gas, despite being fired into protest crowds by police, is a riot control tactic that "the Chemical Weapon Convention [of 1997] outlawed."[1] This cyberpunk dress-up was symbolic social commentary on the state of a nation in which justice does not reach many of its own citizens. In the same week of civil unrest, another US protester appeared as Batman's infamous nemesis Joker, smiling and dancing in the chaos. Another fitting gesture for the first generation of US citizens to realize that a cyberpunk dystopia like Batman's Gotham City may be here and now.

During the Black Lives Matter protests, Polish video game developer CD Projekt Red was still taking preorders for its controversial cyberpunk action role-playing video game, *Cyberpunk 2077* (2020). Eight million people preordered copies of the game, which released in September 2020.[2] In the open-world role-playing game, players choose their own actions in a sprawling cyberpunk city through the eyes of V (the story's protagonist) and a plethora of gameplay decisions. Of the five dynamic endings that punctuate this edgy interactive jaunt through a megacorporate future California, two are defaults, which result in the protagonist either going along with the corporation's commands or taking their own life. Other endings are similarly grim. The final ending—a *hidden* one—comes only to players who single-handedly attack and defeat the corporate Arasaka Tower, with its many crooks and bosses. Those who don't die (in-game) in the process have their choice of two outcomes: to upload their character's essence into cyberspace forever, or to return to their daily life at great personal loss. In true cyberpunk fashion, the game teaches that corporations will ruin the lives of all in their efforts to uphold an inner circle of elitists with God complexes. Yet, if you risk it all to blow up their headquarters and kill everyone unwise enough to work for them, your life could be comparatively pleasant again. That's if you survive, of course. And if you don't? You might rest well in some vague afterlife. If stories like these are trying to say "act now to avoid outcomes as hopeless as this," the message is too often lost in translation.

Cyberpunk works are also prone to the problem of Orientalism in their depictions of Asian culture. In November 2020, Alexis Ong criticized *Cyberpunk 2077* for just such offenses: "After CDPR released a look at the Asian Tyger Claws gang, many are rightly concerned about the sloppy decision to mash together Chinese and Japanese motifs for a cheap, fast idiom."[3] She also criticized the cyberpunk movement's bad habit of Orientalism overall. She wrote: "And while anxiety about China has been present in Western cyberpunk literature since the 1990s, we're only seeing more of it in go-to cyberpunk branding today."[4] Wondering why this tendency exists, Ong pondered, "Maybe the simplest answer is because . . . cyberpunk stuff looks good."[5] Perhaps Western audiences feel drawn to whitewashed Asian techno-futures because it allows them to indulge in exoticism, and then take comfort in an Asian future that speaks their language (read: is colonized). Deep socioeconomic fears run between the West and East, particularly the United States and China. Neither nation is a golden example of fruitful history, present, or near-future policy. But when the cause for concern about Asian dominance comes from a racist place, only problematic fiction can manifest. When we see a slick cyberpunk Neo Tokyo, devoid of Asian people, the creators of that film have likely fallen prey to a worldview rooted in white supremacy. A phantom fear of Asian otherness in Western minds is often culturally engrained. In any case (ignorance or supremacy), this ghost must be laid to rest, not provoked by new narratives that say that a "cool future" is one where Asian culture is merely a conquered accessory to a more-colonized future.

The deep-seated fears of the Asian other linger in today's cyberpunk works. The problem rhymes with the anti-Asian rhetoric that emerged from the shadows in March 2021, when a shooting in the Atlanta area left eight people dead. Six were of Asian descent. FBI director Chris Wray's initial assessment of the tragedy invited anti-Asian rhetoric to rise in the United States: "While the [suspect's] motive remains still under investigation at the moment, it does not appear that the motive was racially motivated."[6] One week later, US Senator Tammy Duckworth voiced concern about Director Wray's statements, which she said "only fuel stigmas about race, gender, and sex work."[7] "It looks racially motivated to me," Senator Duckworth, herself Asian American, told CBS's *Face the Nation*. The shootings added to "a spike in hate crimes since March 2020 when then-President Donald Trump began referring to COVID-19 as the 'China virus.' "[8]

To combat racism between people and our cultures and systems, it is important to imagine inclusive near futures in our storytelling going forward. Cyberpunk storytellers can and should break their nasty habit of Orientalism when crafting their worlds. Solarpunks create from an inclusive foundation. While they are not immune to using otherness for props and cheap bad-guy motifs, solarpunk visionaries avoid exploiting and abusing cultures and identities. Solarpunk is in many ways a new leaf turning over, but its default inclusivity and social self-awareness are its greatest assets in refreshing the future of worldbuilding and storytelling. In 2021, Eurocentrism still influences the future of culture (and, by extension, the world) more than other perspectives.

Crafting inclusive futures in fiction is one way to show that a diverse future will work out splendidly. Supremacists and garden-variety racists typically fear diversity. Diversifying our visions of the future gives people an engaging form of exposure therapy to help them relinquish those unjust and misinformed aversions to the otherness (the goodness and richness) in different identities in the world.

One additional critique of cyberpunk and other dystopic fiction is that dismal future fiction is passé—or at least overdone. Seth MacFarlane must have agreed when he spoke with the Television Critics Association in 2017, expressing how his *Star Trek*–style show, *The Orville* (2017), would buck the trend. "It can't all be *The Hunger Games*," he critiqued. "There has to be an aspirational blueprint for [a future] where we get our shit together."[9] The *Hollywood Reporter* detailed the motivation behind his comments: "[MacFarlane] is sick of pop culture painting a uniformly bleak vision of the future, and [*The Orville*] is not going to contribute to that."[10] Two years earlier, American Canadian science fiction writer Madeline Ashby offered a gentler critique: "Dystopia is very useful in grappling with the world as it exists. It's a . . . way of talking about things that are already happening in practice. But [with] more optimistic stories . . . you can imagine a future that you actually want."[11] Indeed, the solarpunk movement is growing along with Ashby's advice when it imagines more fruitful futures that people hope to build now. Perhaps that's because climate concerns in our actual world have worn us down with a not-so-fictitious variety of burnout: apocalypse fatigue.

People experience apocalypse fatigue when they are overstimulated by climate change alarmism and feel helpless to do anything about it. UC Berkeley's *Greater Good* magazine highlighted the issue in a 2018 interview with psychologist, economist, and Norwegian Parliament representative Per Espen Stoknes. Stoknes remarked: "If you overdo the threat of catastrophe, you make people feel fear or guilt or a combination. But these two emotions are passive. They make people disconnect and avoid the topic rather than engage with it."[12] Stoknes explained how social norms are a greater source of influence to inspire people to take climate action than any other motivator. Stoknes urged creators to use pop culture as a catalyst for this shift: "[Social norms] can be amplified if they can be combined with better storytelling, too. The story of the apocalypse disengages people. But there are other stories that seem to be more engaging—like the story of smarter, more resource-efficient growth, where we reduce waste while improving our lives."[13] The connection between storytelling and fruitful societal transformation is not new but it is often overlooked. Solarpunks do not forget this important amplifier.

The growing sense of fatigue for dystopian speculation, coupled with real-life climate despair, has primed the next generations for the opposite of cultural masochism. Audiences will grow tired of seeing the world fall apart in their favorite stories. Soon, the irreverence of Gen X and millennials will give way to Gen Z and Gen Alpha's hope and proactivity. Staff at the Annie E. Casey Foundation emphasized this in a blog post about Generation Alpha: "Pre-pandemic, experts projected that Generation Alpha kids would follow in the activist footsteps of Generation Z and keep sustainability near the top of their priority list."[14] Because of COVID-19's effects on this new generation, its inherent "radical reset of societal norms could further intensify this age group's interest in reimagining a greener, healthier world."[15] Perhaps there's a poetic irony in how Gen A starts the generational alphabet anew after Gen Z. We can be confident that these two generations will be highly receptive to and engaged by the solarpunk movement, whether in story or in practice.

Structurally, solarpunk has multiple arms: one is a visual aesthetic, another is a literary subgenre, still another is a platform for real-world involvement. All arms have integrations with a cluster of micro-movements nearby to solarpunk like biopunk, hopepunk, cli-fi, and eco-fiction, as well as adjacent climate activism practices like permaculture, slow fashion, and upcycling. The many movements and their monikers will coalesce into larger, simpler ones as cultural interest grows. Solarpunk's own name may face further critique. The term may not endure as larger audiences continue to question its alleged inaccuracies. There is a bottleneck between how people expect solarpunk stories to be and what solarpunk's definition allows them to be. Pressure is building at that bottleneck, and solarpunk may soon outgrow its own niche name.

Bloggers and visionaries started the solarpunk movement in 2008 and grew it to a sapling stage throughout the 2010s on Tumblr and other platforms. Today, the movement provokes thought and action in a way cyberpunk cannot. I define solarpunk as an optimistic imagining of our own future on Earth, where renewable energies and policy do their best to sustain a more fair society built upon ecocentric economies. Conflict and tension center on struggles to find and keep a balance in the seven conflicts (person vs. nature, self, technology, destiny, the supernatural, society, and other people) as they apply to the actual world. The "-punk" affix of solarpunk comes when people act on what is necessary to protect the climate and its human and nonhuman communities. Most solarpunk fiction imagines a world where the problems of climate crisis become adaptable in the imagined future of planet Earth. Solarpunk envisions a mutualistic relationship between the human and nonhuman. Utopianism can serve as inspiration or catalyst to solarpunk ideas and action, though solarpunk does not rhyme perfectly with the utopian. Even ecotopias are not without their struggles to sustain or defend the relative balance of a climate-stable world. Heroines who save the day in solarpunk tales may help to guard their solar-powered cities from ecofascist attackers. They may sabotage ecoterrorist groups holding natural resources hostage to leverage their own demands. Other solarpunk stories might show the interpersonal struggles of militant guerrilla gardening squadrons risking their personal freedoms to carry out seed-bombing missions. They might lose their lives trying to re-green abandoned private or government land. There's no shortage of potential drama, but loss of life in solarpunk speculative works should be at the hands of antagonists far more than its revolutionaries and freedom fighters. This is not *Star Wars* or *Blade Runner*, and there should be a scaling difference between how tragedy, struggle, combat, sacrifice and victory are defined in solarpunk works.

Not all future thinkers are aboard this solar-powered train or riding its anticapitalist tracks. In 2015, cyberpunk enthusiast Lidia Zuin claimed solarpunk is not for her, writing: "Cyberpunk is about survival, finding strength and opportunity in adversity, recreating [and] rewriting history: hacking."[16] She also argued that cyberpunk "is about finding beauty in ugliness . . . [and] is about taste, mindset, and point of view, not quality or utility."[17] Solarpunk need not diminish or replace cyberpunk and its warnings against corporate regimes. The same goes for the general dystopian speculative. Zuin is right to defend the smoky-metallic fragrance of cyberpunk story worlds that caution against *allowing* such inhumane outcomes where capitalism can continue unfettered. Solarpunks imagine how the world might soon be if we dismantle the corporate apocalypse *now*. The two ends of this spectrum can coexist in the arts and entertainment spheres. They attract a similar crowd through two opposite types of reinforcement. Cyberpunk, when perceived as a cautionary tale, is negative reinforcement for its audiences, while solarpunk is positive reinforcement. Solarpunk fosters optimism and teaches practical methods of establishing sustainability, renewable energies, and egalitarian societies. Cyberpunk and cli-fi (that's apocalyptic climate fiction) don't present strategies for improving the actual world.

Other critics dismiss solarpunk when they cannot find a "punk" feature in its foundational boundaries that would suit their own definition of what "punk" means. Lee Konstantinou, an associate professor of English literature at the University of Maryland, wrote a critique of solarpunk's literary arm: "If you retain the hope of writing fiction that confronts readers with new ways of thinking about their relationship to the future—our future—you may need to drop the -punk suffix."[18] Indeed, solarpunk has not shown the staunch tear-it-all-down mantras we associate with the punk subculture. Solarpunk goes against the entirety of our global status quo, more than the actual punk movement ever did. Solarpunks are in relentless opposition to late-stage capitalism. They are in unwavering pursuit of social, economic, and environmental justice. They are intrepid in their innovations toward sustainability in energy policy and an inherently fair approach to progressive reform. Solarpunk's game plan is to rebuild communities and infrastructure and to influence policy and wealth distribution to better serve human and nonhuman life on Earth. The trajectory of the solarpunk movement is to inspire people into cocreating a biomimetic (or at least ecocentric) model of the human-nature relationship—without forgetting human-to-human reciprocity. That is a fruitful revolution.

While significant full-length solarpunk works of fiction have yet to make a mark on popular culture, solarpunks often retroactively tag existing works that check its boxes. Take Kim Stanley Robinson's climate fiction works, such as his *Mars Trilogy* (1992, 1993, 1996) and his 2017 novel *New York 2140*. In these works, Robinson shows humanity making the best of inhospitable climate scenarios, whether on Mars or on Earth. Robinson also acknowledged the rise of solarpunk: "There's a group of young writers who call themselves solarpunk, and what they're trying is all about adaptation."[19] Solarpunk's resident creatives today are crafting hundreds of solarpunk worlds and works, targeting multimedia (even transmedia) presentations of all sorts. Solarpunk works range from literature to video games, music to tabletop and card games, even crypto-art pieces and mixed-reality experiences. When a few of these stories have caught the eye of Generation Alpha in the mid-2020s, the culture of that time will consider solarpunk anchored within it. How will our way of life, then, respond to significant solarpunk works? Our culture is likely to mimic reactions to today's well-circulated solarpunk anthologies. Two examples are *Glass and Gardens: Solarpunk Summers* (2018), edited by Sarena Ulibarri, and *Sunvault: Stories of Solarpunk and Eco-Speculation* (2017), edited by Phoebe Wagner and Brontë Christopher Wieland. There were skeptics and critics; those unenthused by the ecological possibilities described and depicted in these future worlds. yet most critics of these early solarpunk collections were vocal about how refreshing and uplifting they can be.

The authors and visionaries of solarpunk fiction often discover a valuable side effect of building story worlds in this style. To write their captivating, semirealistic depictions of how the world could do better, these creators are searching for plausible climate solutions now. While speculative fiction doesn't mandate believable and practical technology at every turn, the early solarpunk communities insisted that its worlds should be possible, if not plausible. Jennifer Mae Hamilton said it best in her 2019 article on solarpunk: "The focus on the cultural change that will . . . accompany the full transition to renewable energy is the defining feature of solarpunk."[20] Together, researchers and professionals could tackle the implementations of the climate scenarios and hypotheses required to craft compelling fiction. As with Stoknes's emphasis on storytelling as an amplifier for social revolution around the issue, climate researchers and professionals can benefit from solarpunk authors and activists. With tectonic-scale problems breathing down their necks, scientists cannot afford not to look for ways to bridge hard climate data with soft skills that enchant. Entertainment industry folks can't afford to ignore a fresh approach at holding the hair-thin attentions of their audiences throughout the 2020s. Gen Alpha will pine for stories with greener horizons. It's a win-win for the creators, producers, and artists with the courage to tell a new tale.

Most of today's storytelling relies on dismal dystopias to shock audiences into paying attention (or just paying). Dystopian stories inspire their audiences with fear, limitation, and notions of impending doom. This is a cultural fight-or-flight response. Actions performed from a state of anxiety seek to preserve the self, not one's environment. It is true today that attention spans may be shorter than ever, and thus the visceral approach in cyberpunk and postapocalyptic stories is a primal way to keep them. We can find it in the harrowing class inequity of cyberpunk television series like *Snowpiercer* (2020). Still, the morals of too-late-now scenarios are falling on distracted ears. It's just killing time, for most—especially during the pandemic months of 2020–2021. We could address this problem at the cultural level. We can switch to something new and novel, no longer repackaging tired, defeatist notions that might get little response from Generations Z and Alpha. Fear-mongering tactics may keep viewers watching (and advertisers bidding) in the short term, but solarpunk storytelling can enchant and inspire viewers in the medium and long terms. Solarpunk stories still show struggles. It's just that the edge-of-your-seat drama typically takes place in the name of altering, sustaining, or defending the living world and its ecosystems.

Solarpunk fiction and solarpunk activism have been growing under the same umbrella term in a hybridized manner since 2017. Although this dynamic puts a lot of proverbial campers in one tent, it keeps storytellers bound to near-future speculation. It keeps more pragmatic activist types from losing their soft senses. After all, solarpunk is not about primitivism and survival in the odds of eco-apocalypse. It's about imagining a better, more sustainable future of planet Earth where ecofascism and other life-depriving beliefs get weeded out from the gardens of society. It's about discovering innovative, anticapitalist ways of achieving that type of world. But the key emphasis in this essay lies in how we can accomplish this without becoming violent extremists, enacting harm to others in the climate's name. This is close to, if not synonymous with, the ecofascist notions on the rise worldwide as climate change becomes climate crisis at the dawn of the Anthropocene. As solarpunks we can help eco-revolutionaries dismantle systems of worldwide exploitation without ourselves becoming a source of malevolence.

Solarpunk is, in all forms, a fruitful revolution because it exhibits values, economics, politics, culture, and lifestyles that would keep our actual world abundant and fulfilling. The movement, still a sapling, is reaching maturation along with Generation Alpha who, I predict, will appreciate it. Solarpunk is a legitimate cultural opponent of patriarchal late-stage capitalism. It inspires climate hope in our contemporary cultural narrative, where disheartened and downtrodden communities—human and nonhuman—need them most. In 2019, calls for climate action came from ninety-three-year-old Sir David Attenborough (to no one's surprise) yet also from a sixteen-year-old Swedish environmental activist, Greta Thunberg. A subculture that demands ecological optimism and fair economic reform is valuable in these rattled moments of history. We cannot all be Thunberg and Attenborough. The common person needs inspiration on how to contribute to a better future with their own strengths and purposes. We need stories that show plausible outcomes of climate action and can express our desires as individuals in the Anthropocene. No revolution ever made a change without many individuals supporting their leaders. There was only one Neo in *The Matrix*, only one Motoko in *Ghost in the Shell*. In reality, the impact one fictional hero can have relies on thousands of small, consistent heroic acts by community-minded people. The same holds true when comparing protagonists in solarpunk stories and real-life heroes ready to make change. As the Anthropocene makes itself known—bringing the greatest global discomfort to humanity in recorded history—solarpunk stories will restore cultural hope in our future.

We all have a place in a solarpunk future of Earth—even those opposed to its outcomes. Not all of us could be *the* hero of the world's own solarpunk future. But for perhaps the first time in a countercultural movement, all of us can *be heroes*. We can be heroes for doing our own part in our own community—hero's journey not required. This sentiment is anticlimactic for any kneeler to kings or presidents or tycoons. Any fan of blowing up Death Stars and wiping out thousands of sorry employees. To solarpunks, the notion that we are a collective of cooperative heroes (as opposed to individuals with savior complexes) is fuel to the fires burning in our hearts, and the hearts of millions who could accomplish far more in a solarpunk victory than beneath the suffocating weight of late-stage capitalism. Our revolution is fulfilling. It is prepared and purposeful—not murderous nor exclusionary nor ecofascist. It is sustainable, fair, and just. Much to the chagrin of fossil fuel barons—of defeatists, supremacists, and capitalists—it is fruitful.

Notes

1. McKenzie Sadeghi, "Fact Check: It's True Tear Gas Is a Chemical Weapon Banned in War," *USA Today*, June 6, 2020, https://www.usatoday.com/story/news/fact check/2020/06/06/fact-check-its-true-tear-gas-chemical-weapon-banned-war/3156448001/.
2. Hirun Cryer, "Cyberpunk 2077 Pre-Orders Went over 8 Million Worldwide, CD Projekt Reveals," *Gamesradar+*, December 2020, https://www.gamesradar.com/cyberpunk-2077-pre-orders-went-over-8-million-worldwide-cd-projekt-reveals/.
3. Alexis Ong, "Fear of a Yellow Planet: Why We Need to Actually Understand Cyberpunk," *Fanbyte*, November 18, 2020, https://www.fanbyte.com/features/fear-of-a-yellow-planet-why-we-need-to-actually-understand-cyberpunk/.
4. Ong, "Fear of a Yellow Planet."
5. Ong, "Fear of a Yellow Planet."
6. Carrie Johnson, " 'We're Going to Keep Digging,' FBI Director Wray Says of Capitol Siege," *NPR*, March 18, 2021, https://www.npr.org/2021/03/18/978193998/were-going-to-keep-digging-fbi-director-wray-says-of-capitol-siege.
7. Sarah N. Lynch and Valerie Volcovici, "Atlanta Shooting of Asian Women Was Racially Motivated, U.S. Senator Says," *Reuters*, March 21, 2021, https://www.reuters.com/article/us-crime-georgia-spas/atlanta-shooting-of-asian-women-was-racially-motivated-u-s-senator-says-idUSKBN2BD0LW.
8. Lynch and Volcovici, "Atlanta Shooting."
9. Mikey O'Connell, "Seth MacFarlane Says He's Sick of Bleak, Dystopian Sci-Fi," *Hollywood Reporter*, August 8, 2017, https://www.hollywoodreporter.com/tv/tv-news/orville-seth-mcfarlane-says-hes-sick-bleak-dystopian-sci-fi-1027907/.
10. O'Connell, "Seth MacFarlane."
11. Maddie Crum, "Forget Dystopias, These Sci-Fi Writers Opt For Optimism Instead," *HuffPost*, November 10, 2015, https://www.huffpost.com/entry/techno-optimism-sci-fi_n_56394cffe4b0411d306eceed.
12. Jill Suttie, "How to Overcome 'Apocalypse Fatigue' around Climate Change," *Greater Good*, February 23, 2018, https://greatergood.berkeley.edu/article/item/how_to_overcome_apocalypse_fatigue_around_climate_change.
13. Suttie, "How to Overcome."
14. "What Is Generation Alpha?," Annie E. Casey Foundation, November 4, 2020, https://www.aecf.org/blog/what-is-generation-alpha/.
15. "What Is Generation Alpha?"
16. Lidia Zuin, "No (Bright) Future for Me: Solarpunk Is Not the New Cyberpunk," Medium, February 9, 2016, https://www.medium.com/wirehead/no-bright-future-for-me-solarpunk-is-not-the-new-cyberpunk-e0493b5667aa.

17. Zuin, "No (Bright) Future for Me."
18. Lee Konstantinou, "Our Sci-Fi Is Broken, and Hopepunk—Whatever That Is—Can't Fix It," *Slate*, January 15, 2019, https://www.slate.com/technology/2019/01/hopepunk-cyberpunk-solarpunk-science-fiction-broken.html.
19. Sally Adee, "The Power of Good," *New Scientist*, June 10, 2017, https://www.sciencedirect.com/science/article/abs/pii/S0262407917311223.
20. Jennifer Hamilton, "Explainer: 'Solarpunk,' or How to Be an Optimistic Radical," *The Conversation*, August 28, 2019, https://www.theconversation.com/explainer-solarpunk-or-how-to-be-an-optimistic-radical-80275.

PART 4

ingenuity

Solarpunk Ingenuity and DIY Projects

Phoebe Wagner

Ingenuity: Publishing and Solarpunk

One thing that drew us to solarpunk in 2015 was the genre's focus on the need to imagine, which leads to action, as presented in the do-it-yourself pieces in this part. Solarpunk recognizes that we can't make change without imagining it first. To a writer—or any creator—such a call to action feels as important as the makers and designers that later implement these imaginings. But the older we become and the more we read, it seems like we've imagined this all before. We've imagined the creeping extent of racism and how to uproot and dismantle it in the bibliographies of James Baldwin, Angela Davis, Octavia E. Butler; the impact of Indigenous genocide and what recovery might look like in *Ceremony* (1977) by Leslie Marmon Silko, *Love Medicine* (1984) by Louise Erdrich, and *Braiding Sweetgrass* (2013) by Robin Wall Kimmerer; resisting and overthrowing of corrupt governments in *1984* (1949) by George Orwell, *The Dispossessed* (1974) by Ursula K. Le Guin, and *The Hunger Games* (2008) by Suzanne Collins; how we might engage with nonhumans in *Wild Animals I Have Known* (1898) by Ernest Thompson Seton, *Watership Down* (1972) by Richard Adams, and *The Overstory* (2018) by Richard Powers. That's not even touching our imaginations of the future—utopic and dystopic—that line the science fiction section of the library.

We've been told that novels in particular have an empathetic power that can change minds. And they certainly do—we owe much of our current views to authors like Ursula K. Le Guin and Octavia E. Butler. Yet that change is slow, incremental, and individual. To paraphrase Wendell Berry, it's planting sequoias. We don't have time to watch sequoias grow. Just like we don't have time to cast a vote and wait, or, as Rob Nixon explains, "Because preventative or remedial environmental legislation typically targets slow violence, it cannot deliver dependable electoral cycle results, even though those results

may ultimately be life saving. . . . Many politicians—and indeed many voters—
routinely treat environmental action as critical yet not urgent."[1] In some ways,
the idea that literature will make change feels like the timeworn insistence on
voting. Yes, voting, particularly at the local level, can make change—and we've
certainly seen historic votes that shook up the status quo, for better and for
worse, just as there have been books with sizable impact, making the world
better and worse. This isn't a call to stop writing or to stop writing the story
that matters to you, but it does question the role of storytelling *right now*.

In the solarpunk community, there's always been talk of publishing *the*
solarpunk book that will inspire people and introduce the genre to the general
populace. In 2015, we agreed that we needed more novels that engage with
environmental and social justice while still telling good, imaginative, inventive
stories that reach and resonate with a large readership. That desire operates on
a few key assumptions. First, the assumption that a book published through
traditional pathways (or discovered through traditional means such as large
retailers like Amazon and Barnes & Noble) can simultaneously be intensely
popular and revolutionary.

Let's take the *Hunger Games* as an example. Suzanne Collins claims the
series inspiration came from the Iraq War: "I was flipping through the chan-
nels one night between reality television programs and actual footage of
the Iraq War, when the idea came to me. . . . For [*The Hunger Games* series], I
wanted a completely new world and a different angle into the just-war [theory]
debate."[2] Setting aside the issues with the series, the books are often cited on
social media as part of the interest in revolution for younger millennials and
Generation Z. The series values revolution while fighting against poverty, corruption, government control, environmental damage, and class, but the books
and subsequent movies were quickly eaten up in the capitalist machine as fast
fashion pumped out "Down with the Capital!" T-shirts and mockingjay socks,
pins, and bags. This is not a criticism of fandom culture but an attempt to
show what would happen if a solarpunk text truly resonated with the public.
That a series so obviously critical of capitalist power structures can so quickly
and effectively be defanged by the very system it's attacking shows the major
tension between revolutionary writing and traditional publishing. There's no
room for meaningful critique among so much waste, or, as Le Guin's anarchist
revolutionary writes, "Excess is excrement."[3]

The second assumption relies on finding a Big Five publisher like Penguin
for a solarpunk novel, which would be necessary for wide-reaching popularity.
Yet those publishers do not share the values that a solarpunk novel should
embody. Let's consider literature—and, by extension, publishing—as part of

an occupying and nationalizing force in the so-called United States. Richard Ohmann questions this issue when examining the role of college humanities courses: "Why, in spite of much good will and intelligence on our part, and in spite of the great works lined up in marching formation on our bookshelves, did the humanities as we practiced them often fail to humanize, or succeed in humanizing a few at the expense of the many?"[4] This question remains vital as it demonstrates that even someone practicing progressive methodology like Ohmann (a Marxist) can easily slip into teaching a canon meant to maintain the hegemony of capitalism and white supremacy. Intelligence or good intentions have little to do with rejecting this hegemony. Rather, one must recognize the institutions upholding hegemony and work outside those them, deconstructing them. Being college-educated, an artist, or a solarpunk does not automatically allow a person to step outside these intuitions because they are so foundational to our cultural thinking. For example, calls to reform (rather than abolish) the police in the summer of 2020 represented many people's inability to think beyond an institution cultural woven into US society (through the police's hegemonic role to support capital, property, and white supremacy). The publishing and subsequent teaching of literature is part of creating this hegemony: "The humanities, like schools and universities within which they are practiced, have contributed through the hundred years of our profession's existence to this hegemonic process. . . . The effect—unintended [by professors] of course—is to sustain the *illusion* of equal opportunity."[5] For example, Eve Tuck and K. Wayne Yang demonstrate how the commonly taught and still popular *Leatherstocking Tales* (1823–1841) by James Fenimore Cooper recreates this hegemonic experience:

> In addition to fabricating historical memory, the [*Leatherstocking*] *Tales* serve to generate historical amnesia. The books were published between 1823–1841, at the height of the Jacksonian period with the Indian Removal Act of 1830 and subsequent Trail of Tears 1831–1837. During this time, 46,000 Native Americans were removed from their homelands, opening 25 million acres of land for re-settlement. The *Tales* are not only silent on Indian Removal but narrate the Indian as vanishing in an earlier time frame, and thus Indigenous people are already dead prior to removal.[6]

Tuck and Yang continue their examination of the *Tales* throughout their essay "Decolonization Is Not a Metaphor" (2012), and a key takeaway is that this popular text not only erased historical fact but did so in a way that served white male readers in the US while invalidating Indigenous readers. This "historical amnesia" serves the continued occupation of Indigenous lands by the US as detailed in a book *still* in print, taught, and read today. This discussion is not meant to dictate what should be published and read but to question why solarpunk creators—writing stories in opposition to these hegemonic white supremacist, nationalizing institutions—still hope for a solarpunk novel to be published by the same institutions their stories stand in opposition to.

Recently, the inequality inherent in publishing has been more exposed. Publishing is based on systems of continued oppression, even as projects like We Need Diverse Books, founded by Ellen Oh and Malinda Lo, and #PublishingPaidMe, started by L. L. McKinney, do amazing work. Yet foundational to that work is pointing out that publishing is still hegemonic. In a 2019 survey, the Diversity Baseline Survey demonstrated the issue remained: "The [original] 2015 survey reported that overall, 79 percent of people who work in publishing self-report as White. Given the sample size difference, this 3 percent change [reported in 2019] in White employees does not meet the bar for statistically significant change. . . . In other words, the field is just as White today as it was four years ago."[7] This survey does not diminish the work of organizations working for change in publishing. Rather, publishing is a capitalist enterprise, and capitalism is inherently connected to white supremacy through colonization, genocide, and slavery. As a capitalist institution, publishing will not easily change its white hegemony, as that goes against its very nature. This lack of change shows that publishers are happy to cash in on the writing of people of color, such as Angie Thomas or Ta-Nehisi Coates, but care little for institutional change that would threaten the industry's white supremacy.

Finally, publishing is designed as a highly wasteful industry. Paper usage alone makes the traditional publishing industry unsustainable.[8] While such ventures are commendable, using recycled paper does not acknowledge that, like all international institutions, publishing requires oil. Imre Szeman notes that while oil is rarely the subject of fiction, the substance is required in order for fiction as we know it to survive: "World literature . . . embodies and exemplifies the expectation and desire for more that characterizes the culture of surplus. What happens to literature when we can't have any more, because the energy that has enabled petromodernity and petroculture is—or is about to be—no longer available to us?"[9] Szeman's point is hard for book lovers to hear but hits home—our own bookshelves hold more books than we have read or have need of. As writers and editors, we love the feeling of holding physical books and long for even more publications. Yet how much of this longing—by us and other solarpunks—is merely cultural yearnings of the capitalist system? Ultimately, we must recognize that publishing, especially traditional Big Publishing, is unsustainable and part of an imperialist oil culture.

We've written before that solarpunk must be anticolonial and decolonial, must be anti-racist, and must seek environmental justice.[10] These ideals are largely absent from the publishing industry, even as activists, artists, and editors strive to make it a better place. Again, this isn't a call to stop seeking traditional publishing for creative work but to question why solarpunks should seek that avenue when it does not meet the genre's ideals and even undermines them. There is an inherent compromise to be made in seeking traditional or well-respected routes of publication. We must ask if that compromise is worth the potential upside, and we must also seek or create alternative methods if the answer turns out to be no.

One thing solarpunk storytelling can do right now is question and experiment with the current accepted forms of storytelling. Writers such as Rob Nixon and Amitav Ghosh have interrogated how we tell stories of the climate crisis, coming to the conclusion that current forms of narrative often can't capture the needed range to truly explain or explore what's happening. Ghosh acknowledges it as "the peculiar forms of resistance that climate change presents to what is now regarded as serious fiction."[11] In other words, as solarpunk creators, we don't *have to* focus on the market or the most marketable way to tell a story. Ghosh is right—the climate crisis doesn't lend itself to the types of stories we prefer in the US. There is nothing for the hero to "win" or "defeat." There is not ultimate success. There is no technological miracle for someone to discover. In other words, there is no way for a story that truly engages with the complexities of the climate crisis to become popular in US entertainment as the industry currently exists.

Collecting and Sharing the Carrier Bag

What might solarpunk storytelling look like? Scholars and writers have called for the form of storytelling to change in order to address environmental issues. In particular, Ursula K. Le Guin discusses an alternative to Joseph Campbell's *The Hero's Journey* (1990), which is often utilized in US storytelling. Instead, Le Guin offers her Carrier Bag Theory of fiction. First, the idea of the hero has to be redefined: "And *hero*, in Virginia Woolf's dictionary, is 'bottle.' The hero as bottle, a stringent reevaluation. I now propose the bottle as hero."[12] With the hero redefined as "a thing that holds something else" rather than a heroic killer, Le Guin continues:

> If, however, one avoids the linear, progressive, Time's-(killing)-arrow mode of the Techno-Heroic, and redefines technology and science as primarily cultural carrier bag rather than weapon of domination, one pleasant side effect is that science fiction can be seen as a far less rigid, narrow field, not necessarily Promethean or apocalyptic at all, and in fact less a mythological genre than a realistic one.[13]

In some ways, solarpunk is exactly that: a carrier bag of theories, fixes, transformations, ideas, strategies all meant to help in some places while being potentially useless in others. This type of story—indeed, this type of living—refuses the idea that progress is linear, that modernity means advancement, that ingenuity means evolution. Instead, Le Guin describes this type of living, and storytelling, as a space for holding:

> If it is a human thing to do to put something you want, because it's useful, edible, or beautiful, into a bag, or a basket, or a bit of rolled bark or leaf, or a net woven of your own hair, or what have you, and then take it home with you, home being another, larger kind of pouch or bag, a container for people, and then later on you take it out and eat it or share it or store it up for winter in a solider container or put it in the medicine bundle or the shrine or the museum, the holy place, the area that contains what is sacred, and then next day you probably do much the same again—if to do that is human, if that's what it takes, then I am a human being after all. Fully, freely, gladly, for the first time.[14]

In many ways, the solarpunk genre mirrors this idea as it has been most successful in the anthology form. Anthologies allow readers to page through a collection of voices and stories rather than strap in for a single novel. The diversity of voices supports the solarpunk idea of community, and telling different stories allows readers to choose what resonates with them and their situation. Similarly, solarpunk has always acknowledged that there is not a singular fix for social inequality or environmental degradation—each community must assess what is needed. We can all give and take from the carrier bag of story.

Similarly, addressing the climate crisis means addressing community in a way not prevalent in fiction. A singular hero going on a quest to save his rural town isn't going to cut it. How do the stakes change when the climate crisis is transforming a community? Is it possible to truly have a heroic figure in that moment? If solarpunk creators instead focus on specific needs or communities that they can contribute to, solarpunk has the chance to impact communities in a positive way rather than become a fad.

The question becomes, then, what does that story look like? We don't know, but other underground art movements suggest that art grows from community and activism, whether it's Grandmaster Flash DJing in the South Bronx or a local punk band shouting about racist transit operators. The intersectionality of solarpunk remains part of the draw as a genre and broader movement, but the transition from solarpunk as literature to solarpunk as an active, transformative choice means practitioners must become multifaceted even as the climate crisis and social justice issues call for various talents and experiences. Barbara Smith put it this way when speaking about the disconnect between academia and activism in the feminist movement: "I began to recognize what I call . . . academic feminists: women who teach, research, and publish about women, but who are not involved in any way in making radical social and political change."[15] Similarly, there's an almost academic brand of solarpunk floating around where people are trying to write the first solarpunk book but aren't engaging in helping their communities make systemic change.

This type of solarpunk is evident in the focus on gardening as way to be a "solarpunk," which we recognized when reading submissions for our fiction anthology *Sunvault: Stories of Solarpunk & Eco-Speculation* (2017). While we weren't sure what types of stories we would receive, we did expect, and encounter, a lot of gardening stories. Gardening has long been a way to learn more about food systems, lessen carbon footprints, grow organic foods, and transform what might otherwise be a lawn into a multispecies space. These are all good things, but starting a personal garden, or even a community garden with a few friends or in a neighborhood, is an extremely privileged engagement with the environment and with solarpunk ideology. More gardens are not what we mean by transforming the climate crisis. That being said, normalizing gardening for those with the privilege to have the space, tools, time, and physical ability is well and good, but that is often an individual response to climate change rather than a community response. Rather, how can we and our communities live in just relationship with each other and the nonhumans around us? How can we prepare our communities to adapt to crisis, such as an ice storm in Texas or a pandemic?

So let's get inventive with the stories we tell. Let's allow that work to grow and flourish from our actions in the community, not just our fears and frustration with the news cycle or personal experiences. Some great speculative fiction has been written through such influences, such as that by Jewelle L. Gomez, a well-known Black lesbian activist. Gomez wrote *The Gilda Stories* (1991), one of the earlier speculative novels to focus on queer relationships and people of color, embodying much of what critics and activists like Barbara Smith and Barbara Christian were searching for in fiction by Black queer women. Even though the novel pushed boundaries, Gomez used the form of the vampire story to explore and demonstrate her activism: "Even as I explained that *The Gilda Stories* would be a lesbian-feminist interpretation of vampires, not simply a story about a charming serial killer, people found the idea hard to accept."[16] Unsurprisingly, the book was published by a small feminist and activist-oriented press called Firebrand Publishing, since closed. Rather than cater to a big publisher's expectations, solarpunk stories should grow from a carrier bag of experiences, including activism and community work, not only our personal gardens.

Punk Expectations

Much of solarpunk's inventiveness is characterized by the "-punk" aspect. While the validity of solarpunk's claim to the punk affix is often challenged, the do-it-yourself nature of community resistance and transformation during the climate crisis suggest a punk ethos. Similarly, the way that solarpunk stories have been published so far also suggests a rather punk outlook, as most anthologies are from small presses often founded and run by their editor-in-chief. What makes the punk part of solarpunk necessary is the need for it to move beyond literature, just as many punks do more than drink beer at basement shows. There is an inherent action in being a punk, even if it's as small as designing patches or buttons. Part of that activeness comes from being outside the support systems of the normalized, capitalist institutions. If a regular venue won't book a punk band, then a house show or a basement show is just as viable (and always more fun). Similarly, the anticapitalist ideals of solarpunk mean that it should never be profitable, so if traditional publishing venues aren't an option, then what other DIY avenues open up?

When people criticize or question the validity of the -punk affix, they fail to recognize how deeply institutionalized environmental degradation has become since the Industrial Revolution. Our current society is built on oppressive and exploitative systems that are causing the climate crisis, and to transform the crisis, we must work to undermine and work outside those systems, whether it's capitalism or ecofascism. Yes, solarpunk is founded on the idea of hope, but it's hope through action, which feels very punk. David Beer describes the punk scene as "seek[ing] to foster its own discomfort and to find creative ways of expressing it."[17] A similar description could be applied to solarpunk stories, as writers find what angers them and then write about it in a way to transform the situation and give hope. Solarpunk writing also fosters discomfort through the envisioning of futures that are attainable only through radical action to create cultures and communities incompatible with what we have known and how we have lived thus far.

Where solarpunk could serve to learn from the punk scene is in the transformation from a music genre to a lifestyle to a principal ideology. In punk, there's room for the individual and the community. Individual style even contributes to the community, be it designing a patch, hosting a house show, or bringing a unique approach to street art. Being punk doesn't mean just headbanging and power chords but a cleverness, a get-the-job-done-with-what-you-got attitude. A learning attitude—how do we screen print shirts for cheap? How do I fix this broken amp? How do I fix the potholes in the road that are ruining my wheels? How do I help feed the houseless around the corner? How do I make sure my friends have a roof over their heads? To be punk means to recognize that the government is not looking out for you or your friends, so what are you going to do about it?

Punk is also inherently *fun*. Not necessarily fun in the sense of playing a video game or watching Netflix, but there's a sense of energy and enthusiasm that comes when a bunch of punks gather, whether it's to listen to music or cover up the latest fascist propaganda posted around town. With this sense of fun comes power. As adrienne maree brown describes it, "I have seen, over and over, the connection between tuning into what brings aliveness into our systems and being able to access personal, relational and communal power."[18]

Honestly, that's one of the best parts about being a solarpunk creator—to focus on actions that bring joy, not just as an individual but as a community. Learning ways to combine the two—that's where the ingenuity comes in. In the US, capitalism is so engrained that we are programmed to believe something a person is good at or enjoys should be turned into profit. To reclaim that enjoyment, and even give it as a gift to the community, is to reject and undermine our current culture around the arts, entertainment, and community storytelling. Ingenuity shouldn't just be about how to get ahead, how to make the most in a system of false scarcity. It's about cheating a system designed to hold people down, about making the community better just because you can, about singing or playing music not as a platform but strictly for the way it connects you to yourself, about building a fort not because it makes anything better but because it's fun.

DIY Beginnings

While we focused on publishing as an example of where solarpunk could turn to the DIY as an alternative, the following pieces focus on growing, foraging, mending, and building. The pieces in this part tackle solarpunk ingenuity from the structural issues, such as the need for multispecies spaces, to individual actions such as permaculture and DIY mending. While this part is one of our favorites with advice, blueprints, and knowhow to break away from consumerist practices here in the US, we want to emphasize that individual response will not change the climate crisis. "Doing it yourself" is often a privileged ability that is too often slung around without considering race, class, and the patriarchy. What we hope the following pieces do is inspire and inform. We hope these pages are torn out and passed around or instructions texted to friends. We hope more ideas are scribbled in the margins and in the back pages. We hope you make a book of your own with blueprints and recipes for *your* community. We at least hope these DIY projects make you smile or inspire you to daydream.

Too often, corporations return the problem of the climate crisis to the 99 percent. The climate crisis is not caused by suburban families failing to recycle. The climate crisis is caused by giant corporations, oil companies, and big box stores choosing profit over the living world. This cannot be said enough: it is not your fault, or your neighbor's, or your community's. Yet individual action can be useful in considering the cultural systems we have been pulled into without choice. No matter how small the change, individual and community action can help us rethink our relationships with the living world. Even small actions, such as removing ableist, racist, sexist, or speciesist language from our vocabulary, can affect how we think about and relate to the world.

For others, DIY action is future-thinking to what skills might be necessary during societal unrest, such as being able to mend clothes if stores are limited in inventory as we saw in 2020 (see the step-by-step guide for mending by Sari Fordham). Or planting food-growing trees for the next generation. In "Appalachian Solarpunk: Growing Trees from Seed for the Plant Revolution," Vance Mullis and Joy Lew offer step-by-step instructions on how to grow trees that will produce food. While planting trees is a great way for any community to support the living world, planting chestnuts and hazelnuts not only sequesters carbon but provides food for generations of humans and nonhumans alike. Planting noninvasive species is always future-thinking, but planting edible trees, as Mullis and Lew suggest, recognizes the needs of coming generations to have a different, more community-based relationship with food.

Michael J. DeLuca also tackles where our food comes from. While foraging is not feasible for everyone—nor does it replace the need for better community access to fresh food in oppressed communities—it does change an individual's relationship to both food and the living world. Foraging requires us to slow down and use our senses in a way that disrupts the capitalist food systems we are required to rely on in the US. Foraging, when done with awareness, is often beneficial to plants and increases our connection to the living world. As DeLuca writes, "I'm not prepping for doomsday, just building resilience."

The part ends with a visual representation of how to create and maintain multispecies spaces. Christoph D. D. Rupprecht, Aoi Yoshida, and Lihua Cui demonstrate a design concept for supporting humans and the more-than-human: where food can be grown for all, places to rest and play, water and a variety of native species to promote regrowth and resilience. These spaces can be created now, but the authors imagine these sites as a way to reclaim vacancy as cities shrink. By reframing vacant lots and green spaces as locations for multispecies communities, we can shift thinking away from the human/nonhuman binary toward community that works together in order for all to survive and thrive.

The following DIY pieces feature one of the best parts of the DIY subculture—sharing knowledge. These authors are practitioners, writers, academics, menders, storytellers, and so on. We hope these pieces will inspire structural changes, communal changes, and personal changes. While there is not a single ingenious fix waiting to reverse climate change or systemic oppression, there are plenty of ways to innovate as our ideas of industry, progress, and modernity transform in the wake of the climate crisis. These pieces present ways to take individual action, but even more vital, they encourage doers to think differently about basic necessities too often forgotten. By changing how we view our connection to the living world, we can change our personal response and reaction to the climate crisis from one of fear to adaptation.

Notes

1. Rob Nixon, *Slow Violence and the Environmentalism of the Poor* (Cambridge, MA: Harvard University Press, 2011), 9.
2. David Levithan, "Suzanne Collins Talks about 'The Hunger Games,' the Books and the Movies," *New York Times*, October 18, 2018, https://nyti.ms/2QXylP3.
3. Ursula K. Le Guin, *The Dispossessed: An Ambiguous Utopia* (New York: Harper Voyager, 1974), 98.

4.   Richard M. Ohmann, *Politics of Letters* (Middletown, CT: Wesleyan University Press, 1987), 5.

5.   Ohmann, *Politics*, 8.

6.   Eve Tuck and K. Wayne Yang, "Decolonization Is Not a Metaphor," *Decolonization: Indigeneity, Education & Society* 1, no. 1 (2012): 16.

7.   "Where Is the Diversity in Publishing? The 2019 Diversity Baseline Survey Results," *The Open Book Blog*, Lee and Low Books, January 28, 2020, https://blog.leeandlow.com/2020/01/28/2019diversitybaselinesurvey/.

8.   Though some authors are utilizing recycled paper, such as Richard Powers's *The Overstory*'s first paperback printing, which was "printed on 100 percent recycled paper[,] . . . sav[ing] 637 trees" in addition to reducing water, solid waste, and greenhouse gas emissions. Richard Powers, *The Overstory: A Novel* (New York: W. W. Norton & Company, 2018), vi.

9.   Imre Szeman, "Conjectures on World Energy Literature: Or, What Is Petroculture?" *Journal of Postcolonial Writing* 53, no 3 (May 2017): 286.

10.   See Phoebe Wagner and Brontë Christopher Wieland, "Sunvaulting: Five Years on a Path toward a Literature of Environmental Resilience," *About Place Journal*, May 1, 2020, https://aboutplacejournal.org/issues/practices-of-hope/how-to-do-things-in-turbulent-times/phoebe-wagner-bronte-wieland/; Phoebe Wagner and Brontë Christopher Wieland, "Solarpunks & Storytelling in the Capitalocene," *American Book Review* 41 (September 2020): 14–15.

11.   Amitav Ghosh, *The Great Derangement: Climate Change and the Unthinkable* (Chicago: University of Chicago Press, 2016), 9.

12.   Ursula K. Le Guin, *Dancing at the Edge of the World: Thoughts on Words, Women, Places* (New York: Grove Press, 1989), 166.

13.   Le Guin, *Dancing at the Edge*, 170.

14.   Le Guin, *Dancing at the Edge*, 168.

15.   Barbara Smith, *The Truth That Never Hurts: Writings on Race, Gender, and Freedom* (New Brunswick, NJ: Rutgers University Press, 1998), 97.

16.   Jewelle Gomez, *The Gilda Stories*, 2nd ed. (Ithaca, NY: Firebrand Books, 2005), xii.

17.   David Beer, *Punk Sociology* (London: Palgrave Macmillan, 2014), 29.

18.   adrienne maree brown, "Introduction," in *Pleasure Activism: The Politics of Feeling Good* (Chico, CA: AK Press, 2019), Kindle.

CHAPTER 13

Visible Mending: A Recipe for Beautiful and Sustainable Clothing

Sari Fordham

According to the United Nations Environment Programme, our clothes account for 10 percent of greenhouse gases and 20 percent of water usage.[1] When we eventually throw them away (or even drop them off at a thrift store), 80 percent of our clothing ends up in landfills or is burned, as estimated by the advocacy group re/make.[2] There's a better, more beautiful way.

Visible mending honors the resources that go into our clothing and celebrates the history of a piece and the repair process. It can take the form of embroidery, darning, or a patch. Patching jeans is the fastest, and most fascinating, entry into the world of visible mending. And really, who doesn't have a pair of jeans with an unwanted tear? You don't need experience to hand-mend your clothes; you just need a relaxed mindset. Imperfections will be part of the final product's charm. Your hands, not a machine, created something new.

What You Need

Sewing needles
Sturdy thread
Sharp scissors
A pair of jeans you want to patch
The patch—created from used clothing or fabric
Sashiko needles (optional)
Sashiko thread (optional)
Thimble (optional)

A word on sashiko. It's a Japanese form of embroidery that traditionally uses blue or white thread and longer needles, allowing the mender to gather several stitches in one go. Sashiko thread is well suited for visible mending because it's thicker and more durable. A lot of visible patching draws inspiration from sashiko, and if you can afford the thread and needles, I recommend using them. However, you certainly don't need them in order to create beautiful visible mending.

Getting Started with Your Visible Patch

1. Gather your sewing materials, selecting a thread color that will visually contrast to the jeans you're mending. If you're not using sashiko thread, regular cotton thread with a heavier weight is a good alternative. Cotton is durable, and therefore will hold your patch in place, and it is kinder to the Earth than polyester.
2. Select fabric for the patch. This fabric should be of equal sturdiness to the item you wish to repair. I keep a small box of clothing to use as patches. These are clothes that are too damaged (or unloved) to be repaired. Sadly, it has not been hard to keep such a box filled, though when I see cheap jeans in a thrift store, I will buy them to use for patching. Denim makes excellent patch material, especially when patching jeans.
3. Cut the loose threads from the hole in your jeans and decide whether you want to hand-hem around the hole or leave the edges raw. A raw edge will look more informal, but the mend will hold up the same. I like the tidiness of sewing around the hole, but it is an aesthetic choice, not a utilitarian one.
4. Place the patch fabric over the hole to measure it and cut a generous (no, even more generous) patch.
5. Place the patch behind the hole and use basting stitches or safety pins to hold the patch to the jeans in the exact place you want it. I prefer basting stitches—a quick stitch around the edge of the patch—because safety pins are awkward to sew over. Since you will be removing the basting stitches at the end of your mend, it's best to choose thread that's a different color than the thread you will use for your visible mend.
6. Decide on a stitch pattern for your mend. The patch, especially if it is denim, is not what will make your mend interesting. Your stitching will. An easy and visually striking pattern is a box with lines. Think of a square or rectangular garden plot with furrows. That's your patch design.
7. First, use your sturdy thread to sew a large box (or garden plot) around the area you're mending. You'll use a simple running stitch for this box. A running stitch is one that comes in and out of fabric in a straight line. If you have seen a cartoon character hand-sewing something, this is the stitch they're using.

8. Then, inside the garden, you'll create the furrows with either vertical or horizontal running stitches. The decision between vertical and horizontal is entirely visual. Both make for comfortable patches. Tip: When sewing your running stitches, don't pull the thread too taut. Let the thread have a bit of give in each line. This way, the finished fabric will be able to bend naturally and the patch won't be puckered.
9. Don't try to complete the patch with one long line of thread. It will get tangled. Words will be spoken. It's much better to work with less thread and embrace the opportunity to show off your needle-threading chops. Tip: Before I tie off the thread, I like to anchor the knot to the backside of the patch by grabbing a bit of fabric with the needle and then tying my knot.
10. When you've completed your rows of stitching, tie the final knot, remove the basting stitch, and enjoy your enhanced clothing item. Now that you're hooked on sustainable clothes and the joy of creating your own fixes, let's talk about darning socks!

Useful Resources

Briscoe, Susan. *Ultimate Sashiko Sourcebook: Patterns, Projects, and Inspiration*. Newton Abbot: David & Charles, 2005.

Cardon, Jenny Wilding. *Visible Mending: Artful Stitchery to Repair and Refresh Your Favorite Things*. That Patchwork Place, 2018.

Lewis-Fitzgerald, Erin. *Modern Mending: Minimize Waste and Maximize Style*. Kent: Search Press, 2021.

Marquez, Jessica. *Make and Mend: Sashiko-Inspired Embroidery Projects to Customize and Repair Textiles and Decorate Your Home*. New York: Watson-Guptill, 2018.

Montenegro, Nina, and Sonya Montenegro. *Mending Life: A Handbook for Repairing Clothes and Hearts*. Seattle: Sasquatch Books, 2020.

Noguchi, Hikaru. *Darning: Repair Make Mend*. Gloucestershire: Quickthorn, 2020.

Rodabaugh, Katrina. *Mending Matters: Stitch, Patch, and Repair Your Favorite Denim & More*. New York: Harry N. Abrams, 2018.

Notes

1. "Putting the Brakes on Fast Fashion," *UN Environment Programme*, November 12, 2018, https://www.unep.org/news-and-stories/story/putting-brakes-fast-fashion.
2. Allison McCarthy, "Are Our Clothes Doomed for the Landfill?," *re/make*, March 22, 2018, https://remake.world/stories/news/are-our-clothes-doomed-for-the-landfill/.

CHAPTER 14

Appalachian Solarpunk: Growing Trees from Seed for the Plant Revolution

Vance Mullis and Joy Lew

To grow the forests and forest cities of tomorrow, we need plants today. Traditional horticultural growing methods use black plastic pots, a variety of soilless mixes, or a large area of land. We're here to share with you the materials and methods we have been experimenting with that are cheap, accessible, environmentally conscious, and grow healthy trees and shrubs. We are part of a large experimental plant-growing community in the Asheville, North Carolina, area. We run a small wholesale nursery specializing in disease-resistant fruit and nut trees and shrubs and have been involved in numerous nonprofit plant projects in the southeast US, including at Living Web Farms. We have over forty years of experience raising plants, with an eye toward innovative practices and advanced genetics.

Plant Revolution!

The Green Revolution of the 1960s fed the world, but it did not feed the soil. It was based on predominantly annual crops, bred for drought and disease resistance, but as a result of this revolution we became overly dependent on annual tillage and pesticide application, both of which are unsustainable practices in the long run. If we're going to build a revolutionary and sustainable system, it has to be based on perennial crops that feed into the soil food web and sequester our carbon. These plants will feed the soil, the community, and the world.

Why Trees and Shrubs?

Our future depends on us getting as much carbon out of the atmosphere as quickly as possible. While solar panels and green tech can prevent carbon from entering the atmosphere in the first place, they cannot remove carbon that is already there. Trees and shrubs—particularly those with vigorous, deep root systems—can efficiently sequester the carbon, that is, pull carbon from the atmosphere and store it deep in the soil. While the carbon in the trunk of a tree can be lost to a chainsaw or a forest fire, carbon that is exuded from the plant roots remains in the soil, as it is incorporated into the soil ecosystem through soil-dwelling microbes and various layers of the soil food web. This is one of the few reliable ways to prevent the carbon from reentering the atmosphere.

Unfortunately, deforestation across the world has devastating environmental impacts—loss of biodiversity, loss of habitat, erosion, disturbing regional hydrological cycles, and impacting carbon sequestration. The destructive colonial practice of clear-cut deforestation on the East Coast has been massive and ongoing, replacing the forest management practices and food forests of numerous Indigenous tribes. While not all of us have the power to stop this deforestation, we can do something about the other side of the equation—planting trees.

China is currently reforesting on a massive scale. They have been perfecting how to grow trees using the least materials possible, as cheaply as possible. Taking note of their new methods, we've been trying them out at our food forest here in the southern Appalachians. Food forests can provide a diversity of food, sequester carbon, and provide important wildlife habitat.

Growing Basics

All plants want two basic things for their roots—water and air. They also prefer for their roots to be cool in the heat of summer. Traditionally, plants grown in black plastic pots can struggle in the heat and sun, and as our summers are getting hotter, they are increasingly struggling to survive the hotter months without supplemental water.

The first part of this new growing technique is nonwoven fabric bags. These mesh bags are very lightweight, allow for better air flow to the roots, and are cooler in the sun than hot black plastic pots, are cheaper, take a small fraction of material to create, and are cheaper to ship. Many of the mesh bags are biodegradable. This means you can plant your tree seed in the mesh bag, let it grow for at least a few months to get established, and then plant it directly where you want it to go. It's ideal for guerrilla gardening edible trees or for any other growing projects you might have. How biodegradable these bags are depends on which company manufactures them and the polymers involved. Some of our best bags are branded Root Pouch, which are 100 percent recycled plastic bottles and cotton. We use these for apple trees that take multiple seasons to properly develop before planting. The thinner white mesh bags are acquired through Ali

Fig. 14.1. Happy, blight-resistant hazelnuts in white mesh bags.

Express, directly from China. We use these for trees and shrubs that can be quickly grown and planted out in a single season. In the future, these would be good candidates for local 3-D printing projects on a large scale, particularly using some of the new biodegradable polymers developed for that technology.

Keep in mind: the nonwoven part matters. Woven things will eventually strangle plant roots, unless they quickly biodegrade, but nonwoven fabrics won't, because the plant roots (and other critters) can push right through. So while you can grow plants in old cotton T-shirts or socks—which will easily biodegrade—if you try to grow them in old cotton-poly shirts or socks, the plants will eventually struggle as the woven fibers girdle the roots.

What makes particular nonwoven bags biodegradable? It's a combination of UV exposure (sunlight), starch (plant sugars), and planting it in the ground (soil microorganisms). We have gone back and dug up old bags out of the ground, and they do degrade.

The second important part of this planting technique is the soil mix. You can easily use compost in the white mesh bags, but we've found a combination of fine pine bark and compost to be excellent for growing hazelnuts and chestnuts in particular. This mix is much cheaper than buying traditional soilless potting mixes. What mix to use depends on what you're growing. As this is

Fig. 14.2. Sprouting chestnut seeds on a reusable microfiber cloth in a repurposed plastic clamshell container. Critters find these and other nut trees to be delicious; planting them in bags gives them time to safely establish themselves.

an experimental project, we are currently testing out new mixes and refining them, but we welcome collaboration, as we need lots more trees, and lots more cheap trees, to aid in the Plant Revolution. For any given plant, we find that it is important to test out multiple different soil formulations and growing conditions to discover what works best for that species. Be courageous! Try new things! Fortune favors the bold!

A note on soil mixes: growing trees in pots versus growing them in white mesh bags. For growing trees in black pots, a good basic mix is 5-1-1, which is 5 parts pine bark fines, 1 part peat, 1 part perlite. When growing in bags, they're already highly aerated, so you don't need to add perlite, and can use a muckier mix. Generally we do 5-1-1 with 5 parts pine bark, 1 part peat, and 1 part zeolite-based ionic exchange fertilizer, which we created by reverse engineering some NASA research. That's probably overkill for most folks, so to simplify, you can use straight compost, most basic organic fertilizers, or even just the soil in your area, because that will allow the plants to become accustomed to the soil prior to being transplanted. That's how they're doing it in China. This ensures better transplant success and also makes it much cheaper, since you're just buying a three-cent bag and tree seeds instead of all these other ingredients.

Black pots require a soilless mix, which is mainly used to create better aeration in the root zone, but the white mesh bags allow you to use your local soil.

The third aspect of this technique is that you can grow these tree seeds in bags in small spaces. We like to put them in trays with a few holes punched in the bottom for those seedlings that prefer more aeration and trays with no holes for the water-loving plants. In an area as small as two square feet, you can easily grow ten to twenty tree and shrub seedlings to plant in your local ecosystem. This can be done on a sunny porch or in a backyard. The reason this technique matters so much is that you can grow perennial plants with monster root systems—comparable to the ones you'll find in a hydroponic system—for a fraction of the cost with far less transplant shock.

What to Grow?

We have been focusing our efforts on hazelnuts and chestnuts. These are both edible native (or improved hybrid) species that are of great interest in agroecology and forest gardening. In some cases, the trees have been bred and refined for better-tasting nuts, larger nuts, greater cold tolerance, greater heat tolerance, and greater resistance to pests and diseases. For anyone interested in trying this project, we suggest starting with hazelnuts, as they are more forgiving than the chestnuts.

It is being increasingly acknowledged and appreciated that First Nations tribes practice sophisticated methods of agroecology, which provided abundant food in very low-maintenance, low-energy ways. Unlike annual crops, which are labor-intensive, tree and perennial crops offer food sources to humans and wildlife with relatively minimal labor and low impact on the local soil and ecology. In fact, in many cases, planting these trees and other native species can dramatically increase the health and resilience of local Appalachian ecosystems. These practices informed our methods.

All food systems are based around staple crops. Few crops can fill this niche where they can produce ample staple food and work in a silvicultural system. Hazelnuts have a long history of being able to fulfill this niche, as can be seen in the Holocene pollen records throughout Europe. Hazelnuts were also one of the important tree foods for the local Cherokee tribe.

Why Aren't These Methods Used More Broadly?

Unfortunately, agriculture and horticulture are very slow to change. The overall approach to these fields is very traditional and conservative. The plants are also grown to sell and must be shipped to various locations. The black plastic pots are sturdier than the biodegradable fabric bags and look neater on a table

Fig. 14.3. Happy roots—plants are only six weeks old!

at your local plant nursery or big box store. The vast majority of those black plastic pots will end up in your local landfill, as will the trays they stand in. Until companies and industries are better penalized for the waste that they produce, they have no reason to experiment with newer, more sustainable methods.

Where to Plant?

Plant your baby trees anywhere that you think they might survive. One of the bigger changes in human consciousness that will need to be embraced for the Plant Revolution is people appreciating plants and allowing them space to live. Allowing plants and other wildlife space to exist is a shockingly difficult concept for some individuals to embrace, but our solarpunk future calls for it. Navigating the needs for humans to survive economically by altering the landscape versus allowing nature to thrive is where agroecology can help.

How to Plant?

General planting recommendations: Dig a hole two to three times as wide as your mesh bag and as deep as your bag, but no deeper. If you are trying

Fig. 14.4. Density! You can grow many young trees in small spaces.

to plant in heavy clay, add in soil conditioner with whatever compost or composted manure you can get your hands on, and mix this with the clay. Somewhere around 40 to 50 percent soil conditioner, 0 to 10 percent compost, and 50 percent local clay soil is a decent, affordable recipe. Once you have dug the hole and prepared your soil, you plant your precious mesh bag with a happy seedling, water it as best you can (or plant before a heavy rainstorm), wish your plant a happy life, and go plant the next one. This level of preparation is not always possible, depending on when and where you are planting. One does what one can. During drought, your plants will appreciate it if you can visit them with some water, especially if it is during their first year of establishment.

This might sound complicated. However, once you get into the rhythms of plant life, of the Plant Revolution, it all becomes second nature.

We hope to see you out there.

Fig. 14.5. Hazelnut catkins blooming in winter. They release their pollen and let the wind carry it to other plants, to create the next generation.

Recommended Suppliers

Black mesh bags: Cotton + recycled plastic bottles (PET)

   Greenhouse Megastore: https://www.greenhousemegastore.com
   /containers-trays/bags-pouches/root-pouch-grey-fabric-pot-3-4-year

Crowd-sourced Seed-Sharing Communities

   Chestnuts as a tree crop—Castanea species nut trees: https://www
   .facebook.com/groups/272120753285618/

   Northern Nut Growers Association: https://nutgrowing.org/

Seed Suppliers

   Burnt Ridge Nursery: https://www.burntridgenursery.com/

   Grimo Nut Nursery: http://www.grimonut.com/

   Route 9 Cooperative: https://route9cooperative.com/

Further Reading

Abrams, Marc D., and Gregory J. Nowacki. "Native Americans as Active and Passive
    Promoters of Mast and Fruit Trees in the Eastern USA." *Holocene (Sevenoaks)*
    18, no. 7 (2008): 1123–37.
Ajmeri, J. R., and C. J. Ajmeri. "13—Developments in Nonwovens as Agrotextiles."
    Elsevier Ltd (2016): doi:10.1016/b978-0-08-100575-0.00013-9.
Arkatkar, Ambika, et al. "Degradation of Unpretreated and Thermally Pretreated
    Polypropylene by Soil Consortia." *International Biodeterioration & Biodegrada-
    tion* 63, no. 1 (2009): 106–11.
Arkatkar, Ambika, et al. "Growth of Pseudomonas and Bacillus Biofilms on Pretreated
    Polypropylene Surface." *International Biodeterioration & Biodegradation* 64, no.
    6 (2010): 530–36.
Darr, Alexander. "Agroforestry as Observed by the DeSoto Expedition of 1538." *AFTA*
    24, no. 2 (2018), https://www.aftaweb.org/138–2018-vol-24/volume-24-no
    -2-august-2018/239-agroforestry-as-observed-by-the-desoto-expedition-of
    -1538.html.
Kuneš, Petr, Petr Pokorný, and Petr Šída. "Detection of the Impact of Early Holocene
    Hunter-Gatherers on Vegetation in the Czech Republic, using Multivariate
    Analysis of Pollen Data." *Vegetation History and Archaeobotany* 17, no. 3 (2008):
    269–87.
Lehmann, Johannes, and Markus Kleber. "The Contentious Nature of Soil Organic
    Matter." *Nature* 528, no. 7580 (2015): 60–68.
Living Web Farms. "Nuts as Staple Foods with Osker Brown." YouTube video, December
    18, 2019. https://www.youtube.com/watch?v=CJpitVC4mzs.
Ming, D. W., and E. R. Allen. "Zeoponic Substrates for Space Applications: Advances in
    the Use of Natural Zeolites for Plant Growth." In *Natural Microporous Materials
    in Environmental Technology,* 157–76. New York: Springer, 1999.
Pang, Ming-Meng, Meng-Yan Pun, and Zainal A. M. Ishak. "Degradation Studies during
    Water Absorption, Aerobic Biodegradation, and Soil Burial of Biobased
    Thermoplastic Starch from Agricultural Waste/Polypropylene Blends." *Journal
    of Applied Polymer Science* 129, no. 6 (2013): 3656–64.
Rutter, Phillip. *Growing Hybrid Hazelnuts: The New Resilient Crop for a Changing Climate.*
    White River Junction, VT: Chelsea Green Publishing, 2015.
Warren, Robert J. "Ghosts of Cultivation Past—Native American Dispersal Legacy
    Persists in Tree Distribution." *PLoS One* 11, no. 3 (2016). https://doi.org
    /10.1371/journal.pone.0150707.
Yan, Wong. "China's Forest Shelter Project Dubbed 'Green Great Wall.'" *Xinhuanet*, July
    9, 2006, web.archive.org/web/20080407213655/http://news.xinhuanet.com
    /english/2006-07/09/content_4810897.htm.

CHAPTER 15

Anthrocene Strategy: Foraging

Michael J. DeLuca

Foraging is just one of the ways I'm preparing for a future I can't always see. The future changes so fast these days it's impossible (for me) to keep up, but I try.

Reduced access to materials, food, water. An increase in hostility from some people, the opposite from others; a deep and abiding need to find and make common faith with those others. Increasing unreliability in infrastructure—which is saying something, living here in southeast Michigan after generations of white flight, crumbling tax base, and disaster capitalism. Massively reduced ease, affordability, and justifiability of transportation. An influx of climate refugees. New and worse outbreaks of infectious disease. Invasive bugs, plants, fish wiping out native populations, reducing biodiversity and therefore resilience. Much of this is beyond anybody's control. Cascade effects are already under way, there's no averting what's already happening, the fires, the hurricanes, not even with unlimited political will. The Great Lakes are warming faster than most places, but they're also far away from hurricanes and rising sea levels, comparatively safe from tornadoes, and they're big and wet, generating a kind of captive water cycle that cushions us from drought and temperature extremes. Plus, the cost of living is low due to all the terrible infrastructure, blight, racism, and environmental injustice. I can't claim I had all this figured out when I moved here almost ten years ago. But I'm here now, I'm invested, I'm doing what I can to adapt.

Some of that investment is in technology. I put solar panels on the house, installed an electric car charger, and bought an electric car that just happens to be made in my town. Maybe that will play out into reliable transportation if the grid goes down, maybe not. House-size batteries are expensive, hard to come by, and not yet of sufficient capacity for comfort; electric cars were the same way until very recently. But the car (it's a Bolt) is its own enormous battery, and having practiced with it for a few years, I'm realizing we might be able to get more out of it than transportation. It takes 4 kilowatt-hours to drive a mile; the Bolt can go 250 miles at full charge. It only takes 100 kWh to power my whole house for a month. That's promising. I can look forward to the opportunity to adapt further, to the possibilities opened up by the prospect of relying entirely on that system—if that's how the future goes. In the meantime, I've got other plates spinning.

I've been teaching myself to grow and forage food, medicine, and tools, in hopes of being able to better support my family—and contribute to supporting a community—in the event of a global economic collapse engendered by the climate crisis. I'm nowhere close to self-sufficiency, operating on a tiny scale, but I think of it as building a store of possibilities, proofs of concept. I want to know what's available and how to take advantage of it, to reduce my dependence on mass-produced goods mailed to me in single-use packaging by corporations with awful, exploitative labor practices and massive carbon footprints, and to develop a wealth of experience I can share when things get worse. I'm not prepping for doomsday, just building resilience. I try to expand on what I enjoy, what I'm already good at. It doesn't feel like work. In fact, it feels like the best kind of play: creative, productive, collaborative. I spend a lot of time in the woods and fields, the brooksides, the edgelands. I watch, I invest, I learn patterns, I try to anticipate. As I figure out what thrives in this climate now, invasive and otherwise, I figure out what I can use it for and adapt what I can grow in my own garden based on that knowledge, and to compliment it.

Actually, I can think of all this as technology, too—technology of a different kind, older, neglected, discredited, and thus forgotten by an unsustainable, energy-glutted society because it requires investment of patience and time rather than exploitation of resources.

What follows are some highlights of my learning process.

––––––

There's an abandoned apple orchard on state land a mile from my house. In a good year, knobby heirloom Red Delicious crabs pile up under thickets of blackberry canes and invasive Russian olive, attracting yellowjackets, deer, and me. I prune the trees, I clear ground underneath them, I learn the cycles of wet and dry years and the trees' accompanying tendency toward biennial yield. I bike to the orchard, fill panniers to overflowing, and bike home, over and over until I've got bushels piled up in my basement, enough to get pressed at the local cider mill. Red Delicious, even these generations-old precursors now half wild, produce a sweet but insipid cider lacking the acids and tannins necessary to provide a welcoming environment for fermentation and stable shelf life. So I look around for acids and tannins. I've planted a few varietal cider apple trees in my tiny yard, I tend them, learn from them; eventually they'll produce enough to blend with. Meanwhile, I forage Siberian crabapples and wild Oregon grapes, both small but sweet and very tart. They need to be pressed separately, by hand, not to clog up the mill machinery. I experiment with Staghorn sumac and spruce tips, both abundant, high in tannins and vitamin C, both used for that purpose, among many others, by Ojibwe and other Native people before imperialism and colonialism all but obliterated those traditions. Yeast can be had anywhere—from the skins of apples or grapes—and can be propagated endlessly.

After a few years of observation, practice, and experimentation, I can make reliably, actually delicious hard apple cider that lasts through the off years, for which the only cost or carbon footprint is the effort and two dollars per gallon for the pressing.

Fox Grape Cider

Wild apples, enough to produce 3/4 gallon of cider, about 1 and 1/2 pecks
1/2 gallon Siberian crabapples, yield 1 quart juice
2 cups wild fox grapes, yield 3/4 cup juice
1/2 cup sourdough starter
1 oz local wildflower honey (for bottling)

Harvest fruit as it ripens—here at Michigan's 42nd parallel in 2019, that's the second week in October. The grapes can be pressed immediately; apples should cure a few weeks in a cool, dark place for maximum yield. At home I crush fruit in a big metal pot using a section of red oak, then press a quart or so at a time using cheesecloth, a metal colander, and a full gallon jug for a weight.

Combine all the juice in a gallon glass jug (the kind they sell table wine in). Add sourdough starter and stir thoroughly to combine. Seal with a drilled rubber cork and an airlock (available at any homebrew supply for two dollars), store in a cool, dark place and allow to ferment for a few months until the liquid has clarified, or gone from cloudy to clear, then siphon the liquid off the sediment into a new glass jug. Consider adding a tablespoon or two of dried wild or homegrown herbs such as yarrow, sumac, bee balm, hyssop, lavender, or coriander. Age anywhere from two months to a year, then siphon off into a clean vessel for bottling. Heat half a cup of the fermented cider over low heat, add honey, and stir until dissolved. Allow to cool, combine with the rest of the cider, mix thoroughly, then siphon it all into clean glass bottles and seal. I like Grolsch-style bottles with wired-on ceramic stoppers; they can be reused endlessly with zero waste. The small infusion of sugar from the honey will allow the residual yeast to work in the bottle and carbonate. Store in a dark, cool place anywhere from six months to six years—or longer; that's just the longest I've managed to make mine last.

————————

Apparently my town also used to have black walnut orchards, even before the apple orchards, because there are big, old, second- or even third-generation black walnut trees everywhere, including my neighbors' yards. They're native, but they're basically weed trees now, colonizing lawns and disturbed ground where nobody wants them. The walnuts end up everywhere underfoot, staining everything they touch, leaching allelopathic biochemicals into the soil, inhibiting the growth of plants like cucumber and peas, considered more desirable according to contemporary gardening sensibilities; every spring and fall I hear the neighbors complaining about it. I take it as a challenge: another living thing I can learn to coexist with. I can't beat them, so I might as well garden around them. Nightshades, brassicas, onions, and helianthus all seem to do pretty well, as it turns out. And this past summer, I decided I'd make more of an effort—not to try and beat them, nor merely to coexist, but to join them.

Black walnuts are edible, obviously. They don't even need to be roasted, just hulled and dried. Shelling them takes a little effort; a hammer works, if you've got a stone to brace them against, or, failing that, a vise, and then a chopstick or nail to push out the good bits. With a little practice, they're delicious: like regular walnuts, only more so. It took me maybe three tries to acquire the taste; after that I couldn't get enough. That left the sticky, smelly, intensely brown-staining hulls. With a little thinking I realized I could mulch with them, as long as I saved them for around the house foundation, paths, and other places I don't want plants.

I also knew they could be used to make ink. I'd never made ink. I'd never even used any but the kind that comes in ballpoint pens and toner cartridges— most of which, it turns out, is made from petroleum. And most of those pens are "disposable." Suddenly I had ample reason to try. Not to mention the pure romance of writing with homemade ink, which struck me as something of a siren song in this age of disposable tech.

Black Walnut Ink

Hulls from 20 ripe, intact black walnuts, about 1 quart, harvested either just
    before or just after they fall; late September in southeast Michigan
A nonreactive stockpot, stainless steel or enamel or else it will stain
Water, enough to cover, about 1 quart
Cheap alcohol as a preservative and evaporant (helps the ink to dry); I used
    vodka. About 1 cup.

Wear gloves. The thick green outer hulls should split off the ripe walnuts after
one good smack with a hammer. Pile them in the stockpot, cover with water,
bring to a boil, then remove the lid and simmer, mashing the contents down
occasionally with a piece of wood, until the liquid is thickened and reduced to
near-viscousness. This takes a while, hours, and is inexact—if you want ink
for a platen press, it's got to have the consistency of grape jelly; if you want it
for dyeing clothes, you're going to need to add water later. Remove the hulls
from the liquid when it's getting close and save them for mulch—but be careful to avoid dripping on anything you don't want stained brown. Allow the
liquid to cool fully, then test for consistency. I made a quill from a foraged
turkey feather, using kitchen shears to cut a sharp, angled tip. If needed, cook
the ink down some more, or add water and stir well to loosen it. At this stage,
the liquid should be somewhat thicker than the intended final product. When
it's about right, decant carefully into resealable jars (narrow necks help prevent spillage), filling them a bit less than halfway. Top the jars up with alcohol,
seal and shake to combine, then test again and adjust accordingly.

When you're satisfied, label and date the jars using their contents. The ink
should keep indefinitely.

———

Garlic mustard is an intimately familiar invasive species for many in north-
eastern North America. It forms huge monocultures, choking out native flow-
ering herbs in spring and discouraging the wildlife that depend on them. It
can take advantage of black walnut allelochemicals, colonizing where other
plants can't. Like many invasives, it's edible, but globalized food culture isn't
exactly making room for it. Also, it tastes like its name. Not exactly inviting,
depending on your palate.

Another abundant edible spring green whose innate attributes make it
repugnant to globalist food culture, stinging nettle hurts astonishingly for

fifteen minutes after contact with bare skin, but it's nutritious, delicious, and native to North America and has thousands of years of culinary history.

It turns out these two competing herbs synergize remarkably.

Every late April/early May, when garlic mustard and nettle are both getting leafy and robust but haven't yet flowered, I take my gardening gloves, a knife, and a couple of giant cloth bags down to the long-neglected brookside to harvest. I pull up garlic mustard by the root, armloads of it. I carefully trim the top few florets of leaves from the bushiest nettle stalks the way I would with mint or basil, leaving the roots and stems intact, encouraging new growth, ending up with armloads of that too. I'm helping to keep the two plant colonies, native and invasive, in equilibrium. Then I pack it all into my bike panniers and take it home to make pesto.

Stinging Nettle and Garlic Mustard Pesto

2 quarts stinging nettle leaves, tightly packed
2 quarts garlic mustard leaves, tightly packed
1/4 cup olive oil
1/2 cup pine nuts, walnuts, black walnuts, or pecans
1 tbsp local wildflower honey
1 tsp salt

Pesto by no means requires basil. The word just means "ground up with a mortar and pestle" in Genoese; it's a name for a process by which a ton of fresh, perishable herbs can be concentrated and made to last. Globalism trains our palates to expect a certain thing, but I've found all that pretty easy—and rewarding—to unlearn. I'll get back to you when I've figured out how to eat Japanese knotweed.

In the meantime: separate the garlic mustard leaves and soft green stems from the woodier lower stems and roots, and leave the latter somewhere to dry out so they can be safely composted. Wash all the greens. To de-sting the nettles, throw them in a pot of boiling water just until they wilt and the water turns a beautiful emerald green, no more than a minute. (You can make dye from that water, much concentrated, though I've not tried it yet. You can also just drink it—nettle tea is full of nutrients and tastes rather like liquid Earth; I prefer it with honey and plenty of ice.) Strain out the nettles and press them dry. Then combine nettles, garlic mustard, and the rest of the ingredients in a giant mortar and pestle if you've got one, a food processor if you don't, and mash it into a wet, aromatic paste, and store in an airtight pint jar. You can pour a thin layer of oil over the top to prevent oxidation, but unlike basil pesto, this won't turn brown at the drop of a hat and will keep six months or more. And you can amend this recipe to include practically any other edible greens from the garden or the woods, invasive or otherwise—I've tried black mustard greens, dandelion greens, onion greens, chives, lambs' quarters, sheep sorrel, mint. Nettle makes a great base for a blend with stronger-flavored herbs because it's so mild. Basil pesto usually includes garlic—the garlic mustard takes its place here, but I often add some anyway, because I love garlic and I grow it, in the form of scapes, which start coming up at the same time of year. On the other hand, garlic mustard also adds a lot of bitterness, which the honey is there to counteract. The end result is savory and complex, excellent on sandwiches, pasta, and pizza.

I've not attempted to be exhaustive here, just to give an impression of my outlook and approach, a gesture in the direction of work that's yet to be done, reaching back toward a slower existence, lighter upon the Earth and more attentive to its patterns, invested in and interdependent with the natural processes around me, not above them. I'm always experimenting, failing, and internalizing lessons. There are always more new-to-me, ancient, marginalized technologies to explore: foraging, wildcrafting, composting, permaculture, hugelkultur, coppicing and pollarding, herbal medicine, rainwater and graywater catchment, replacing fossil-fuel-powered tools with manual ones, mending clothes, repairing everything instead of replacing, scavenging, learning and teaching others, developing symbiotic, mutually beneficial relationships with other living things.

What I've managed so far is a drop in the bucket. I know it isn't enough. I'm not going to eradicate garlic mustard eating a couple of armloads a year, even if I convince twenty of my neighbors to join me. I've no idea whether those wild apple trees will keep producing reliably amid all these weather extremes. I'm not at subsistence level with any of it—food, ink, alcohol, energy. I still need the grid. But I'm taking a tiny load off the global food network, adding a tiny cushion of self-sufficiency for my family and community in case things fall apart. And I'm still going, still learning, teaching myself the skills to adapt further as needed. And teaching others to do the same. Building resilience, in hopes that whichever future actually arrives, these skills, and the practice of acquiring them, will help us to adapt.

Further Reading

Buhner, Stephen Harrod. *Sacred and Herbal Healing Beers*. Boulder, CO: Brewers
    Publications, 1998.
Del Tredici, Peter. *Wild Urban Plants of the Northeast*. Ithaca, NY: Cornell UP, 2010.
Katz, Sandor Ellix. *Wild Fermentation*. White River Junction, VT: Chelsea Green
    Publishing Company, 2003.
Proulx, Annie. *Cider: Making, Using & Enjoying Sweet & Hard Cider*. North Adams, MA:
    Storey Publishing, 2003.
Pursell, JJ. *Master Recipes from the Herbal Apothecary*. Portland, OR: Timber Press, 2019.
Toensmeier, Eric. *Perennial Vegetables*. White River Junction, VT: Chelsea Green
    Publishing Company, 2007.

CHAPTER 16

Multispecies Community Garden: A More-Than-Human Design Concept Proposal for Well-Being in Shrinking Cities

Christoph D. D. Rupprecht, Aoi Yoshida, and Lihua Cui

In the Japanese context of depopulation and postgrowth society, this research rethinks everyday life and neighborhood greening in shrinking regional cities from a multispecies perspective (more-than-human coexistence). With the goal of using vacant lots as products of increased urban spongification for socio-ecological restoration, we propose a design concept of a space co-created and enjoyed by a diversity of life-forms. Here, we think through the concept using a site from Iwakura (Kyoto) from construction to twenty-five years of dynamically changing and diversifying environment.

Iwakura, Sakyo Ward, Kyoto City

Living urban fabric, flourishing neighborhood
Depopulation and society's postgrowth transformation are driving an increase in vacant lots. The Multispecies Community Garden concept adds the joys of gardening in everyday life to a wider vision of an expanding ecological network of green and blue spaces: a living urban fabric for a flourishing neighborhood.

What does "multispecies" mean?

The multispecies (also: more-than-human) concept "acknowledges the inter-connectedness and inseparability of humans and other life forms"1 and is "attentive to the agency of other-than human species, whether they are plants, animals, fungi, bacteria, or even viruses."2 Landscape in particular cannot be created by humans alone, but must be understood as formed in an ongoing process of co-creation: a multispecies commons.

Why not try to imagine exploring the city through the eyes of a bee or butterfly?

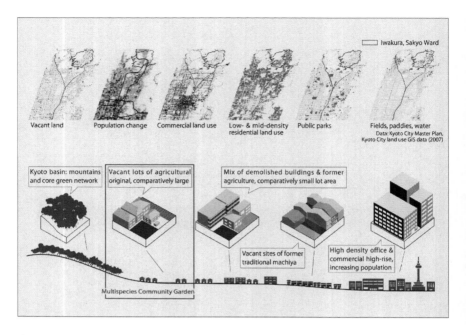

Iwakura, Sakyo Ward

Vacant land Population change Commercial land use Low- & mid-density residential land use Public parks Fields, paddies, water
Data: Kyoto City Master Plan, Kyoto City land use GIS data (2007)

Kyoto basin: mountains and core green network

Vacant lots of agricultural original, comparatively large

Mix of demolished buildings & former agriculture, comparatively small lot area

Vacant sites of former traditional machiya

High density office & commercial high-rise, increasing population

Multispecies Community Garden

Current state of Kyoto City & vacant land characteristics based on spatial unit types

To understand the characteristics of vacant land in Kyoto City, we combined land use data analysis with fieldwork on the ground to identify spatial unit types. The study area, Iwakura (Sakyo Ward), featured many vacant lots formerly used for agriculture and comparatively large in size. Surrounding them were mostly detached houses with very limited garden area.

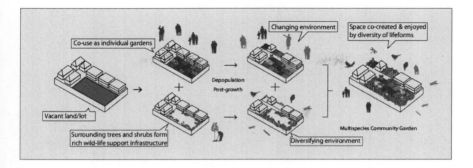

Concept

The vacant lot is transformed into a space co-created and enjoyed by a diversity of life-forms. Within it, space turns into private gardens with individual lots. These are surrounded by community-planted and cared-for trees, which form the basis of a rich habitat for other wildlife. As depopulation and postgrowth society change the city, both inside garden spaces and surrounding green space mature over time.

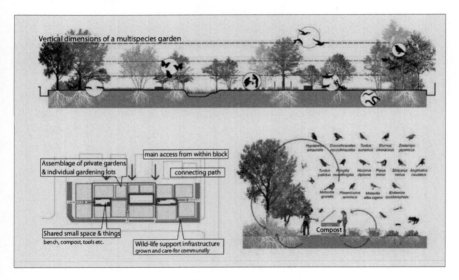

Structure and Cycle

A garden unfolding both horizontally and vertically as a stratified green space: upper levels frequented by birds, mid- to lower levels by insects, a ground-level home to human activities, a subterranean level of soil life, all in constant interchange.Individual gardening preferences drive horizontal diversity. Individual gardening preferences drive horizontal diversity. A compost serves as the hub of garden-internal nutrient cycling.

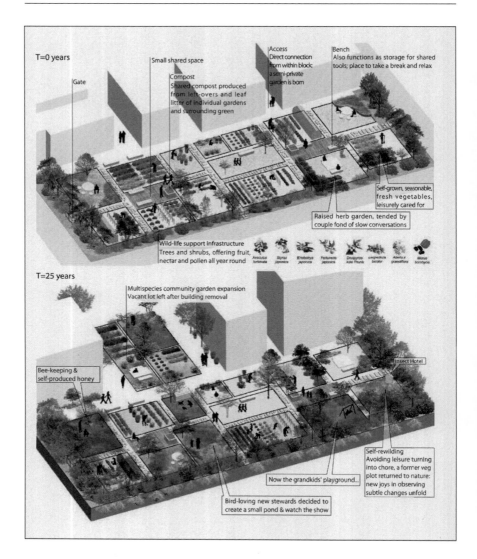

T=0 years

Gate

Small shared space

Compost
Shared compost produced from left-overs and leaf litter of individual gardens and surrounding green

Access
Direct connection from within block: a semi-private garden is born

Bench
Also functions as storage for shared tools; place to take a break and relax

Self-grown, seasonable, fresh vegetables, leisurely cared for

Raised herb garden, tended by couple fond of slow conversations

Wild-life support Infrastructure
Trees and shrubs, offering fruit, nectar and pollen all year round

Aesculus turbinata *Styrax japonica* *Ehretobrya japonica* *Fortunella japonica* *Diospyros kaki Thunb* *Lespedeza bicolor* *Abelia x grandiflora* *Morus bombycis*

T=25 years

Multispecies community garden expansion
Vacant lot left after building removal

Bee-keeping & self-produced honey

Insect Hotel

Self-rewilding
Avoiding leisure turning into chore, a former veg plot returned to nature: new joys in observing subtle changes unfold

Now the grandkids' playground...

Bird-loving new stewards decided to create a small pond & watch the show

Dynamically changing and diversifying environment

Imagining twenty-five years having gone by, we considered how the environment might have changed. As the concept is based on individual gardens, so would individuals' changing interests and ideas be reflected in the environment. A home for a diverse community of life emerges from this diversity. We thus propose this design concept as one possibility for life with vacant lots in regional cities and grassroots-created local identity.

Challenges for the Future

- Making: transition method and process from individual to shared ownership, toolkit for selection of vacant lot and appropriate vegetation
- Managing: flexible self-management based on co-ownership, sustainable membership system, representing nonhuman stakeholder interests
- Spreading: links with climate adaptation, disaster preparation, urban and green planning; certification for payments for eco-services (PES) etc.

Acknowledgments

We thank friends, colleagues, and fellow solarpunks for support and inspiration. This research was supported by the FEAST Project (14200116), Research Institute for Humanity and Nature, and JSPS KAKENHI grants 17K08179, 18K18602, and 20K15552.

Notes

1. Locke, Piers, and Ursula Muenster, "Multispecies Ethnography," In *Oxford Bibliographies in Anthropology* (2015): https://doi.org/10.1093/obo/9780199766567 -0130.
2. Katsumi Okuno, "Jinruigaku no genzai, karamiau shutachi, fuantei na 'shu,' " *Ékrits* (2019): http://ekrits.jp/2019/04/3061/.

CONCLUSION

Looking Forward

Phoebe Wagner and Brontë Christopher Wieland

In our original idea for this almanac, we hoped to have a slim volume full of recipes and blueprints and community-building plans. Yes, we have some of that, and we are so excited for the ideas that have been shared, but what we noticed is a gap between solarpunk ideas and actual implementations of these practices. Many solarpunks and people interested in solarpunk are theorizing online and in person. We've witnessed it and contributed to it. Solarpunk literature initially grew out of hope for a different future and the belief that before that future could exist, we had to imagine it. Yet as environmental degradation continues at drastic levels and social support for impacted groups remains negligible, literature and imagination are not enough—at least not right now. We worry that one reason solarpunk has struggled to make this leap from imagination to action is not so much because of obscurity—books, articles, conference presentations, meet-ups, classes all suggest solarpunk has a presence. Rather, we worry people are waiting and hoping for a piece of solarpunk literature or media to go mainstream, much like cyberpunk did with *Blade Runner* (1982). We wonder if this lack of manifestation in solarpunk off the page is rooted in longing for a solarpunk bible, a singular voice that points the way forward.

But, as we have mentioned elsewhere in this book and in other writings, we must question the role storytelling—even a story as potentially revolutionary as a solarpunk novel—plays in the present. Do stories make the type of change we need right now? Can we tell stories that decenter the individual and meaningfully treat interconnectedness while intellectual property standards constrict authorship to discrete units? Can we learn to see stories as gifts? Can we afford to decentralize storytelling from major venues—be it large publishers, Hollywood studios, or corporate silos like Instagram and YouTube—while even well-known artists struggle to make ends meet through these venues? Who do our stories not reach? And how do we stop the radical messaging of storytelling from becoming sanitized by the actions of those who see them as merely profitable?

Stories help us envision, imagine, critique, and normalize other ways of being, but so do direct actions. Going forward, we want to explore how we can tell stories of other worlds and other futures through our decisions, relationships, practices, and more. We believe that now, as much as ever, it is crucial for storytellers to practice what we preach, and vice versa. If telling stories and building structures of resistance have each individually changed our world, then we can't wait to see what we can accomplish when we learn to treat stories and actions as sides of the same coin, as strategies that can be yoked together for even greater effect and change.

We know the end goals for survival—global net-zero carbon dioxide emissions by 2050—but we also recognize that most individuals and communities have no ability to impact our chances of reaching that goal. What's left is to prepare for either situation, whether carbon dioxide emissions slow down or not. The COVID-19 pandemic has shown us that drastic change is possible, that our communities will rise to the occasion, and that, in supporting each other, we have more power than is obvious or even acknowledged. Much like environmentalism at large, the next step is much harder and often comes with privilege. Few people can go vegan, commute by bike, forage, garden, use public transit—and so on. We all have heard these talking points. And we all know that individual-oriented actions have little net power in the face of systemic and structural inequalities and abuses. What comes next is building structural opposition to the systems that are exploiting our environments and building structures that work directly for our communities. As solarpunks, we must understand our role in this process as one of support. Instead of seeking a popular novel to act as a monolith for a solarpunk future or seeking to impose our personal structures on the world as a whole, let's examine how we can work with the communities we are already a part of—as always, human and more-than-human. We've done our best in this book to show what ideas underlie this strategy and how solarpunks are already doing these things, but we don't attempt to offer a set and static route that must be taken to achieve our goals. To do so would be to fail to understand the world around us, both socially and environmentally, as a massive and complex ecology.

Solarpunks don't need a list of ten commandments, we need to show up wherever, whenever, and however we can—be it putting our bodies on the line at protests, dedicating our time to feeding those around us, providing child-care, distributing resources we have in abundance, telling stories, etc. And we need to understand this as an act of gift-giving that it is our responsibility to undertake.

To that end, we want to offer one more recipe. We want to see more almanac-like things. More collections of old recipes with local or abundant ingredients; more ways to use our daily by-products; grandmother's instructions on how to repair a tractor; your cousin's best wood-sanding technique; how you taught yourself to install solar panels; your best friend's immune-supporting tea blend; your favorite way to use edible nonnative plants; your sister's fire-starting tips; how your community made roof gardens; how to attend and advocate at city hall meetings; how to build resource networks; how to fix a bike; how to make paper and books; ad infinitum.

We believe everyone reading this book has something they can add to the list. Something worth sharing that will help a community survive and thrive. While many guides exist online in various forms, we see little harm in redundancy, and we see great value in collecting these ideas as a practice of gift-giving and resilience. So, here are two different ways to start collecting notes toward our futures. Below are Phoebe and Brontë's tips on creating your own anthology to be published traditionally (through a press) or as a zine (printed yourself in small quantities).

Step 1: Find the need you can speak to. Is there a group that has been overlooked in the media or oppressed systemically by the government? How might an anthology of fiction or nonfiction raise awareness? Maybe the need is how to fix roads and homes in your community's neglected neighborhood—is there a way you could compile designs or ideas to help with those repairs? Or has your community found ways of supporting itself that you think might be beneficial for others to learn from?

Step 2: Don't go it alone. An anthology or collection is about a group of voices and talents—a community in itself. Consider bringing on a coeditor or several! Don't feel like you have to do it by yourself. Find other people to share the struggle and the fun with! Everyone will bring different skills and insights to the experience. Consider your own skill set. If you don't enjoy proofreading for typos, then consider what other role you could fulfill in the process, even if it's just helping to refine ideas or distribute zines. You don't have to be a writer to be part of the process.

Step 3: What's the purpose and audience of your anthology or collection? These key ideas will help you decide whether you should look for a publisher to print your book or make a zine that you print and distribute yourself. If the audience is your local community or an adjacent one, then a traditional publisher probably isn't the right choice. It might be more effective to find a smaller local publisher or create a zine. If your audience or purpose is larger—if, for example, you're discussing strategies of opposition to police brutality across the country—then a traditional publisher might be right for you.

Step 4: Now that you have a sense of your audience and best publishing/printing outlet, here are two paths to completing the manuscript.

To print your own books or zines: you have complete autonomy! Your book or zine can be as simple as you like or need, or as complex as you have the time and will for. We've seen and loved everything from simple printed computer paper folded in half to small volumes handbound between mushroom-leather covers and individually illustrated with homemade inks. There are no rules, which is to your benefit. These volumes can be distributed by hand, left in local galleries, makerspaces, co-ops, or free libraries.

How to find a publisher: What other books, anthologies, or authors have inspired your interest in this topic? See if the publisher of those books and authors might be open to something like your anthology. This information is usually available online under their submission guidelines. Always check the website first! A large publisher (like Penguin) often won't be interested in an anthology unless there's a big name attached or an agent, but smaller publishers (like our first publisher, Joanne Merriam at Upper Rubber Boot Books) will sometimes be open to anthologies or collections by editors outside of the publishing company. If a publisher is looking for pitches for anthologies or collections, the publisher will state that clearly on their website. If you find a publisher that seems like a good fit and they are looking for anthology pitches, follow the guidelines to make your pitch. If guidelines aren't posted, email them and ask any questions you might have. And, as always in the writing world, if at first you receive a rejection, submit again to a new venue!

We look forward to seeing what you create, whether it's a new anthology, a free zine, extra protest signs, masks, low-tech websites, communes, abolition legislation, and everything beyond what we can imagine. Resistance through creating outside of the boundaries of capitalist, colonial, white supremacist systems should be fun. Once we remove ourselves from those systems, those boundaries, the possibility for creation no longer follows the market or what will sell but rather what is engaging to us and our communities. Solarpunk has always been about hope—not just the emotion but the action that necessitates and is necessitated by hope. This type of large, systemic change can feel overwhelmingly impossible, but that's exactly how the people in power want us to feel. As Ursula K. Le Guin said: "We live in capitalism, its power seems inescapable—but then, so did the divine right of kings."[1]

We hope the voices and visions in this almanac have inspired you. Environmental and social change is coming—whether to harm or to uplift depends on how we dismantle the systems holding us down and how we transform our communities.

Notes

1. Ursula K. Le Guin, "Speech in Acceptance of the National Book Foundation Medal for Distinguished Contribution to American Letters," Ursulakleguin.com, November 19, 2014, https://www.ursulakleguin.com/nbf-medal.

CONTRIBUTORS

Gabriel Aliaga received his MS from the University of Nevada, Reno, and works as an exploration geologist focused on gold. Born to Bolivian immigrants in Chicago, Gabe now lives in Reno with his wyfe, dog, and two cats.

Navarre Bartz is a recovering academic writing about the intersection of technology, society, and the environment. Originally hailing from the hills of Missouri, he now lives in Virginia with his wife, child, and feline overlords. His work has previously appeared on the Science Fiction and Fantasy Writers of America blog. You can find more of his musings at solarpunkstation.com.

Octavia Cade is a New Zealand writer with a PhD in science communication. Her academic work on ecosystems in speculative fiction includes "Entering the Ecosystem: Human Identity, Biology, and Horror" in *Critical Essays on the Intersection of Horror and Philosophy* (McFarland, forthcoming); "Microbiology and Microcosms: Ecosystem and the Body in *Shriek: An Afterword*" in *Surreal Entanglements* (Routledge, 2021); and "Humans as Ecological Actors in Post-Apocalyptic Literature" in *MOSF Journal of Science Fiction*. She has won three Sir Julius Vogel awards and was the 2020 writer in residence at Massey University.

The Commando Jugendstil is a solarpunk creative collective: we do projects in which we try to conjugate technology and art with the idea of transforming the city in its sustainable version. Simultaneously, our projects also focus on co-designing solutions with local communities to stimulate a just transition that can spark from the ground up. Together with Tales from the EV we have published several pieces of fiction and essays. Additionally, we created solarpunk cover art for *Revista MaMuT* vol. 6, *Ecologia Politica* vol. 57, and a monograph on the just transition by *Altreconomia* (forthcoming). Our illustration "The Floating Village" recently won a solarpunk contest organized by Italian speculative fiction publisher Future Fiction. We are also trying to bring solarpunk praxis into real life with the projects "Milano, Cartoline da un Futuro Possibile," funded by the European Commission and Fondazione Cariplo and implemented by Punto.Sud, and "The Town That Could Be," a time travel journal from Reading 2045, funded by Transition Bounce Forward and The National Lottery Community Fund.

Lihua Cui is a PhD student from Kyoto University. She has been working on urban green space since her master's study, and currently focuses on microclimate and thermal comfort of urban green space. Cui has a great passion for sustainable urban environments, especially in an Asian context. Her study interests include urban agriculture, agricultural landscape conservation, edible landscape, and children's green space use.

Kris De Decker is the author of *Low-tech Magazine*, an online publication that refuses to assume that every problem has a high-tech solution. Since 2018, *Low-tech Magazine* has run on a self-hosted solar-powered server, and since 2019 it is also available in print. De Decker also wrote for the Demand Centre at Lancaster University (UK), which researches energy demand in relation to social practices, and is the cofounder of the Human Power Plant, an art project that investigates the possibilities of human power production in a modern society. Before creating *Low-tech Magazine* in 2007, De Decker reported on cutting-edge science and technology as a freelance journalist for newspapers and magazines. He was born in Belgium and lives in Spain.

Michael J. DeLuca lives in the rapidly suburbifying postindustrial woodlands north of Detroit with partner, kid, cats, and microbes. He is the publisher of *Reckoning*, a journal of creative writing on environmental justice. His short fiction has appeared in *Beneath Ceaseless Skies*, *Apex*, *Mythic Delirium*, and lots of other places. His novella, *Night Roll*, released by Stelliform Press in October 2020, was a finalist for the Crawford award.

Sari Fordham teaches at La Sierra University, and her writing appears in a number of journals, including the *Chattahoochee Review*, *Green Mountains Review*, and *Brevity*. Her memoir *Wait for God to Notice* is about growing up in Uganda, a country now devastated by deforestation. She believes we are all responsible for disrupting the systems that create climate change. Mending is both a creative pursuit and a reminder that our smallest actions can make a difference. Find her at www.sarifordham.com.

Susan Haris is a doctoral candidate in literature and philosophy at the Indian Institute of Technology, Delhi, and a Fulbright-Nehru visiting researcher at the University of California, Santa Cruz. She is a Culture and Animals Foundation grantee and the fall fellow for the Nature, Art and Habitat Residency (NAHR).

Margaret Killjoy is a transfeminine author, musician, and podcaster currently living in a self-built cabin in the Appalachian mountains. She is the author of the Danielle Cain series of novellas, published by Tor.com, and is the host of the community and individual preparedness podcast *Live Like the World Is Dying*. Her most popular band is probably the feminist black metal trio Feminazgûl. She can be found complaining about things on Twitter @magpiekilljoy, and you can support her work on Patreon.

Michał Krawczyk is a doctoral candidate in the Environmental Futures Research Institute at Griffith University; within the ecological humanities, he combines ethnographic research with ecocinema to create a portfolio of moving images on permacultural forms of dwelling (https://vimeo.com /earthcare). His recent audiovisual project with Giulia Lepori is the short *LAND/SCAPE* (2020), a multispecies collaboration between humans and donkeys. Their ecocinematic meditation *How Does a Bark Feel Like?* (2020) featured in the exhibition *CLIMATE CARE: Reimagining Shared Planetary Futures* at Vienna Biennale 2021. He is a volunteer, gardener, and storyteller through bioregional practices of world making.

Petra Kuppers is a disability culture activist and a community performance artist. She creates participatory community performance environments that think/feel into public space, tenderness, site-specific art, access, and experimentation. Petra grounds herself in disability culture methods and uses ecosomatics, performance, and speculative writing to engage audiences toward more socially just and enjoyable futures. Her book of queer/crip short stories, *Ice Bar*, appeared in 2018, and her third poetry collection, *Gut Botany*, was named one of the top ten US poetry books of 2020 by the New York Public Library. Her next academic book is *Eco Soma: Pain and Joy in Speculative Performance Encounters* (University of Minnesota Press, 2022). She teaches at the University of Michigan and on Goddard College's low-residency MFA in Interdisciplinary Arts.

Giulia Lepori is a doctoral candidate in the School of Humanities, Languages, and Social Science at Griffith University; within the ecological humanities, she works on the regeneration of the imaginaries of water, plants, food, and waste through human and more-than-human forms of communication as experienced in a permacultural site. Her recent audiovisual project with Michał Krawczyk is the short *LAND/SCAPE* (2020), a multispecies collaboration between humans and donkeys. Their ecocinematic meditation *How Does* *a Bark Feel Like?* (2020) features in the exhibition *CLIMATE CARE: Reimagining Shared Planetary Futures* at Vienna Biennale 2021. She is a volunteer, gardener, and storyteller through bioregional practices of world making.

Joy Lew is a professional horticulturist with a passion for native, edible, and medicinal species. She co-owns Critter Cove Farm, a food forest and small wholesale plant nursery in the southern Appalachians. Previously she co-ran the Kirkwood Urban Forest and Community Garden, a seven-plus-acre community garden and food forest in Atlanta, Georgia. Joy is a refugee from academia, and when her hands aren't in the soil, she's either teaching, researching, writing, photographing, or helping to run a variety of online solarpunk and gardening spaces. She happily shares her life with the brilliant and unconventional Vance Mullis and their three cats.

Connor D. Louiselle is a creative producer working to create, write, and develop the Sunkeeper Storyworld, an original solarpunk-inspired universe. Connor believes solarpunk narratives serve as beacons of intention for those who co-create an ecocentric Earth. When Connor helped lead a Microsoft Social Innovation Camp in Silicon Valley, he saw that the next generations envision sustainable, accessible, and inclusive futures. Connor's experience in creative direction helps him weave story magic into experiences that will someday soon renew hope in the better climate and involvement in a better society. Connor is pursuing a degree in sustainable parks, recreation, and tourism at Michigan State University.

Vance Mullis is a lifelong horticulturist, experimental agroecologist, and orchardist. Vance co-owns Critter Cove Farm, a food forest and small wholesale plant nursery in the southern Appalachians. Previously he helped develop the Kirkwood Urban Forest and Community Garden, a seven-plus-acre community garden and food forest in Atlanta, Georgia. Vance is a refugee from academia, and when his hands aren't in the soil, he is providing consultations, researching, or tinkering with the passive solar retrofit of his home using recycled materials. A restless innovator, he is currently trialing Geneva rootstocks to help create the next generation of more resilient apple trees. He happily shares his life with the savvy and seed-obsessed Joy Lew and their three cats.

Christoph D. D. Rupprecht is a geographer, associate professor at the Department of Environmental Design, Faculty of Collaborative Regional

Innovation at Ehime University, Japan. When he's not researching and teaching multispecies sustainability, food, agriculture, green space, degrowth, and solarpunk, you might find him reading science fiction, hanging out with plants, trying to make cheese, or taking a nap. He believes the imagination holds the key for jointly building sustainable and just futures for all life, and hopes his coedited solarpunk anthology *Multispecies Cities* (World Weaver Press, 2021) is a tiny step in this direction.

Craig Stevenson is a queer neurodivergent guy who fell in love with solarpunk the moment he learned of its existence. Since then, he has used his well-practiced talent of daydreaming to blog about all the possible futures before us.

Tales from the EV is an Italian collective of speculative fiction writers. Our members are engaged in climate justice activism with Earth Strike UK and the Green New Deal for Europe campaign. Our collaboration with Commando Jugendstil has already resulted in the publication of four solarpunk short stories: "Midsummer Night's Heist" in *Glass and Gardens: Solarpunk Summers* (World Weaver Press), "Fermentos Criativos" in *RevistaMaMuT* vol. 6, "Viam Inveniemus Aut Faciemus" in *Glass and Gardens: Solarpunk Winters* (World Weaver Press), and "Under Pressure" in *And Lately the Sun* (Calyx Press), plus two essays published by *Reckoning Magazine* and one speculative essay published on the website of the Green New Deal for Europe campaign.

Phoebe Wagner holds an MFA in creative writing and environment and currently is a PhD candidate studying environmental literature at University of Nevada, Reno. She has published fiction in *PANK*, *Diabolical Plots*, and *AURELIA LEO*—among others. She is the coeditor of *Sunvault: Stories of Solarpunk & Eco-Speculation* (Upper Rubber Boot Books). Follow her work at phoebe-wagner.com.

Brontë Christopher Wieland has a lot of books to read and games to play, a banjo he's slowly getting better at playing, an MFA in creative writing and environment, and a countably infinite number of unfinished projects.

Aoi Yoshida is the founder of AOI Landscape Design. Aoi is interested in exploring better relationships between nature and humans and how to combine research, analysis, and spatial design. She believes landscape architecture is one powerful way of designing rich relations between various elements, from human life to water to biodiversity to infrastructure and more. She studied environmental science with specialization in phytosociology at Yokohama National University in Japan and holds a master's degree in city planning from the Department of Urban Engineering at the University of Tokyo. Since graduating, she worked at GLAC Co., Ltd in Tokyo, joined the master of landscape design at the Academy van Bouwkunst (AvB) of Amsterdam as a guest student, and worked at H+N+S landscape architecture in the Netherlands before setting up AOI Landscape Design in 2019.